D0505974

Gloucestershire

people and history

Gloucestershire

people and history

Richard Sale

The Crowood Press

First published in 2002 by
The Crowood Press Ltd
Ramsbury, Marlborough
Wiltshire SN8 2HR

www.crowood.com

© Richard Sale 2002

All rights reserved. No part of this publication may be reproduced or transmit-
ted in any form or by any means, electronic or mechanical, including photocopy,
recording, or any information storage and retrieval system, without permission
in writing from the publishers.

British Library Cataloguing-in-Publication Data
A catalogue record for this book is available from the British Library.

ISBN 1 86126 533 6

All photographs by Richard Sale except:

p22 Gloucestershire Newspapers Limited
p41 and p44 Gloucester City Museum and Art Gallery
p49 Woodchester Parish Council
p55 Corinium Museum, Cirencester
p163, p165, p192 and p193 Dean Heritage Centre
p207 Gloucestershire County Cricket Club
p208 Cheltenham Museum and Art Gallery (The Bridgeman Art Library)
p213 Nathan Sale

Frontispiece: Duntisbourne Abbots

Map on page 8 by John Richards, reproduced from Ordnance Survey mapping
on behalf of The Controller of Her Majesty's Stationery Office © Crown
copyright MC100038003

Typeset by Carreg Limited, Ross-on-Wye, Herefordshire

Printed and bound in Spain by Mateu Cromo, Madrid

CONTENTS

INTRODUCTION

Set between the Midlands and the south-west (the ancient Saxon kingdoms of Mercia and Wessex) and on the border between Wales and England, Gloucestershire was often also at the crossroads of history. The county has played a part in the history of England that other counties might envy. The critical battle between the Saxons and the Celts was fought within Gloucestershire's borders, as was the battle that ended the Wars of the Roses and the final battle of the Civil War. Wool from Cotswold sheep fuelled the economy of medieval England, and the coal and iron from the Forest of Dean were crucial to the new industrial age.

Gloucestershire has some of the finest churches in England, wonderful old villages, a spa town and excellent modern developments. It has, in the Cotswolds, one of Britain's most beautiful areas, not to mention one of the finest remaining forests in the country and a share of the Wye Valley, the loveliest river valley in the land.

This book explores all these aspects of the county. Starting with its earliest, prehistoric settlers, it moves through the Roman era – scratch Gloucestershire and find Rome, an old saying goes. The Saxons, who named the county and defined its borders, were followed by the Normans, whose early kings used Gloucester as one of the centres of their new realm. Then through the medieval period to the Civil War, where much significant action took place within the county. Following the Restoration, the events of the late seventeenth and eighteenth centuries are examined in terms of their role in defining the way in which the county developed. The Industrial Revolution and Gloucestershire's role in it, leads on to the modern county, which has been moulded in part by the conflicts of the twentieth century.

In starting such a project it was necessary first to define the county, a simple enough task it

might be thought. Not so. When the Saxons defined the borders of Gloucestershire, though they used several criteria, logic was not one of them. But once defined, the borders remained (with very minor changes) intact for almost a thousand years. Then in 1974, for reasons that were soon seen to be as illogical as the Saxon penwork, the county border was redrawn, removing the southern part of Gloucestershire to help make up the new county of Avon. In keeping with the faintly ludicrous concept, the spoken media chose to refer to the new county not as A-ven, with no accent on the second syllable in keeping with the Celtic word *afon* (river) from which it derives, but as A-von, with a heavily accented second syllable, just like the cosmetics company. Avon's demise was unlamented, but failed to restore Gloucestershire to its former glory, South Gloucestershire being created as a self-contained unit.

This book ignores the vagaries of local government and deals with proper Gloucestershire, the old county. It also includes Bristol, which will shock some purists. The inclusion was not made lightly, but in recognition of the influence the city's existence has had on the county, particularly its southern section.

The county's history is offered chronologically except where to fragment a topic whose story developed over centuries would have been illogical. By necessity, the approach has been broad-brushed. Whole books have been written on certain aspects of Gloucestershire's history, even on individual villages. As a consequence of that approach, the book is not a gazetteer of county towns and villages. Aspects of many are included, but some villages will have been excluded altogether. That is not to imply they are without interest. Every village in Gloucestershire has its tale to tell, but, sadly, in a book of finite length this has not always been the place to tell it.

The Forest of Dean.

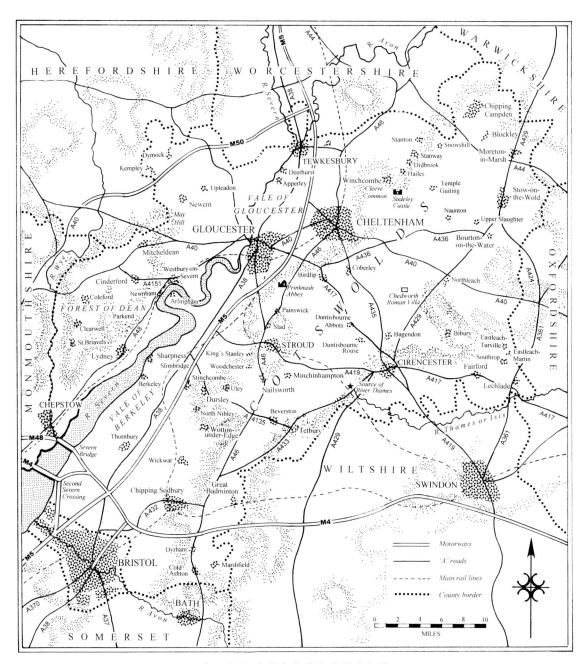

GLOUCESTERSHIRE

GLOUCESTERSHIRE CURIOS

Many places in the county have curious festivals and events, some of which have survived into modern times despite origins lost in ancient times. Some of these events are great fun – the Tetbury woolsack races, and the brick and rolling-pin throwing at Stroud – but others have a greater significance.

Unlike the Olympick games on Dover's Hill near Chipping Campden, which have a well-defined history (*see* page 136), the origins of the cheese-rolling at Cooper's Hill are lost in antiquity. It is known that similar events took place elsewhere, usually where there were springs at the bottom of the slope, as there are at Cooper's Hill. At some of these places a wheel was rolled, and in one instance at least, the wheel had been set alight, so it is likely that the rolled object symbolised the sun. The ceremony originally took place at midsummer and is thought to be pagan in origin, intended to arrest the fading sun and ensure its return the following year. The Cooper's Hill festival is now held at the spring Bank Holiday when the contestants perpetuate the age-old tradition of chasing cheeses down the 200m (650ft) 1-in-1 slope.

In the past the programme was more extensive. At one nineteenth-century festival the events included:

2 cheeses to be ron for
1 plain cake to be green for
1 plain cake to be jumpt in the bag for
Horings to be dipt in the toob for
Set of ribbons to be danced for
Shimey to be ron for
Belt to be rosled for
A bladder of snuff to be chatred for by hold wimming

The first item is the traditional cheese-rolling event; the second is grinning (gurning) through a horse-collar, still a feature of similar festivals in the Lake District; the third is a mystery, perhaps more hilarious for being so; the fourth is dipping for oranges in a tub; the fifth and seventh are dancing and wrestling for the ribbons and belt worn by the master of ceremonies; the sixth is a girls' race for a chemise; and the last involves old women talking loudly or long for the reward of a bag of snuff.

The bread and cheese ceremony at St Briavels is also of an unknown origin. Each Whit Sunday, after the evening service, small pieces of bread and cheese are thrown to the villagers from the Pound Wall outside the church. It is suggested that the ceremony might date from the seventeenth century when alms for the poor were distributed, but the true origin is by no means certain. Anciently the Free Miners kept the bread and cheese as they were thought to bring luck – something much needed by miners.

Close to Cooper's Hill, at Painswick, the church is host to a curious annual clipping ceremony. The church, which has one of the finest collections of table tombs in Britain, is also notable for the fine yew trees in its churchyard. Legend has it that there are only ninety-nine trees, and that if a hundredth is planted, one will die to maintain the same number. As the trees are such a feature, and so well maintained, it is usually assumed that they are involved in the clipping ceremony, but this is not the case.

Clipping derives from the Saxon word *ycleping* (to encircle or embrace). The children of the village encircle the church while they dance and sing hymns. The first recorded clipping ceremony took place in 1897, but this was probably the revival of an ancient tradition rather than an innovation. The ceremony, which is not unique to Painswick, takes place in September, which suggests that its origins lie in a very early pagan agricultural rite that was incorporated into the early Christian festivals.

1. GEOLOGY AND GEOGRAPHY

The rocks beneath Wales and Scotland are the oldest in Great Britain; the further south and east a traveller journeys, the younger the rocks he encounters. This is a simplification of course, as the earth movements of prehistory created a complex pattern of rock types. But it is a simplification that works, allowing the geologist to define the River Severn as a border, not just between England and Wales, but also between an area of ancient rocks and one of much younger strata. Gloucestershire, which straddles the Severn, is one of the most geologically varied counties in Britain. With the exception of the Ordovician and Permian, Gloucestershire has areas of exposed rock representing every geological period from the Cambrian through to the Cretaceous – a remarkable range within the confines of the county boundaries.

Geologically, the county can be considered as three regions, divided by the River Severn. However, they are less uniform than the strata-age model might suggest – the earth has had plenty of time to complicate the simple processes of geology.

The Forest of Dean

The Rocks Beneath

The Forest of Dean covers a relatively high, dissected plateau that lies to the west of a line linking the Malverns, May Hill and the River Severn. Geologically, this line defines the boundary between the Palaeozoic (ancient life) rocks of Wales and the Mesozoic (middle life) rocks of England. As an aside, where this boundary – which, though not a straight line, is both almost straight and very abrupt – crosses the Severn the step it creates in the river's bed is a contributing factor to the existence of the Severn Bore.

The rocks of Wales include Pre-Cambrian strata of igneous (volcanic) origin, which are among the oldest in the world. On to these, the rocks of the Palaeozoic era were laid down. Cambrian rocks, the earliest of that era, were laid down beneath a vast but relatively shallow sea, which extended from America's eastern coast to Scandinavia. Though there is a small area of exposed Cambrian strata near Berkeley, nothing remains west of the Severn.

Towards the end of the Silurian period, earth movements created St George's Land, which stretched from Ireland across Wales and through Gloucestershire to central England. To the south of this lay the inland Devon Sea. As St George's Land was semi-arid, the rivers draining into the Devon Sea brought sediments that were red-brown in colour, which led to the creation of the distinctively rust-coloured Old Red Sandstone of which the hills of the Brecon Beacons National Park are formed. Old Red Sandstone is also the base rock of the Forest of Dean, forming a ledge that encircles the raised plateau. Though there is nothing in the Dean area to compare with the glorious Old Red Sandstone scenery a few kilometres to the west, the rock does colour the soil of the ledge and was used to construct the imposing 'House of Correction' in Littledean in 1790.

Following the laying down of the sandstones, the entire area sank below the waves of a warm, clear, shallow sea. The accumulation of dead shellfish and other creatures on the sea bed formed the fossil-packed limestones of the Carboniferous period, rocks that vary in colour from white to a pink-tinged grey. The Carboniferous and Permian periods were times of significant earth movements which folded the land beneath the sea. The folding created a ridge of Silurian strata, of which May Hill is an expo-

The Devil's Chimney, Leckhampton Hill.

It is doubtful whether the poachers and other local miscreants that found themselves incarcerated in Littledean gaol found the building anywhere near as attractive as the geologists who now visit the site. No longer a gaol, the building is now the records depository of an insurance group.

sure, and ridges of Old Red Sandstone that run north-south along Dean's eastern edge. It also exposed the limestone at Symonds Yat, creating the basis for one of the most picturesque sites in Gloucestershire (and Britain).

Coal and Iron

Towards the end of the Carboniferous period, the land was lifted above the sea. The uplifted ridges caused by the earth movements created a lower-lying triangle of land into which rivers discharged on their way to a sea that now lay well to the south. The vast triangle became a swamp with luxuriant vegetation such as giant club mosses, horse-tail trees, seed and tree ferns. The poor drainage and acidic soil of the area provided exactly the right conditions for peat formation, the peat being compressed over aeons of geological time to create the coal of the Dean coalfields as well as that of the Bristol and Somerset coalfields to the south. The strata of later geological periods that overtopped the coal measures have been eroded, so the coal-bearing strata are the surface rocks across much of Dean.

Also of geological significance was the early Permian period when the area was a desert. Weathering produced iron-rich surface deposits, which were eventually washed underground

The strata of the Old Red Sandstone ridges are beautifully exposed at Wilderness Quarry on the southern end of Breakheart Hill, Mitcheldean. The 60-degree tip of the bedded rock is an impressive illustration of the immense power of the forces that shape the earth.

where they accumulated as brown haematite. On the western side of the Dean, the haematite deposits were close to the surface, while on the eastern side they were much lower. It was these accumulations of haematite, with iron contents of up to 65 per cent, which were later to be exploited by the Dean iron miners.

Rock Outcrops

The major landscape feature of the Forest of Dean is, of course, the forest itself. However, within the forest, close to Symond's Yat, there are a number of rock outcrops which are well worth visiting both to see the rocks and to

understand the context of the legends associated with them.

The Suck Stone, north-west of the village of Staunton, is a block of quartz conglomerate (a rock of the Old Red Sandstone series), which has fallen from the Near Hearkening Rocks and is, at approximately 4,000 tonnes, probably the biggest such block in Britain. The Hearkening Rocks – 'Near', close to the Suck Stone, and 'Far', closer to the Wye – are said to have been used by gamekeepers listening for poachers in the wood, hence the name. It is claimed that the concave surfaces of the rocks amplify the forest sounds, and that taps made on one rock can be heard at the other, which would have made the

THE BUCK STONE

Close to Staunton is the Buck Stone. This was once a logan and is steeped in legend. Logans are boulders which, as a result of weathering, rest so delicately on the underlying rock bed that the slightest touch causes them to rock. All logans, and there are numerous examples in Britain, were held in awe by locals and were usually thought to foretell the future to anyone wise enough to 'read' the rocking.

There are several versions as to how the stone came to be so-named. According to legend, the stone was a sacred Druid site and its name dates from the times of the Celtic priesthood. During the Roman invasion, the senior Druid dreamed that the advance of the foreign army would be halted if the creature found at the stone that morning was sacrificed to the Celtic gods. When the Druids arrived, they were horrified to find a young man sitting on the stone. The Druids explained their mission, and the young man realised that he would have to die to save the Celtic homeland from Rome. But just as the sacrifice was about to take place, a buck dashed out of the forest and leapt on to the stone. The buck was immediately caught and sacrificed, and the young man survived to become a hero of the resistance.

However, according to another story, King John who was hunting in the forest, decided to execute a member of his retinue who had displeased him. Moved by the pleading of the rest of the hunting party, he agreed not to hang the man if a fine buck was killed during the day's sport – and one duly was, close to the Buck Stone.

Today the Buck Stone no longer rocks, having been overturned by vandals (said to have been a group of London actors appearing at Monmouth) in June 1885. Though replaced in its original position, the delicate balance could not be restored. Nonetheless, the stone is still thought to be a powerful talisman: those who walk around it three times at sunrise are granted a wish, and just touching it confers luck.

The River Wye and Tintern Abbey from the Devil's Pulpit.

SYMONDS YAT

The origin of the name Symonds Yat, one of the finest and most famous viewpoints in Gloucestershire, is difficult to establish. Yat is from the Saxon *gate* (track), but Symonds could derive from Robert Symonds, the seventeenth-century High Sheriff of Herefordshire, or from seamen – there is a local story of a battle against some Norsemen who had sailed up the Wye. The Gloucestershire side of the river to the south of Symonds Yat is called The Slaughter, which would tend to support the battle story, but it is worth recalling that the Slaughter villages of the Cotswolds are named after the sloe trees that grew locally, which also seems a plausible explanation for the Wyeside name.

The view northward from Yat Rock is the highlight of the area, taking in the entirety of a huge horseshoe bend of the River Wye. Although the actual creation method of the deep-cut Wye channel is still debated, it is now generally believed that during the Pleistocene epoch (the most recent geological period, covering approximately the last 1.75 million years), the Wye meandered over a plain about 180m (600ft) higher than the present river bed. Successive falls in the level of the sea into which the Wye drained increased the energy of the water, allowing it to cut deeply into the underlying rock. This created the gorge-like valleys to the east and west of Yat Rock, beneath which, at the closest approach, only 450m (1500ft) separates the two arms of the river. What many visitors do not realise is that Yat Rock itself is pierced by a railway tunnel which, were it much larger, would offer the Wye a short-cut.

pair a good early-warning system for Welsh incursions across the Wye.

Another noteworthy rock outcrop is set high above the Wye, overlooking Tintern Abbey. The Devil's Pulpit, the most prominent feature of a Carboniferous limestone scarp edge, is so-named because the Devil is said to have harangued the monks from it as they built the abbey. This is a superb viewpoint, both of the scarp and the Lower Dolomite Black Cliff across the water.

Scowles

This scenic highlight of Dean is man-made rather than natural, but no less picturesque for that. Miners following the iron ore veins in the limestones of the Carboniferous period excavated canyons and caves in the rock, creating weird formations and sculptures known as 'scowles'. The origin of the word is unclear, but it probably derives from an ancient word for a hollow or, perhaps, for debris. West of Coleford, there is a village called Scowles, but the best examples are to be found in the Devil's Chapel area close to Bream (south of the B4231 Lydney–Bream road). Here, where the forest has reclaimed the old workings, the combination of weird rock

formations – the limestone stained red by rust from the iron-bearing haematite – and shadowing trees, is intriguing and picturesque but sinister enough to justify the name.

The Course of the Wye

The Devil's Pulpit – or, rather, the cliffs of which it forms a part – is where the Wye enters limestone country once again, having left it near Symond's Yat to traverse Old Red Sandstone. From Symonds Yat to the Severn the Wye has carved a deep gorge, most spectacularly so at the great cliffs of Wintour's Leap: the formidable Chepstow castle is built on top of a smaller limestone cliff.

The sinuous curves of the Wye between Tintern and Chepstow are examples of incised meanders where the river's meandering course has been maintained as it cut deeply into the underlying strata. Similar incised meanders are seen at Symonds Yat, but between there and Tintern, on the softer, exposed sandstone, the river's course, though incised, is much straighter.

However, all is not as it seems as a visit to Redbrook/Newland or St Briavels shows. In each case there was, anciently, a meander, but

The Devil's Chapel, the most impressive example of a scowles in Dean.

the river has cut through the short-cut between the two arms. At Redbrook/Newland, the southern meander valley is now occupied by Valley Brook, a tributary of the Wye. The old valley may be followed by public footpath from Newland to Lower Redbrook, the drop of 120m (400ft) between the two giving the scale of the depth of channel cut by the Wye since the meander was lost. The ancient St Briavels' meander is less dramatic, but equally distinct and can also be followed on foot.

The Severn Vale

The Rocks Beneath

The iron deposits of the Forest of Dean were cre-ated during the early stages of the Permian period, which brought the Palaeozoic era to an end. The Triassic period of the Mesozoic era began about 250 million years ago. Both dinosaurs and cynodonts (the ancestors of mammals) made their first appearance around this time. The rocks of the Triassic form the scenery and one edge of the boundary between the middle life rocks of the River Severn and the older rocks of Dean and the Welsh borderlands. Geologically, the most interesting Triassic rocks are those exposed by the Severn as it cuts its way through them.

The cliffs on the left bank of the river below Wainlode Hill, north-west of Norton, show the transition from the red of the oldest rocks to the 'tea green' of the youngest. The striking colours

MAY HILL

It might seem strange to include May Hill in the Severn Vale, as its height would appear to associate it with the Forest of Dean rather than the low-lying Vale landscape. Nonetheless, it is quite geologically distinct from Dean. Technically, May Hill is an 'inlier', a region of old rock set among newer ones. In this case the old rock is Silurian, the hill representing the principal Silurian rock of Gloucestershire.

May Hill is one of the most distinctive landmarks in the county, its summit topped by a pine copse, the trees of which overtop the somewhat forlorn trig point. The hill is also a wonderful viewpoint, which has now been secured by the National Trust. To the north are the Malverns; to the east, the solid wall of the Cotswold Edge. Southwards is the Forest of Dean, while to the west are the Old Red Sandstone peaks of the Brecon Beacons National Park.

are due to the rocks having been laid down when the area was a near-desert, the lack of rain allowing colourful minerals to remain *in situ* rather than to be dissolved and washed away. At Westbury-on-Severn, the Garden Cliff on the Severn's right (northern) bank offers an even more striking slice through the strata. The cliff is topped by what is called the 'Bone Bed', a black shale formed at the bottom of an enclosed, stagnant lagoon, rich in marine reptiles and lung-fish. The abundance of fossils in the shale beds gave them their name. Gastropods, fish teeth and, much more exciting, the vertebrae and teeth of ichthyosaurs and plesiosaurs are found in these beds.

The same rocks are exposed in the cliffs at Aust. Those waiting patiently for the Aust–Beachley ferry before the opening of the bridge had both time and opportunity to admire the strata beds. Nowadays, it is well worthwhile

The Severn and the long wall of the Cotswolds from May Hill.

The Garden Cliff, Westbury-on-Severn.

taking the time to view the rocks before crossing the bridge, as this fine sight is easily missed. The fragile-looking cliffs at Aust might alarm some who gaze at the massive bridge structure: in fact the bridge supports are set in the Carboniferous limestone of Aust Rock and Great Ulverstone.

Overlaying the Triassic strata, and now exposed to the east, are the rocks of the Jurassic period. These rocks, laid down when dinosaurs roamed the earth, are the predominant Gloucestershire rock – the basis of the Cotswolds, and the stone of which the beautiful villages, which are the hallmark of the area, are built.

In the Severn Vale, the first rocks of this period were laid down below a muddy sea. When exposed, this mud formed clay called Blue Lias, in which ammonites, the well-known spiral fossils, are often found. Occasionally the ammonites are 'pyritized', the fossil being replaced by iron pyrites (iron sulphide). This 'fool's gold', so-called because many are fooled into believing they have discovered the real thing, turns the fossil into something of real beauty.

The Blue Lias is best seen at Hock Cliff, on the left bank of the river near the hamlet of Fretherne (at the start of the Arlingham Loop), but recently the instability of the cliff has led to access being restricted. Here, the beds of limestone are separated by bands of clay and shale. Ammonites can be found here, together with belemnites (squid-like creatures) and gryphaea (ancient oysters).

A gryphaea from Hock Cliff. The characteristic shape of these fossils has led to them being referred to as 'devil's toenails'. In medieval times, gryphaea were powdered into whey and given to cattle as a medicine. Presumably, though the basic element was calcium rather than magnesium, the solution worked as an antacid, though quite why the gryphaea were chosen as a source, rather than any handful of the friable clay layer is a mystery. The clay itself was collected as an early form of cement and was later quarried on a commercial basis.

Ice-Age Terraces

During the Ice Ages of the Pleistocene epoch, which began about $1^3/_4$ million years ago, the ice sheets reached as far south as Gloucestershire. In the warmer periods between them, the meltwaters filled the River Severn, powering the cutting of deep channels into the underlying Triassic/lower Jurassic strata as well as broadening the river. The effect of successive periods of fast, violent flow followed by slower, gentler flow, created a series of terraces in the Severn's valley. Each terrace was coated with a layer of fertile alluvial debris and then left, quite literally, high and dry. The terraces are best seen between Gloucester and Tewkesbury, where villages such as Sandhurst, Hasfield and Apperley stand on the ancient river beds, the local land sculpted by old meanders.

Below Gloucester, the flood plain of the river is covered with the same fertile alluvial debris. The width of the flood plain is an indication of

Floods near Gloucester. The flood waters in the year 2000 were not only very high, but lasted a long time.

the ease with which the Severn floods. The largely impermeable rocks of the river's upper reaches cause a rapid run-off of rain, which is rapidly transferred downstream, seriously increasing the river's volume. In recent years, the increase in violent and unpredictable storms attributed to global warming has led to severe flooding of the land adjacent to the lower reaches of the Severn. The width and speed of the river at these times provides an indication of the conditions which led to terrace formation, though the niceties of such a lesson in observational geography are unlikely to raise much enthusiasm in those directly affected.

The Severn Vale, viewed from May Hill, is a patchwork of fields and villages – and the cathedral city of Gloucester – through which the river makes a succession of lazy, silver meanders. Most impressive of all the meanders is the Arlingham Bend. Although this may be seen from May Hill, it is better viewed from the Cinderford to Newnham road. The horseshoe meander itself, despite its elegance and form, is the product of very ordinary circumstances. In any broad plain, a river will develop a sinuous form. This may be due to a lack of uniformity of the underlying strata or a more complex process called divagation, which has to do with flow rate and river-bottom friction. Either way, once a curve has formed, the river tends to strike the outer curve bank harder than the inner, causing undercutting and a gradual smoothing of the curve and widening of the meander. Place four curves close together and a horseshoe bend is created.

The Severn Bore

The River Severn's estuary has the second highest tidal range in the world, the difference between the low- and high-tide marks reaching about 15m (50ft). Maximum tidal ranges (spring tides) occur when the gravitational pulls of the sun and moon are in phase, while minimum ranges (neap tides) occur when they are out of phase. The effect of the sun's gravitational pull is about half that of the moon, and is at a maximum at the summer and winter solstices. The highest spring tides therefore occur at the new moon in July and the full moon in March.

At those times, a tidal surge of water runs along the River Severn towards Gloucester. The narrowing of the river in the section between Sharpness and Tites Point causes the surge to well up as a 'tidal wave' of water advancing upriver against the normal downstream flow. This is the Severn Bore. Officially, the Bore develops near Frampton Sands, at the geological

The Severn Bore. Whereas a few years ago the bore was popular chiefly with spectators interested in nature's spectacle, of late canoeists and surfers have realized the potential for a free ride upstream.

step in the river bed, but the maximum height is reached between Framilode and Stonebench. The latter is a favoured place to watch not only the Bore but also those who attempt to ride it in canoes, or on surfboards and windsurfers. Minsterworth and Overbridge are also good places to view it. The Bore continues beyond Overbridge but much of the tidal energy has been dissipated by then and the spectacle is much reduced.

Though primarily driven by the sun and moon, the size of the Bore is also influenced by wind direction and the amount of water flowing in the river. At its best, the Bore can be 2m (6$^1/_2$ft) high, travelling upstream at a speed of about 16km/h (10mph). The Environment Agency has a website and also produces a leaflet, each of which give details of the year's Bores, together with star ratings for the expected display.

The Cotswolds

The Rocks Beneath

Towards the end of the Triassic period, the sea covered Gloucestershire intermittently. By the early Jurassic period, there was more consistent sea coverage. Beneath this shallow, clear sea in which corals and associated animals flourished, the limestones that form the Cotswolds were laid down. Where it is exposed, the Cotswold Edge – the distinctive, steep escarpment slope – shows the change in rock type from the clay of Blue Lias to the Jurassic limestones. There are several forms of these limestones, but the most important, in terms of creating the Cotswolds as we know them, are the Inferior and Great Oolitic limestones.

The name oolitic derives from the Greek *oion lithos*, egg stone, because of the similarity of the granular rock structure to herring roe. The creation of ooliths – the individual granules – is well understood, as the formation process is at work today in the warm lagoons of Florida and the Bahamas. Evaporation causes the precipita-

> ### COTSWOLD STONE
>
> As a result of the deposition process, Freestone exhibits fairly regularly spaced, horizontal bedding planes. There are also right-angled joints caused by tensions in the rock as it dries after deposition. This bedding and jointing allowed the rock to be extracted in huge blocks. To produce blocks suitable for building, the large blocks were split using the 'tare and feather' method. A line of holes was bored into the stone and two feathers – metal strips with one curved end – were inserted into each. The tare, a metal wedge, was then inserted between the curved feather ends. With a series of such tares and feathers, hammering of individual tares then split the block along the line of holes. Smaller blocks could actually be sawn, as the freshly dug moist stone was still soft, but rapidly developed a hard casing as it dried and weathered. The stone colour, which enhances the beauty of Cotswold villages, varies from quarry to quarry and according to the depth below the soil, but the predominant colour is a pale yellow-brown, tending to grey with age.

tion of calcium carbonate around minute fragments of broken shell and suchlike, forming a series of concentric shells. As the seawater moves, these shelled structures roll on the sea floor and become spherical. Eventually laid down as a tight-packed mass of up to 900 ooliths per cubic centimetre (14,000/cubic inch) and then raised above the sea by earth movements, the ooliths form oolitic limestone.

Limestones are permeable rocks – rocks that allow the downward passage of water. Oolitic limestone is classified as having primary permeability – the rock is porous because water can flow around the ooliths. By contrast, the Carboniferous limestone of the nearby Mendips has secondary permeability – the water flows downwards through joints, cracks and fissures in the crystalline structure. This explains why the Mendips are riddled with caves while the Cotswolds are not, though it is occasionally possible to find small, water-eaten chambers and even stalagmites and stalactites in quarried faces.

A piece of Great Oolite showing the fish-roe-like mass of oolites of which the rock is composed and which gives it its curious name.

Quarry Face, Leckhampton Hill. The face shows the variation from Freestone, at the base, to the ragstone at the top.

Inferior Oolite underlies the northern Cotswolds, reaching a maximum depth around Cheltenham where its 110m (350ft) helps Cleeve Hill attain the highest point of the Cotswolds. The best site at which to observe the rock is Leckhampton Quarry. At the base of the quarried face, the first band of the Oolite is a pisolitic limestone in which the ooliths are as large as peas (hence the name, from the Greek *pison*, pea: the common name is pea grit). There are then two bands of Freestone (Lower and Upper) separated by a thin band of oolitic marl. The name 'freestone' derives from quarrying days: it may refer either to the rock being freely available, or to its being free of fossils and therefore excellent for forming straight-edged, flat-faced building blocks. Lower Freestone was the most sought-after building stone: at Leckhampton the rock band was 40m (130ft) thick and yielded Cheltenham stone. Upper Freestone was also sought after, but was frequently a disappointment because despite being almost devoid of fossils, it was soft and friable, making it unsuitable as a building stone.

Above the Upper Freestone is a layer of ragstone, a fossil-rich rock that weathers to a very uneven – ragged – appearance, making it unsuitable as a building stone unless the knobbly texture is an advantage. Ragstone was chiefly used for dry-stone walling, a distinctive feature of the Cotswold landscape. The construction of dry-stone walls is a craft, as anyone who has tried it will know. A craftsman waller, with a good supply of stone, could erect a standard field wall from base to its vertical topping of 'cocks and hens' at a daily rate of about one chain – the length of a cricket pitch.

In the southern Cotswolds, the Inferior Oolite attains a thickness of only about 10m (35ft) and is overlaid by the Great Oolite. At the base of the Great Oolite is Fuller's Earth, argillaceous (fine-grained) clay, which was to play an important role in the development of the Cotswold wool industry. Next comes a layer of Stonesfield slate, up to 7m (25ft) thick. Stonesfield slate is a sandy limestone, rich in fossils, and though not technically a slate it has acquired the name because it was used to produce the roofing slates of Cotswold houses. Above the slate beds are layers of limestone which have formed some of the most famous building stone of the area, including the honey-coloured Bath stone.

Cotswold Roof Slate

There was a wonderful vocabulary attached to the excavation and cutting of the stone for roofing slates. Slabs of stone that occurred close to the surface were called 'presents' – they were presents from nature – but when these slabs were exhausted, and the quarrymen had to mine more deeply for the stone in excavated pits, the slabs were called 'pendle'. The excavated slabs were 'green' – still damp from the ground, and were earthed over to prevent them from drying out until the first frosts of winter. The slabs were then exposed, the frost splitting them into slates by the same process that wrecks pipes nowadays. In some villages where slate making was an important trade, the church bell was rung on frosty nights to summon all useful hands to the task of exposing the slabs.

The split slab slates were then cut to size. This was the job of the 'slatter', the man who actually excavated the slabs – the man who got the stone – being a 'getter'. The tiles came in a variety of sizes, as the tiles of a row increased in size the further the row was from the ridge. The smallest were 'cocks' or 'tants', the largest the 'long 16'. There were also 'cussems' for the eaves. These were huge and it is not difficult to trace the origin of the name when the effort to hold one in position for nailing is considered. In addition there were 'muffets' or 'muffities', 'becks', 'batchelors', 'wivutts', 'duchesses', 'countesses', 'chilts' and 'wirnetts'.

The problem with Stonesfield slates was their weight. A Cotswold roof is a vast weight of stone, requiring equally huge oak beams to support it. Ultimately, the cost of timber became prohibitive and cheaper slates from Wales and the Lake District were brought in, and then clay tiles replaced the real thing.

A Cotswold slate roof. Though very beautiful and blending totally with the stone of the walls, the vast beams needed to hold the roofs aloft eventually made such roofs uneconomic.

Looking along the Cotswold Edge and into the Severn Vale from Frocester Hill. The outlier of Cam Long Down can be seen, with Stinchcombe Hill beyond.

The Cotswold Edge

To see the true nature of the Cotswolds, any walk close to the Cotswold Edge will suffice; but better is a walk, on a clear day, to the top of May Hill. Looking south-east and east, the observer can enjoy the silvery path traced by the River Severn. Beyond the river is a solid, dark wall. This is the scarp slope of the Cotswolds, the deep valleys cut by rivers draining the upland wolds into the Severn create the illusion of hills (which leads to the often-seen, but incorrect, reference to Cotswold Hills) to a traveller heading north or south through the Cotswolds.

The dip, which slopes east from the Cotswold Edge, is very gentle, ending in the Oxford Vale. Some Cotswold rivers follow the dip towards the River Thames, though most flow west, cutting

through the scarp slope to reach the Severn. The exception is the Bristol Avon, which in its lower reaches defines the end of the Cotswold Edge. The river seems to have been imposed on the present strata after the Mesozoic rocks, on which its course began, had been eroded. The river rises to the north-east of Bristol, then flows east as might be expected, before turning south-west, then west, then north through Bath.

The Edge is dotted along its length with excellent viewpoints from which the Severn Vale, and much beyond the river, can be seen. Also in view from some points are isolated hills – Robinswood Hill, Churchdown, Cam Long Down and Cam Peak (and Bredon Hill too, though it lies over the county border in Worcestershire). These are 'outliers', volumes of rock separated by erosion from the main mass of

Old Father Thames. The Thames is the only major British river which rises in Gloucestershire. Exactly where has been a matter of debate for many years. Some favour Seven Springs, the source of the River Churn. This spot is actually the furthest from the mouth of the Thames and a local tablet inscribed in Latin adds weight to the claim. The accepted source is Thameshead, a little way south-west of Cirencester. This statue of Old Father Thames was erected at Thameshead in 1855. After years of vandalism it was moved to Lechlade where it currently resides.

which they once formed a part. A cap of resistant rock postpones erosion of the outlier itself – in each case here it is marlstone, which forms a terrace close to the base of the scarp along much of the length of the Cotswold Edge. This terrace

is discernible beneath Leckhampton Hill, but is most noticeable at Stinchcombe Hill, which is itself an excellent illustration of outlier formation. The golf course-topped hill is T-shaped in plan, the crossbeam about 1km ($^5/_8$ mile) in length overlooking the Vale; the hill then narrows to a few metres about 600m (650yd) back from the Edge. In time, this narrow piece of land will erode and a new outlier will form. In the same way as the line of existing outliers shows us the old line of the Cotswold Edge, the outlier of Stinchcombe Hill will tell our descendants where the Edge was in our time.

The Spring Line

A visitor to the Cotswolds could not fail to notice that a string of villages lie at the base of the Cotswold Edge. The water percolating down through the porous oolitic limestone of the Cotswolds eventually meets a layer of impervious clay. At this point, it reappears as a spring of

OUTLIERS

Churchdown is often called Churchdown Hill, but that 'doubles-up' its original name of *Cruc Dun* (round hill). By contrast, the name of Robinswood Hill has more recent origins, deriving from the Robins family, former owners. Cam Long Down and Cam Peak owe their names to their shape and the ancient word for 'crooked'.

In Gloucestershire legend, Cam Peak was formed when the Devil decided to dam the Severn in order to flood the county as a punishment for its high ratio of churches to acres. He loaded a wheelbarrow with earth and stones at Dursley and trundled off towards the river. He had not gone far when he was forced to pause for rest. At that point, a cobbler came striding into view, a string of old shoes around his neck. The Devil's grasp of geography was clearly poor as he asked the man how far it was to the river. Smelling a rat, the cobbler replied that he had worn out all the shoes around his neck walking from there. In disgust and dismay, the Devil overturned his barrow, forming Cam Peak.

well-filtered water with a high lime content, ideal for supplying a village. One interesting aspect of village siting is that the Romans chose sites below the spring line so that water could flow through their villas and bathhouses, while the Saxons chose the dry land above.

Dry Valleys

One final feature of the Cotswold landscape is the number of dry valleys, that is valleys that were clearly cut by rivers or streams but which no longer have active waterways. Walkers of the Cotswold Way will recognise Happy Valley, immediately south of Cleeve Common, as fitting this description. There are two theories about the creation of these geological curiosities. The first is that the valleys were carved when rainfall and the local water table (the level of underground water) were much higher; the second favours formation at the end of the last Ice Age when the frozen limestone was impermeable.

GLOUCESTERSHIRE WILDLIFE

Each year the bird watchers of Gloucestershire record over 200 species, while over 300 species have been recorded in total. This seems a huge number, yet it is hardly surprising given the county's range of habitats – forest, estuary and farmland.

The Forest of Dean is home to almost all of Britain's forest birds, including some unusual species such as crossbills and firecrests. It is famous for the peregrines which nest at Symonds Yat, where the raising of the annual brood offers an additional pleasure for visitors to the site.

The Royal Society for the Protection of Birds (RSPB) has reserves within the county, but the most famous bird site is Slimbridge, the original site of the Wildfowl and Wetlands Trust. Founded by Peter (later Sir Peter) Scott – son of the Antarctic explorer Robert Falcon Scott – just after the end of World War II, the site became world famous for its work on the conservation of endangered species, particularly the Hawaiian goose or nene. Today, countless visitors are drawn to see the famous Bewick's swans that travel from Siberia to overwinter on the site's ponds, as well as the thousands of waders that feed on the mudflats exposed by each low tide.

A recent newcomer to the county is the red kite, which has been spotted working the thermals rising up the Cotswold Edge near Cheltenham. It is to be hoped that the kites will soon become a permanent feature of the Gloucestershire landscape.

The Forest of Dean is the county's most extensive wildlife area. Fallow deer, once hunted to the edge of extinction here, have increased in numbers and roe deer are occasionally seen. Of other mammal species, perhaps the most unusual is the dormouse, though the forest is home to several of Britain's rarer bats. Many butterfly species, including the rare white admiral and grizzled skipper may also be found.

Areas of the wood are carpeted with bluebells in spring, and a surprising number of flower species thrive, including sweet woodruff and yellow archangel in older parts of the forest. There are also a number of Britain's more unusual ferns.

Elsewhere, roe deer are a more common sight than might be imagined, while the county's badger population was recently the subject of heated debate over the rights and wrongs of a cull aimed at eradicating bovine tuberculosis.

The county has numerous nature reserves for animals and plants, some administered by Gloucestershire County Council, others by English Nature and the Gloucestershire Wildlife Trust. Most of the reserves are of general interest, while others specialise in a particular species – one such is the Gloucestershire Wildlife Trust reserve close to Lechlade, which is a national centre for the study of dragonflies.

An annually updated leaflet, listing all of Gloucestershire's nature reserves, is available from the County Council.

2. Prehistory

Gloucestershire's Earliest Settlers

The Ice Age was not a single event, but a series of four advances and retreats of the polar ice caps, separated by well-defined interglacial periods when the climate of southern Britain warmed. There were also warmer times, known as interstadials, during the four periods of extensive glaciation.

Each time the ice retreated, vegetation advanced northwards. It is now believed that during the interglacial period following the second Ice Age (the Hoxnian interglacial), ancient man followed the spreading vegetation. The first steps of man on what was to become Gloucestershire occurred about 400,000 years ago, in the middle Palaeolithic period (old Stone Age). The tools used by the county's first residents were fashioned from stone. Flakes were knocked from both sides of a conveniently shaped pebble – usually of flint – to create a sharpened edge that could be used as a knife or axe. These are known as Acheulean tools, after the type-site of St Acheul, near Amiens in southern France. Though the ice of the two Ice Ages that followed the Hoxnian interglacial did not cover Gloucestershire – the county was a frozen tundra during those periods – subsequent glacial meltwaters shifted the tools left behind by the earliest inhabitants, so that nothing can be said about their distribution. There have been a dozen or so late-Palaeolithic finds in the county, all in river gravels, but little can be deduced from them.

It is conjectured that Palaeolithic man lived in the valleys, as the forests would have been filled with dangerous animals, and water was a primary resource. As well as gathering fruits and berries, he would have hunted mammoth, deer and other small prey-animals, and probably scavenged the kills of carnivores. But he was also the potential prey of sabre-toothed cats and other predators.

During the last interglacial, Neanderthals – early humans now thought to have been replaced by Cro-Magnon men – probably visited the county. However, only a very small number of Mousterian tools, the type normally associated with Neanderthals, have been discovered. Taking their name from the type-site of Le Moustier in the Dordogne area of France, the tools were distinctly triangular in shape. Of several possible examples in the county, only one, found near Lechlade, has been confirmed to be a Mousterian tool.

The humans retreated as the ice advanced for the last time, though there is evidence that King Arthur's Cave, just over the river in Herefordshire, was occupied during the early phase of the last Ice Age. Excavations of the cave indicate human habitation from around 60,000 years ago right through to the Bronze Age. Indeed, it is likely that only Kent's Cavern in Devon can claim as long a history as a shelter for man in Britain. The cave's occupants, who may well have hunted and foraged on the Gloucestershire side of the river, shared their world with the woolly rhinoceros, mammoth, bison, and Irish elk.

The Later Stone Age

Southern Britain was resettled about 14,000 years ago, at the end of the last Ice Age. The settlers crossed the land bridge linking south-east England to the continent, but as the ice retreated, meltwater raised the sea level and Britain was cut off from the rest of Europe.

The land, which was dominated by forests of pine and birch in the early post-glacial period, gradually changed to woodlands of elder, beech, elm, hazel and oak. The newcomers, peoples of

The Nympsfield long barrow.

the upper Palaeolithic and Mesolithic (middle Stone Age) cultures, left examples of their flint-work across most of the county, implying a more confident folk and a less hostile environment. The origins of the flint they used also implies a more benign world, one that allowed long-distance trade, though the people were still essentially nomadic hunter-gatherers.

About 4,500 years ago, the Neolithic (new Stone Age) era began. This period is normally associated with the start of farming, and while this is correct, it is an oversimplification. Agriculture has a long history, beginning about 9,000 years ago in India and spreading westwards across Europe. In Gloucestershire, the earliest Neolithic farmers probably shared the land with hunter-gatherer nomads and engaged in the same activities when not working on their farms. The importance of these farming settlements lies in the well-defined and archaeologically significant marks they left on the landscape. Small houses dating back to 3,500 BC have been discovered at Hazleton and Withington. At Hazleton, the site revealed not only a Neolithic house but also Mesolithic flints, suggesting a lengthy occupation of what was clearly a favourite site. The houses were about 5m (16ft) long and 3m (10ft) wide, wooden posts supporting gabled, probably thatched, roofs and walls of wattle and daub. There was an internal hearth and a midden for household rubbish. Both Hazleton and Withington were later used as burial sites.

Causewayed Camps

There are some ten causewayed camps in the county. The camps are so-named because they consisted of a series of ditches linked by short causeways – making them look like a string of sausages – and backed by a wall made of stone excavated from the ditches. The reason for this curious construction is unclear, though the most obvious explanation is defence, which was also a major siting criterion – although there were valley sites, most were on hilltops or promontories of the Cotswold Edge. The camps varied in size

– the site at Eastleach enclosed about 4ha (10 acres), while that at Down Ampney was barely one-sixth of the size.

The best understood causewayed camp is at Crickley Hill, where two parallel rows of linked ditches cut off a spur of the scarp edge to create a well-defended space. The inner, earlier row had four entranceways each with wooden gates. The second, outer, row was constructed later. It was defensively stronger and had two entranceways through the drystone wall behind the ditch. Within the ditches there were houses and a circular stone platform, presumably a ritual site.

The Neolithic people who occupied the Crickley Hill site were well placed to take advantage of the lime-rich soil of the upland Cotswolds to cultivate wheat and barley, while the rich grassland of the Severn Vale was good pasture for cattle and sheep. The beech woods of the Cotswolds were superb for pigs, which ate beechmast and rooted a soil made rich by falling leaves. Clay from the Severn Vale would have been used to make pottery, while the forests would have supplied the wood for baskets and tool shafts.

Neolithic Burial Sites

Some early Neolithic folk buried their dead in rotunda graves – distinctive, cylindrical structures, perhaps with domed tops. The rotunda beneath the Notgrove long barrow was 7m (23ft) in diameter and 80cm (2$\frac{1}{2}$ft) high. At its heart was a cist of local stone slabs, inside which were the remains of a middle-aged man. Another, much smaller rotunda, was detected below the Belas Knap long barrow.

The long barrows themselves are the most distinctive form of Neolithic burial site and the first human constructions to have recognisably altered the landscape (the ditches of causewayed camps having largely filled over the millennia, so that the untrained eye tends to miss them). Long barrows are a feature common to all Neolithic peoples and occur throughout north-west Europe, but the form of these local barrows is so particular that they have been given the specific

The horns and false portal of the Belas Knap long barrow.

classification of 'Severn-Cotswold'. Around seventy long barrows have been identified in Gloucestershire, but none have so far been found in the Forest of Dean or Severn Vale.

The Gloucestershire barrows are not of uniform design, but share common features. They are usually orientated towards the rising sun. The burial chamber consists of massive stone slabs, creating a box structure. Occasionally there are several tombs connected by a slab-formed passageway. The earth mound that gives the barrows their name is rectangular or trapezoidal, and curves at the eastern end to form two horns that protect the entranceway.

The mounds vary in length from 30–100m (100–330ft), but most are around 55m (180ft), the largest being the barrows of Colnpen and Lamborough Banks in the Coln Valley. Belas Knap mound measures 55m (180ft) in length,

with an average width of 14m (45ft) and a height of 4m (13ft). That is 3,000 cubic metres of earth, weighing about 1,500 tons. The sheer effort required to construct such a mound is staggering. Given the thin soil of the area, excavating with stone spades and antler shovels would take a very long time. If the work was just shovelling from ditch to mound, it would have taken at least 5,000 man hours – and could well have taken three or four times longer. A team of ten men might have taken six months. With settlements estimated to have comprised only a few tens of folk at most, this represents a remarkable investment of time and labour – man had certainly moved on from being a subsistence hunter-gatherer – and indicates that death (in general or, more likely, for tribal leaders) had become a momentous event, implying a belief system.

COTSWOLD LONG BARROWS

The easiest long barrow to examine is the Nympsfield site in the Coaley Peak 'park' on Frocester Hill where the mound has been stripped away. Little of the drystone walling is now original but the general layout of the barrow can be seen. Nympsfield has a single pair of side-chambers leading off the entrance passageway.

Belas Knap is a particular form of long barrow in which the apparent entrance is a false portal consisting of a massive door-slab between two uprights with a lintel that was replaced in 1863 when early excavations broke the original. Behind the false door, the remains of an adult and five children were found. Why the false portal replaced the true one is not known, but it is generally assumed to have been an effort to defeat tomb robbers or to confuse evil spirits as to the true position of the dead. Belas Knap has four true chambers, each relatively small, cut into the sides of the barrow away from the false portal. In contrast to the Nympsfield site, the drystone walling of the false portal is original. It looks remarkably similar to modern walling, the

Cotsaller's craft having lasted several thousand years.

The name Hetty Pegler's Tump derives from Hester Pegler, the wife of Henry Pegler who owned the field where the long barrow was situated. The couple, who died in the 1690s, are presumed to have taken an interest in the mound – perhaps the wife supervised an opening of it. Certainly it was opened several times – excavations in the nineteenth century revealed fragments of Roman pottery and a silver groat of Edward IV. It is believed that the site was dug over by men in search of stone, and subsequent attempts at repair have owed more to enthusiasm than to accuracy. The drystone walling of the forecourt horns is probably modern and there seems to have been movement of the upright slabs of the entrance and galleries. There may also have been some re-roofing. Despite the changes, the Tump is worth a visit. No light enters except through the ancient doorway, and water percolating through the roof plopping on to the floor makes it an atmospheric as well as an interesting site.

It is likely that the horns of the long barrows enclosed a forecourt in which rituals took place before interment – excavations have revealed animal bones and charcoal, suggesting ritual feasting or sacrifice. The entrance to the barrows was invariably constricted in some way. Was this to impede grave robbers, to stop evil spirits entering the tomb and attacking the dead, or to stop the spirits of the dead from escaping and pestering the living? We will probably never know. Usually the constriction was a standing stone, but at Windmill Tump, Rodmarton, access to the barrow was through a porthole, a hole cut in a stone slab.

Interments in the long barrows were of uncremated bodies, the dead being buried with grave goods such as beads, flint arrowheads and tools, and pottery. Little enough, but when it is recalled how few possessions the Neolithic peoples actually had, such items are a moving testament to the care taken of the dead.

For reasons that are unclear, the long barrows were eventually blocked or abandoned. Some experts believe that the settled existence of Gloucestershire's Neolithic farmers came under pressure because of poor harvests caused by climatic changes. Others blame the disruption of the established pattern of life on inter-tribal conflict.

Neolithic Ritual Sites

This final phase of the Neolithic era is associated with the emergence of sites that are not directly related to burial. Of these, the most enigmatic is the cursus – a long rectangle formed of parallel ditches and banks. The best example in the county is at Lechlade, though there is little to see at ground level – it was discovered, together with others close to Tewkesbury, by aerial photography. William Stukeley, the eighteenth-century antiquarian, coined the name for such sites because the one he investigated in

The interior of Hetty Pegler's Tump.

Dorset, which measured 10km (6 miles) – the longest in Britain – looked like a horse-racing course. As is usual in cases where the usage cannot be established, such sites are classified as 'ritual', though the nature of the rituals carried out in them is unknown and probably unknowable.

Another curious site from the same period is the long mound on Crickley Hill. This was 100m (330ft) long, 4m (13ft) wide and formed of earth. Beside it, at intervals, lay stone slabs beneath which animal bones were discovered. At each end of the mound were paved or cobbled areas, one semi-circular with a hole for a wooden post, the other circular with a large stone slab at its centre. Again the purpose of the site is unknown.

The Bronze Age

More settled times followed the apparent chaos that saw an end to the long barrow era. Burials were now in round barrows, the most spectacular of which is the Soldier's Grave on the Cotswold Edge above Frocester. Measuring 17m (56ft) in diameter, and 2m (6$\frac{1}{2}$ft) in height, the mound was found to hold a drystone walled, boat-shaped chamber holding the remains of some thirty people.

As the name would suggest, the Bronze Age was a time of transition from the use of stone to metal for tools and weapons. This was a gradual change, as the use of metal – copper rather than bronze at first — took time to spread, the earliest tools and weapons being rare and very precious items.

The Long Stone, Minchinhampton.

The early Bronze Age also marked the beginning of the megalithic ('mighty stone') culture in Britain. This is usually associated with the Beaker people who appear to have originated in the lower Rhine regions. The construction of Stonehenge and Avebury, the greatest monuments of the period to be found in Britain, is generally attributed to them. However, despite the county's proximity to these centres of megalithic culture, there are no comparable sites in Gloucestershire.

There is a henge site at Condicote where two ditches are separated by a bank. The site has a diameter of about 110m (360ft). In the nineteenth century it was claimed that the bank was so steep it could hardly be climbed, but ploughing has now all but erased it and the site can only be clearly seen from the air.

Standing stones, usually called menhirs from the Welsh maen hir (long stone), are frequent features of the British landscape. While impressive examples may be seen close to the

PREHISTORIC MYTH AND MAGIC

The enigmatic nature of many prehistoric sites has inevitably led to associations with the supernatural.

It is said that lifting children over the long stone at Minchinhampton cures them of whooping cough, and that passing them through one of the holes in the stone will protect them from rickets. However, the holes, apparently made by Cromwell's artillery, seem too small for this to be possible. One explanation is that the stone has been confused with the nearby Tinglestone in local legend. The Tinglestone itself has special powers – it is claimed that people dowsing nearby for water often suffer mild electric shocks. According to another piece of local folklore, the stone runs around when it hears a church bell strike midnight. The other long stone, near Staunton/Coleford is said to bleed if it is pin-pricked at midnight on the summer solstice.

The long barrow at Nympsfield used to be avoided as it was thought to carry leprosy. Many locals were afraid to pass close to Belas Knap at night as it was reputedly haunted. Within living memory, visitors have claimed to feel a malignant presence at the site and to have seen objects levitating.

More visual presences are associated with Money Tump, a burial mound near Bisley, which is said to be haunted by headless men. However, it is likely that vested interests lay behind the ghostly appearances. The mound is so-named because treasure was thought to be buried beneath it – many burial mounds have been excavated and standing stones felled by bountyhunters. However, a haunting by headless men would be sure to keep superstitious locals at bay and so allow the diggers to work undisturbed.

Nan Tow's Tump is said to have been named after an old woman living in a nearby house who was believed to be a witch. According to local legend, she was buried standing upright beneath the mound.

county – the Rollright Stones in Oxfordshire and Harold's Stones near Trellech across the River Wye – nothing of that presence exists within Gloucestershire's borders. There is the Long Stone at Minchinhampton, another beside the Coleford–Staunton road, and the Tinglestone near Avening. There are also standing stones near Horton and Boxwell. It is believed that some of these stones marked the entrances to late Neolithic or early Bronze Age cemeteries, but as with many monuments from the period, their true purpose is not understood. The enigmatic nature of such stones increases their appeal and it is no surprise that to some they have a sacred or ritualistic significance.

Few Bronze Age settlement sites have been found in Gloucestershire. However, there are several excellent examples of round barrows and many bronze items have been unearthed. Nan Tow's Tump, beside the A46 (on the east side of the road, a short distance north of the A433 junction) is an impressive 30m (100ft) in diameter, and 3m (10ft) high. Beech Pike Barrow, beside a minor road to Colesbourne, east of Elkstone, is of comparable size. Of the finds, two hoards revealed by ploughing, one at Bourton-on-the-Water, the other at Nottingham Hill, near Bishop's Cleeve, are the finest. The Bourton find was of axe heads, while that at Nottingham Hill included not only tools and weapons but also delicate ornaments. The elegance of design and beautiful construction of Bronze Age weapons indicate a formal or ritual, rather than a practical use.

However, these were still unsettled times, as a burial site on West Littledown Down to the south of Tormarton shows. Two young men had been buried here with little ceremony, their skeletons showing clear evidence of death in battle. One skeleton had a spear hole through the pelvis; the other had a bronze spearhead still lodged in the spine. The skeletons were radiocarbon dated to about 1,000 BC.

Nan Tow's Tump.

The landscape at this time would have looked surprisingly similar to the modern county. It is thought that much of the original tree cover had been cleared, though there was probably more true woodland than today. The common land would have been a larger fraction of the total, and the fields were divided by banks and ditches rather than hedges and walls. The road system was, of course, absent, and the centres of population smaller, but a discernible pattern of settlement was already developing.

The Iron Age

At about the same time as the two young men were killed at Tormarton, the climate of Britain was becoming colder and wetter. Upland areas became inhospitable, and farming more diffi-cult. This led to increased competition for such good agricultural land as remained – in fact, it may have been just such a territorial skirmish that led to the Tormarton deaths.

The beginning of the Iron Age in about 700BC is generally associated with the Hallstatt Celts (named after a town in Austria). Such dates are always subject to discussion and it is likely that there had been limited iron production for many years previously. This technology was brought to Britain in about 1,000BC, when there was an influx of Celtic immigrants from alpine Europe. Despite stories of their warlike nature, they seem to have been settlers rather than conquerors, a horde of bronze and iron tools discovered in Llyn Fawr (in old Glamorgan) implying peaceful co-existence and trade.

Hill Forts

Whether their insecurities were rooted in fear of civil conflict due to the deterioration of the climate or pressure from immigrants, for the first time in many hundreds of years, Gloucestershire people felt the need to defend themselves against the threat of looting and murder. The Iron Age in Gloucestershire was a time of hill fort construction, many examples of which may still be seen throughout the county.

There are two types of hill fort. The first, thought to have been used for stock or food stores, enclosed a very large area and, perhaps of necessity, made as much use as possible of natural defences to avoid the manpower necessary to dig ditches and construct banks. The enclo-

---

CRICKLEY HILL

Excavations at Crickley Hill show that there were camps on the site. The first was Neolithic (*see page 32*). The hill was then deserted for a considerable period until around 600BC when the first Iron-Age camp was completed. This was larger than the earlier one, covering some 3.5ha (9 acres), containing houses for a considerable number of people, together with livestock pens and sheds. It was surrounded by a ditch 2m (6½ft) deep and a rampart 3m (10ft) high with a fenced walkway. The entrance was a straightforward double-gate arrangement, the gates separated by a narrow passageway. It appears that this fort only lasted for between thirty and fifty years before being destroyed by fire.

The third camp was set up on the ruins, probably by reconstructing the walls of the second camp, which had not been totally destroyed. A notable new entrance was built. It was large and circular with high walls topped by fenced walkways all round. A gated doorway led into the walled circle and a second led through the rampart itself. This, as was the usual practice, made an invader turn left between staggered entrances, so exposing his unshielded right side to the defenders. This third camp was also destroyed by fire, presumably during an attack.

---

sure at Nottingham Hill, Gotherington uses the steep scarp slope to defend three sides of a natural spur of the Cotswold Edge, a double ditch/bank system completing the defences of a 49ha (125 acre) site. At Norbury Camp, to the west of Farmington, a natural slope provides adequate protection only on the south side of the rectangular site, necessitating three constructed sides. Not surprisingly, the site is smaller – 32ha (80 acres) and only a single ditch/bank was built.

The second type of hill fort was much smaller, usually less than 4ha (10 acres), and more heavily defended. It may have enclosed a small settlement or have been used as a refuge by farmers living locally.

It is worthwhile exploring what remains of the smaller Gloucestershire hill forts. The best understood is that at Crickley Hill, which has been extensively excavated. Brackenbury Ditches, between North Nibley and Wotton-under-Edge, is the one of the most complete of all, though its complex array of ditches and banks is sometimes difficult to trace on the heavily wooded Cotswold Edge. At Cleeve Cloud, the visitor can identify with the life of defenders dodging slingshots if particularly wayward golfers are at work on the nearby fairways.

The slingshot was responsible for the next generation of hill forts – the ability of attackers to hurl stones long distances required larger, more heavily defended sites with more ditches and ramparts. Again hill sites were preferred, it being easier to gain distance with a stone if slinging downhill. Of these later sites the best are Uleybury, near the village of Uley; Sodbury, between Little Sodbury and Old Sodbury; and Kimsbury on Painswick Hill – the distinctive 'bury' addition to the names being from the Saxon word for a fort. Uleybury, the interior of which is not on a public right of way, encloses 13ha (32 acres), Sodbury about half that, while Kimsbury is smaller still. Rather larger, indeed almost as large as the defended enclosures of the early Iron Age, is the Salmonsbury Fort, part of which is now occupied by Bourton-on-the-

The ramparts of the Sodbury hill fort.

Water. This interesting site is not a hill fort as it uses the rivers Windrush and Dikler as defensive barriers.

Pre-Roman Celtic Britain

In addition to the hill forts, many other Iron Age settlements have been discovered and excavated in the county. The existence of such sites suggests periods of greater stability, particularly towards the end of pre-Roman Celtic Britain. The farmers of the time grew wheat and barley and kept cattle, sheep and pigs just as their Bronze Age forebears had. The fields they cultivated can still be seen – though really only from the air. Celtic field systems have been

identified at Aldsworth and Eastleach, to name but two. There are many others: indeed, the number of such sites implies that the Cotswolds was one of the most heavily populated parts of Britain at that time.

Gloucestershire was also a very affluent area. A horde of almost 150 so-called currency bars, flat ingots of iron, was unearthed at Salmonsbury – the largest find in Britain to date. While probably not used as money, the ingots were almost certainly used for trade. Real money, that is coinage of specific size and pattern, did not arrive in the county until the immediate pre-Roman period. Beautiful jewellery has also been discovered, sometimes as grave goods. A delightful enamelled bronze brooch from Sudeley is now in the British Museum. However, the finest piece, dating from about 50BC, is the Birdlip Mirror – a flat bronze disc with a short handle inlaid with enamel.

During the 200 years preceding the arrival of the Romans, the Celtic Dobunni tribe held an area centred on Gloucestershire, and the dyke systems known as Bagendon Ditches and the Bulwarks at Minchinhampton are ascribed to the time of their control. These sites are believed to be *oppida* (main settlements) of a tribal chief. The dyke system at Bagendon seems disjointed now, but may once have linked natural defences, such as marshes and rivers, to form an enclosed area of approximately 200ha (500 acres). The Bulwarks is a more difficult site to envisage, as the remaining ditches do not seem to be completed by natural features.

What were the people who lived within, and beyond, these dykes like? The Celts had no written language, so their history may only be inferred from that recorded by others. This is not to imply, however, that they were a backward race. As Julius Caesar himself noted, the Druids (Celtic priests) considered it unlawful to commit the tribal tradition to print. Instead, they venerated the spoken word and an oral transmission of history. Many Greeks and Romans, not understanding its significance, saw the reciting of the deeds of past rulers as vainglorious boasting. However, the brilliance of Celtic

The Birdlip Mirror, one of the finest pieces of Celtic jewellery to have been unearthed in Britain. The mirror was made by the lost wax method.

rhetoric came to be respected, many Celts becoming teachers of the art.

Caesar described Celtic men as long haired and moustachioed, their bodies dyed blue with woad. He remarked upon their enthusiasm for fighting and elaborate funeral rites. The latter is certainly borne out by the exquisite nature of the grave goods discovered in Gloucestershire. However, he made no mention of their craft skills, and, rather surprisingly, maintained that the Celts did not grow cereals, living instead on a diet of meat and milk. Similar inaccuracies have led many to consider that Caesar's accounts provide only a partially accurate description of the Celts in Britain at that time.

Other Roman writers write of Britain as a thriving, prosperous country, its inhabitants skilled in the production of pottery and jewellery, linen and woollen cloth, and masters of metalwork. The British woollen cloak, called a *sagum* by the Romans, was particularly prized in the Roman capital, its wearer the epitome of fashion at the end of the millennium. It was a rich and civilised country that Caesar prospected and to which Aulus Plautius led his legions in AD43.

3. ROMAN GLOUCESTERSHIRE

Invasion

A century after Julius Caesar came to Britain, another army – four legions commanded by Aulus Plautius – came not with exploration but conquest in mind.

At one point it seemed as if the invasion was unlikely to go ahead, for there was near-mutiny among the 40–50,000 legionnaires gathered on the French coast near Boulogne (Gesoriacum). A story, probably started by a Celtic Briton, had spread among the Romans that the voyage to Britain would involve sailing close to the edge of the world, and that a slight misjudgement or the wrong wind could send the entire invasion fleet over the edge and into oblivion. The mutiny was narrowly averted and the fleet eventually sailed.

The Romans advanced inland from the fortified beachheads they created in Kent, defeating a British army in a two-day battle close to the River Medway. The Emperor Claudius arrived just before the army crossed the River Thames. He only stayed for sixteen days, but that was long enough to see the 'capital' of Britain at Colchester (Camulodunum) occupied and to accept the surrender of the British tribes. Cassius Dio, a Roman writer, recorded that one of the tribes defeated at Medway was the 'Bodunnu', which is very likely to be an inexact rendering of Dobunni. Though based in Gloucestershire, the Celtic Dobunni tribe would have had sufficient time to reach Kent.

Despite the surrender to Claudius, Britain was far from subdued. The Romans had to fight hard to secure the land, but eventually established a frontier that stretched from Devon to Lincolnshire. It has been suggested that the Romans had initially intended to do no more than secure south-eastern Britain. If so, they would have very rapidly realised that such a strategy was doomed, and the battle to subdue the Celts, initially united under the leadership of Caratacus, had to be continued beyond the frontier.

In Gloucestershire, the Roman frontier pivoted around the natural defence of the Severn, and a fort was placed on the riverbank. At that time, the river's course was a little to the east of today's channel and the fort beside it was at Kingsholm, now a northern suburb of Gloucester, set well back from the river. Though there have been excavations in Kingsholm little is known about the fort except that it seems to have been large. It would have been built of wood, the size indicating that the barracks housed a great number of soldiers, consistent with operations against the troublesome Britons across the Severn.

Kingsholm was set at the forward edge of the first Roman frontier. Behind it was a second fort at Cirencester. Coins of the Dobunni mention two kings, the later of whom was Boduoccus who was either king at the time of the Roman invasion or was installed as a puppet ruler. The other king is identified only by 'Corio' – the first few letters of his name. It is not known if he pre-dated Boduoccus or was supplanted by him when remnants of the Dobunni joined Caratacus' guerrilla struggle against the invaders. Whichever is true, it is Corio…'s name that the Romans gave to their fort – *Corinium Dobunnorum*.

The fort was strategically placed, close to the dyke system at Bagendon, a Dobunni stronghold. It was sufficiently near for the Romans, who were not yet sure of the allegiance of the Dobunni, to keep an eye on their movements without giving the impression of being an occupation force. The fort was south of the present town centre in an area bounded by The Avenue to the north, Watermoor Road to the east and

The hypocaust at the Chedworth Roman villa.

A Roman Tombstone

Excavations at Wotton, south-east of Kingsholm, unearthed two tombstones of legionnaires who were almost certainly stationed at the fort. One, to a soldier of the XXth legion, who died aged forty after thirteen years' service, has since been lost, but the other can still be admired in Gloucester City Museum. It is the tombstone of Rufus Sita, who was also forty when he died. Rufus had served for twenty-two years, his entire adult life. He is likely to have fought his way across France (Gaul) and then been part of the British invasion force. The close-combat nature of warfare in that era means that Rufus had probably seen things likely to make the blood of us modern mortals run cold and our hair turn white. He was a brave, battle-hardened, probably battle-scarred soldier, and his tombstone reflects this. The inscription notes that it was erected 'according to the terms of his will'. It shows him on horseback – he was a trooper of the VIth Thracian Cohort, a part-infantry, part-cavalry unit – trampling an enemy he is about to dispatch with his lance. If he was actually a Thracian, from the Greco-Turkish shores of the Sea of Marmara, then he died a long way from home in a cold, damp country that could hardly have been a more complete contrast to his homeland.

The tombstone of Rufus Sita.

Chester Street to the west. Southwards, it extended about halfway to King Street.

The fort was rectangular, covering about 1.75ha (4$\frac{1}{2}$ acres), defended by ditches and ramparts. The relatively small size implies a garrison of about 500 men. Two excavated tombstones suggest this was a cavalry unit – as with Rufus' tombstone from Wotton, each shows a mounted trooper riding down an enemy infantryman and dispatching him with a lance. The carving is of a much poorer quality, either due to the effects of time, or, and more likely, because the carver was not up to the standard of the Wotton master. These tombstones may be viewed at Cirencester's Corinium Museum – the Rufus tombstone is at Gloucester City Museum.

A road, Ermin Street, was built from the fort to Kingsholm. The line of this can still be traced – as it can with virtually all Roman roads in England. Ermin Street heads north-west from Cirencester, following the line of the old A417, heading arrow-straight to Nettleton, where it is forced by local geography to turn towards

Birdlip. At Birdlip, it descends to continue in a straight line through Brockworth, Hucclecote and Barnwood (the old A417 once more).

The Kingsholm fort was eventually abandoned in favour of another to the south, set on a hill overlooking the last crossing point of the Severn before its tidal reach. There is some doubt about the construction date of the Gloucester fort, but AD60 is the one most favoured by experts. The new fort was centred on The Cross, which is still the centre of the city, the crossing point of the 'gate' streets. Compared to the fort at Cirencester, it was very large, covering 17.5ha (44 acres).

The *Pax Romana* however, was still some way from being established. The rebellion of Boudicca (Boadicea) was in the same year as the fort was built, and major battles were still being fought in Wales and northern England for another two decades. As a result of the continuing conflict in Wales, the Gloucester garrison was eventually moved across the Severn to Caerleon, leaving behind a perfectly serviceable site.

Gloucester and Cirencester

When peace was established, the 'romanisation' of Gloucestershire was completed with the construction of two major towns: Corinium (Cirencester) and Glevum (Gloucester). The full name of Gloucester seems to have been *Nervia Glevensium*, the first word indicating that Gloucester was founded during the time of the Emperor Nerva (AD96–98). The second word apparently derives from a Celtic word meaning 'bright'.

Gloucester was a *colonia*, a town constructed specifically for retired soldiers. Established initially in the old fort site, it was one of only four *colonia* towns in Britain (the others being Colchester, Lincoln and, later, York) and was therefore of considerable importance. The retired soldiers who were Gloucester's first true inhabitants were each allocated space in the old barracks and land close to the fort. In time, the barracks were converted into houses, shops and

workshops and a thriving town developed. By the end of the second century there was a forum (the civic centre of Roman towns), a basilica (town hall), a theatre, and that most recognisably Roman of all buildings – a bath-house. The forum extended for about 100m (330ft) from The Cross and was about 72m (235ft) wide. South of it lay the basilica. The barracks buildings were eventually replaced by an array of fine houses, many of them boasting courtyards, mosaic floors and piped water. The houses would have had tiled roofs from the town's own tilery, each tile stamped RPG, *Rei Publica Glevum*, which can be roughly translated as Gloucester City Council. The tilery is thought to have begun production in about AD120, indicating that by this time Gloucester was a self-governing town of wealthy citizens set in an area of increasingly prosperous farmers.

Gloucester was surrounded by a high stone wall, pierced by four heavily defended gates. Stout wooden doors closed the gates, and the approach to them was overseen from lofty towers. So strongly defended were these entrances that they were to function as town gates for the next 900 years. The last section of the North Gate was (sadly) demolished in 1974. However, the base of the East Gate (which was partially demolished and rebuilt by the Normans) can still be seen through the glass canopy erected above it at the junction of Eastgate Street and Brunswick Road. Around the corner, a relief sculpture portraying incidents from Gloucester's past offers a reasonable representation of the architecture of Roman Glevum (and quite a good one of the early interaction of the Roman legionnaires and members of the Dobunni, though the latter were likely to have been better dressed).

Though Gloucester, being a *colonia*, was an important town in Roman Britain, it was overshadowed within the county by the growth of Cirencester. Though starting as a small fort, a *vicus* (civilian settlement) had been established just to the north by about AD75. This was the *civitas* (administrative centre) of the Dobunni and was laid out on an imposing scale. The basilica was almost 100m (330ft) long and 24m (79ft) wide – cathedral-like in size and appearance. The building was faced with Purbeck marble, which suggests a very prosperous town considering the abundance of local building stone. Ultimately, Cirencester became the second largest town of Roman Britain (after London), and was the capital of *Britannic Prima* when the country was divided into provinces in the fourth century (the others being *Britannia Secunda*, capital at York; *Flavia Caesariensis*, capital at Lincoln, and *Maxima Caesariensis*, capital at London).

Cirencester's defences were not built until the second century, when a ditch and bank were constructed. Entrance to the town was through gates – the Verulamium (St Albans Gate) gave access to the Fosse Way heading north-east, while on the opposite side of the town the Bath Gate gave access to Fosse Way heading south-west towards Bath (*Aquae Sulis*). There would also have been gates on Ermin Street that headed north-west to Gloucester and south-east to Silchester. The Fosse Way gates were stone-built and protected by stone towers, but the earthen defences were not reinforced with stone walls until the third century.

On the north-western side of the basilica was the forum. It measured 108×68m (355×223ft) and was surrounded on all sides by a colonnade. The stone for the forum, and for many of the town's shops and houses, came from a quarry beyond the Bath Gate. Using the hollow produced by quarrying, the Romans created the town amphitheatre by building steep oval banks on which small stone walls were set to create seating. The amphitheatre was 49m (161ft) along its long axis and 41m (134ft) across, and, it is estimated, could seat up to 8,000 people. There is no documentary evidence about the games the citizens enjoyed, but it is known that gladiators were brought to Britain so it is possible that the occasional bloodthirsty spectacle took place. Today the banks of the oval still rise to an impressive 7.5m (25ft).

Cirencester was laid out on the typical Roman grid pattern. Streets were metalled and cambered to allow water to drain into gullies, and lined with shops fronted by arcades so that shoppers and the shop goods were protected from the elements. The houses, occasionally extremely grand houses, were built and decorated in the finest Roman tradition. Some even had their own bath-houses, fires warming the water for a hot bath that would be followed by a cold plunge. Many houses also had underfloor heating – the sophisticated heating system, the hypocaust, funnelled the warm air from a fire outside the house through an array of pillars supporting the floor.

Little of Roman Corinium remains in place. The amphitheatre still stands, together with a good section of the north-east wall in Abbey Grounds park. This wall section includes a square tower, built in the third century when the earthen defences were reinforced, polygonal bastions having been added in the fourth century. But if the remains *in situ* are sparse, the excavated remains, particularly the mosaic floors of the houses, are a reminder of the richness of the Roman Empire.

The Corinium Museum

Roman Corinium is now submerged below modern Cirencester, but at various times during the last 250 years, building work has uncovered the mosaic floors of Roman houses and commercial premises. The *Hunting Dogs* mosaic, found in 1849 during work in Dyer Street, is perhaps the most significant as it led to the foundation of the Corinium Museum in 1856. This award-winning museum houses not only most of the more important finds from the town, but also features tableaux that re-create life in Roman Corinium.

The *Orpheus* mosaic, discovered close to the town at Barton Farm, includes a superb depiction of a tiger. However, the best known is probably the *Hare* mosaic, discovered as recently as 1971. The centrepiece of the work is a delicately rendered hare, surrounded by delightful scrollwork and geometric patterns. The top panel of the mosaic, as displayed, is actually inverted relative to the as-found floor. Such is the quality and distinctive style of the mosaics (now known as the Corinian school) that a master craftsman must have had a workshop in the town, supplying floors for local villa owners.

The Corinium Museum contains much of interest, and also one item which suggests that Christianity had reached the town at a very early date. After Christianity became the official religion of the Empire in 312 it is known that Britain sent representatives of the Christian church to a meeting at Arles in Provence in 314. It has been conjectured that someone from Corinium was among these representatives, though there is no evidence to support this. But what is believed to be an early Christian symbol was discovered scratched into wall plaster uncovered in Victoria Road in 1868.

```
R O T A S
O P E R A
T E N E T
A R E P O
S A T O R
```

The symbol is a word square or acrostic, which reads the same left, right, up or down. Translated it means 'the sower Arepo holds the wheel carefully', which is meaningless. The acrostic may be just a clever play on words, but if the letters are rearranged it becomes:

```
A           P           O
            A
            T
            E
            R
PATERNOSTER
            O
            S
            T
            E
A           R           O
```

Spelling 'Paternoster' twice in the shape of a cross and leaving A and O – Alpha and Omega,

the beginning and the end. It is difficult to know what conclusions to draw, but it seems unlikely that this could be mere coincidence.

Roman Villas

The Roman villa was a farm with outbuildings, individual villas ranging from small farms to elegant country houses and their estates. Cirencester was at the heart of a county studded with a large number of villas, many more than were found around most other towns of Roman Britain. This could be because the Dobunni were quick to exploit the desire of rich merchants to move into this developing area at the edge of the Empire, or, because then as now, the Cotswolds was rich farming land.

The remains of some forty-five villas have been identified, the best of which is one near Chedworth. Beautifully set in the woodland to the north-west of the village, the Chedworth villa is one of the finest in Britain. It was discovered in 1864 when a gamekeeper noticed that debris thrown up by burrowing rabbits included tesserae, the small stones used to construct a mosaic. Excavations revealed the remains of a thirty-two-room villa, the rooms arranged around two courtyards, the outer one at a lower level. The villa had two baths – one for dry heat, the other for steam – and the hypocaust can still be seen. However, the unquestioned highlight of the site are the remains of several mosaics. Each corner of the mosaic in the west wing includes a representation of one of the four seasons. 'Summer' is depicted as a well-fed figure of plenty – a sharp contrast to 'winter', where a cloak-shrouded figure clutches a hare for the evening meal and a branch for the fire. Chedworth Villa is owned by the National Trust and open to the public.

The only other county site that may be viewed is the villa at Great Witcombe. The exterior may be viewed at any reasonable time, the interior only by appointment. The villa is of unusual design, in part because the builder had to allow for springs at the site that, while supplying running water, made foundation work awkward.

The final design, as suggested by the ground plan, involved a porticoed corridor or gallery linking two large wings of family rooms. Heading off the gallery was an octagonal room, believed to have been a family shrine. Rather more elegant than Chedworth, Great Witcombe would have been a marvellous home, the splendour of its design matched by its position – backed by the wooded areas of the Cotswold Edge and overlooking the Severn Vale.

There are so many villa sites in the county that it would be impossible to detail each individually. However, some are worthy of note. A small settlement site at Dorn, to the north of Moreton-in-Marsh, has caused considerable interest among scholars as it appears to have been well defended, yet is set off the Fosse Way. It is believed to have been the home of officials who collected taxes from the locals: then as now, it would seem, such officials were unpopular. A much bigger settlement has been investigated near Kingscote, on the Dursley–Tetbury road. Again this lies off a major road, but it is known that the Romans also had a system of minor roads, so perhaps it was served by one of those. The Kingscote site is large, about 30ha (75 acres), and was almost certainly a village of farmers. Unlike the Dorn site, it was undefended and has buildings that appear to have been barns and a mill. The beautiful mosaic lifted from the floor of one of the Kingscote houses can now be seen in Cirencester's Corinium Museum.

Of the villas, rather than settlements, that at Spoonley Wood near Winchcombe deserves mention. Like Great Witcombe, it has two wings and a gallery (though not in the same pattern), but differs in having no direct access between the wings. This strange arrangement might suggest a grown child having taken over a wing as a separate home, while still helping on the farm. There are other good sites at Hucclecote and Frocester, but the most interesting of all is at Woodchester – a site that can no longer been seen.

The Woodchester villa may more appropriately be called a palace – on excavation, sixty-four rooms were identified arranged around three courtyards. It is most famous for its mosaic pavement, a square with sides of 14m (46ft), the

MOSAICS

One of the dominating features of Gloucestershire's villas are the mosaics that cover the floors of the living areas. Mosaics were first found in late first-century Roman Britain, examples found in Gloucestershire dating from a little later when the Corinian school of mosaic artists was at work in the county.

The basis of any mosaic was the tessera, a cube of stone or brick, different types of stone or clay being used to give a limited range of colours. Extra or bolder colours could be created by using glass or pottery fragments. The designs for mosaics were created as patterns – the similarities between the Orpheus pavements from Woodchester and Corinium, and in the overall form suggest that the Corinian artists worked from a limited number of basic designs.

There are thought to have been two methods of construction. In the first, the basic pattern would be drawn on to the fresh substrata (a lime mortar) at the site. On-site working required the tesserae to be made at the site as the design sometimes required non-standard sizes. The piles of tesserae debris found during excavations indicate that this was the preferred procedure. The alternative was to create the whole floor at the studio as a series of manageable sections that were then laid at site to complete the work. This had the advantage of studio working, but the disadvantage that joining the sections could reveal discontinuities in the design.

It is believed that the finest work of the Corinian mosaic school was in the fourth century, a time when Roman Britain was extremely prosperous and great works could be commissioned. The mosaics at Chedworth, the Woodchester pavement, and almost all the works in the Corinium Museum date from this time.

The engraving of the Woodchester pavement which Samuel Lysons made for his book, published in 1797. The centrepiece of the pavement is thought to have been a fountain, its water fed by lead piping, the theft of which may have caused initial damage. Later damage was caused by grave digging. The shaded sections of the pavement were assumptions made by Lysons as to the original design.

largest mosaic so far discovered in northern Europe. It was known to exist in the late seventeenth century, but was not completely uncovered until 1794 when the antiquarian Samuel Lysons revealed its size and beauty to an amazed world. At its centre was a figure of Orpheus playing his lyre, the figure breaking into a surrounding circle of birds. Beyond a patterned circle was another of animals, this arrangement of circles being set in a large square of geometric forms. It is estimated that 1.5 million tesserae were required to complete the masterpiece. The size and fragility of the pavement meant that raising it was impossible and it was re-covered to preserve it. Although uncovered at irregular intervals since, there are currently no plans either for its permanent display or for a temporary unearthing. A full-size replica has been constructed and is occasionally on show in the county.

Roman Dean

It is almost certain that the iron ore of Dean was worked in pre-Roman times – indeed, it is probable that Celtic tribes trading locally-produced iron was what first alerted the Romans to the area's potential. However, it was the Romans who, typically, extracted the ore in a more systematic way. By the second century, Roman iron production had been moved from its original centre in Sussex to Dean.

Although the scowles at Devil's Chapel are believed to be Roman in origin, there is little direct evidence for Roman iron mining in Dean other than the circumstantial evidence of a road system. There were Roman villas at Littledean, Mitcheldean, Lydney and St Briavels, and a road certainly headed west from Gloucester towards Mitcheldean. Another Roman road ran parallel to the Severn linking Chepstow (Striguil) to Lydney, passing through Littledean to reach Mitcheldean and then continuing to Ariconium (near Weston under Penyard), just over the county border in Herefordshire.

There must have been a strong incentive to drive a road through the forest and iron ore extraction was the probable reason for doing so. Side roads deep into the forest lead off from Dean Road and hordes of Roman coins have been found close to mining sites in the Dean. Ariconium itself was a major town where, it is believed, the Dean iron was fashioned into tools

The Dean Road. Cobbled sections of the road are still visible beside the modern road near Blackpool Bridge, though as they are partially hidden in the grass and somewhat unprepossessing they are often overlooked. The Roman road system in Britain is often cited as evidence of the advanced culture of the Empire and while that is true and that it also assisted in (relatively) rapid troop movements, the Romans also expanded the use of rivers for the carriage of goods. An interesting statistic on the use of roads for commercial traffic is that a half-ton load carried along a road had doubled in price after 500km, a strong incentive to look for alternatives.

and weapons. A section of the original Dean road is still visible near Blackpool Bridge, a little way south of the Dean Heritage Centre.

Roman Temples

The religion the Roman conquerors brought with them was the 'state religion' of a pantheon of gods headed by Jupiter. As Romano-Britain developed, the gods of the Britons were incorporated into this religion, sometimes being equated to, or associated with, the classical gods, but occasionally as gods in their own right.

At Lydney, within the ramparts of an ancient hill fort in Lydney Park, a temple was erected to Nodens, the Celtic god of hunting and healing. The temple itself was rectangular, measuring 24 × 18m (79 × 59ft) and housed three shrines. Nearby, a series of linked buildings that formed a residential complex and bath-house were grouped around a large courtyard. It is thought that the complex was for the accommodation of travellers arriving to worship or sacrifice at the temple, and also for the sick seeking help from Nodens. A number of votive offerings have been unearthed, as have a large number of coins, which reinforces the 'hotel' nature of the complex. One of the offerings, a bronze sheet with a letter-punched inscription notes that 'Flavius Blandinus, drill instructor, gladly fulfils his vow'.

The temple is believed to have been built around AD350, which is interesting as it means that some fifty years after the adoption of Christianity by Constantine and the representation of the British church at the Council of Arles, the old religion was still thriving in Britain.

Other temple sites have been excavated at Wycomb and Bourton-on-the-Water, and there is also a site close to the Chedworth villa.

Life in Roman Gloucestershire

Life in Roman Britain was well ordered. The country was divided into *civitates* (areas of local government). Most of Gloucestershire fell into *Civitas Dobunnorum* (land of the Dobunni), with its capital at Cirencester. The exact nature of the governance of the *civitas* is not well understood, but seems to have comprised an *ordo* (ruling council), headed by two or three pairs of executive officers who acted as magistrates and controlled local finances. One of these officers was the chairman of the *ordo*. The *civitas* was divided into *pagi* (tax districts).

Although many of the people living in Cirencester were Dobunni, there would also have been some from other parts of the Empire. Gloucester, as a *colonia*, comprised old soldiers together with merchants and craftsmen from all over Europe who had moved to Britain to seek their fortunes or escape their pasts.

The Romans improved the transport system, the existing 'roads' being little more than muddy tracks. Planned by military engineers and built by soldiers, the well-drained gravelled roads (only the important ones were paved) are legendary. Fosse Way is traceable throughout its journey across Gloucestershire, from Bath to Cirencester and north through Stow and Moreton. For much of that distance it is still the basis of a major road. Where it is not, south of Kemble, it can still be followed and forms the county boundary.

It was along these roads that much of the trade which made Roman Britain prosperous travelled. By the early fourth century, Britain was one of the wealthiest places in the Empire, and it is from this period that the great villas date. Roman Britain continued to prosper after the barbarian hordes had begun to chip away at the Empire in mainland Europe. The Picts and Scots invaded in AD367, but were beaten back without doing much damage.

However, the European threat meant that the army maintained in Britain was eventually withdrawn to Gaul. In AD408, soon after the withdrawal, Britain was threatened by the Saxons. Realising that an appeal to Rome for assistance would fall on deaf ears, the Celtic leadership expelled Roman officials from the country, effectively making a unilateral declaration of independence from the Empire. In AD410, the Emperor Honorius wrote to the British and acknowledged the reality of the loss of the province by advising them that they should organise their own defence. Still Roman in outlook and habit, Britain was on its own.

4. The Saxons and the Birth of Gloucestershire

The Saxons in Britain

Gloucestershire in the late Roman period was a prosperous place, the shire folk rich enough to build large, expensive villas and to furnish them in equally lavish style. The retreat of the Empire and banishment of Roman officials had a serious economic impact, as the prosperity depended on the trade and civic order the Romans had been fundamental in maintaining. But those difficulties alone would not explain the steep decline in prosperity, nor why the Romano-British population decreased by almost three-quarters in the fifth and sixth centuries. Although the Saxon invasion is often held to blame, it is unlikely that they could have arrived in sufficient numbers to annihilate such a sizeable portion of the population. Admittedly, the Saxons had formed a section of the barbarians who threatened Rome's gates, and they were less economically and culturally sophisticated than the Romano-British people, but they were not a murderous pagan rabble.

Whatever caused the decline in population and prosperity, the theory that the remaining inhabitants of Britain reverted to the tribalism of their Celtic ancestors is given credibility by the famous story of Vortigern. Vortigern, whose name means leader or warrior king, was a Celtic leader in the early fifth century. It is said that under pressure from a more powerful leader to defeat a rival tribe, Vortigern employed Jute mercenaries from mainland Europe led by the brothers Hengist and Horsa. The Jutes came from what is now Jutland (north Denmark) and were one of the three tribes that were to become the new rulers of Britain. The others were the Angles, from Angeln (southern Denmark) and the Saxons of northern Germany. Though the invaders are often referred to as Anglo-Saxons, it is Saxon that has become the shorthand name for the period and the newcomers, even though it is not clear what the Saxons actually called themselves.

It is likely that Saxons were living in Kent even before the Romans departed, though in tolerably small numbers, peacefully co-existing with their neighbours. However, the Jute mercenaries, once paid off for their work, would have needed land of their own in order to survive if they did not go home. This is almost certainly the reason for the early clashes between the Saxons and the existing population. Having secured a bridgehead in Kent, they would have invited family and friends to join them. This increased local tension and led, inexorably, to a western migration of the Saxons. Vortigern had discovered, as many later would also, that the problem with invited armies is that they stay.

King Arthur

The western march of the Saxons was halted in the early years of the sixth century by a shadowy figure – Arthur. It is probable that Arthur existed – though not, of course, as the romantic king of legend – but facts about him are few. Though Gloucestershire legend has it that he was crowned king of Britain at Woodchester, he was not, in fact, a king but a *dux bellorum* (warlord).

Arthur's most famous victory was at Mount Badon in the early sixth century, a battle that halted Saxon progress for a generation. But then Arthur fell victim to the internecine feuding that did the Celts so much damage and he was killed at the Battle of Camluan together with Mordred (his renegade nephew in most versions of the tale).

The Harrowing of Hell, Bristol Cathedral.

The whereabouts of Mount Badon has been debated for centuries, but expert opinion favours the Wiltshire Downs – the Ridgeway being an obvious route for an invading army as it allows the invader to hold the high ground. Liddington Castle is now thought to be the most likely site. Camluan is trickier as 'cam' is an ancient word for crooked and was frequently applied to rivers and land features. Cam Long Down or Cam Peak have been suggested – as it is said that Arthur camped the night before the battle on the west bank of the Severn and that the battle took place at noon, the idea has some merit, but it must be remembered that the sources for the Arthurian legend are sparse and occasionally dubious.

THE DARK AGES

What exactly happened in the fifth and sixth centuries is still debated, with new theories being proposed at regular intervals. It was recently suggested that an eruption of Krakatoa in about AD535 caused a dust cloud to block out the sun. The Roman Procopius noted that for a whole year the sun was no brighter than the moon. Such a 'nuclear winter' would mean poor harvests, leading in turn to starvation, epidemics and a general breakdown of society. The Roman, Aztec and Mayan civilizations all ended at about this time.

Those who are sceptical about such catastrophe theories suggest that Romano-Britain's decline in prosperity and decrease in population was due to a combination of circumstances. As trade with Europe all but ceased, wealth declined. No new coins were minted and the money supply ended. As the rich became poorer, the artisans supplying them with luxury goods became jobless. Raids from the Picts in the north and from across the sea plundered the diminishing wealth. It is also possible that plague may have depopulated the country.

Some or all of these factors could have led the population to revert to the tribalism of their Celtic ancestors, forming small, belligerent tribes who were individually too weak to counter a Saxon invasion.

The Battle of Dyrham

With Arthur dead, the Saxons could pick up their spears and head west again. The *Anglo-Saxon Chronicle* for the year AD577 records that 'Cuthwine and Ceawlin fought against Farinmail, at the place called Dyrham, and they captured three of their cities, Gloucester, Cirencester and Bath (Acemanes)'. Behind this simple sentence lie events that shaped England. Details of the battle are limited, but it seems that Ceawlin, King of the West Saxons (or Wessex as it became known), cut the Cirencester–Bath road and camped in the hill fort on Hinton Hill, which forced the Celts to act.

Perhaps they attacked before being sufficiently prepared – whatever the reason for the defeat, it had profound implications. The Celts became divided, some being pushed back into Cornwall, from where many migrated to found the 'mini-Britain' of Brittany. Others were eventually forced into Wales, where the rugged terrain and intemperate weather enabled them to resist further advances. Though other English battles are more famous, the importance of this sixth-century battle in southern Gloucestershire should not be underestimated.

Although there is no memorial at the site, the hill is worth visiting to see the ancient strip-lynchet field system. The lynchets, literally 'low banks', were terraced slopes used for cultivation and may be either Saxon or medieval in origin.

Saxon Gloucestershire

Although the Forest of Dean remained an independent Celtic area, and there would have been Celts living in the Saxon-controlled towns and villages, Gloucestershire was a Saxon county at the beginning of the seventh century. The Saxons renamed Gloucester and Cirencester, adding *ceastor* (a walled place or fort) to the Roman names of Glevum and Corinium so that they became Gleaceastor and Corinceastor.

Burials sites from the period – mainly found in the eastern Cotswolds – tell us much about the new settlers. They were pagans, worshipping

This brooch, from a burial site at Lechlade, belonged to a young woman of about eighteen. Her jewellery also contained a circle of glass beads which had held her hair back, saucer brooches at each end of a string of amber and blue glass bead strings, silver rings on her fingers, bronze dress pins, a bone comb and an ivory ring which probably closed the neck of a cloth bag. Inspired by the richness of these goods, the excavators named her Mrs Getty!

COTSWOLD

The derivation of the name 'Cotswold' is disputed, but one plausible suggestion is that in Saxon times a man named Cod (it would have been pronounced 'code'), established a farm above Winchcombe, near the source of the Windrush. In time, the place became known as Cod's Wold (Cod's high land). Not only the land bore his name, local villages also reflected his importance in the area: Codswell, Codestan (now Cutsdean) and Naunton Cotswold (which has now dropped the second part of its name).

The name Cotswold was originally used only for the area of land near the source of the Windrush, but gradually it came to encompass more and more of the wolds. By 1791 we hear that Bisley, a little north of Stroud, was 'the last parish of that division of the county (Gloucestershire) called Cotswold'. Eventually, the name was used to describe all the scarp-top land from Chipping Campden to Wotton-under-Edge, where the Southwolds took over. However, since there is no break in the geology and only a slight, but significant, change in scenery, the Cotswolds is now taken as the name for all the uplands as far south as the Avon valley at Bath.

a collection of gods that, according to their mythology, created the Saxon race and controlled natural events. Woden was the supreme god; Tui, the god of war; Thunor, the god of thunder; and Frig, the mother goddess. These gods have come down to us as the days of the week – Wednesday, Tuesday, Thursday and Friday – and are coincident with the Norse gods, just as the Roman and Greek pantheons were (more or less) identical. The Saxons also had a moon goddess called Eostre whose feast was absorbed in the Christian calendar as Easter.

The grave goods of the Saxons reveal a highly artistic people. The finest objects, such as the Sutton Hoo helmet and the Kingston brooch, are from elsewhere in Britain, but some of the Gloucestershire graves have yielded beautiful pieces. A square-headed brooch and a gilt-bronze belt buckle decorated with a garnet slab

were excavated at Fairford, the largest Saxon cemetery found in the county to date. A number of 'saucer' brooches (gilt brooches, named after the shape) were discovered at the same site. These finds are now in Oxford's Ashmolean Museum. Both the Fairford cemetery and another at Lechlade have also yielded items in glass and amber, together with domestic utensils such as cauldrons and bowls.

The Saxons may have taken over the Roman houses they found locally, but they were not skilled builders and it is likely these establishments soon fell into a state of disrepair. The Saxons lived a more frugal life, erecting *grubenhäuser* (sunken huts). These houses are thought to have been suspended above excavated oblong pits to prevent the wooden floors from rotting. Horizontal poles would have supported both the roof and walls of wattle and daub. A central fire was used for cooking and to provide warmth, the smoke percolating outwards through the thatch keeping vermin in check. Though wooden and thatched – and therefore far removed from the stone-built, tile-roofed Roman villas – these houses would have been very comfortable. Lack of sophistication should never be mistaken for a primitive lifestyle – it is worthwhile remembering that the people who lived in these huts produced *Beowulf*.

Both sexes wore tunics; long ones for the women, short for the men, who also wore leggings in winter. The fashion in hair length varied. At the time of the Norman Conquest, men had shoulder-length hair, which led to much ridicule from the close-cropped Normans who considered them effeminate.

The Saxons worked the land, growing barley, oats, wheat and rye, vegetables and some fruit. The vast quantities of apple pips found at some sites suggest the use of apples to produce cider. There were also vineyards, particularly in the Severn Vale. They used crop rotation to preserve the fertility of the soil, fields lying fallow every second or third year. Cattle would have grazed the fallow field, manuring it at the same time. Later, the Saxons also farmed sheep, particularly on the Cotswolds – forerunners of the indus-

Cleeve Common. The common is one of the last pieces of common land – original high wold – on the Cotswolds. Cleeve Hill is also the highest point of the Cotswolds. The hill is topped by an Iron Age hill fort, its ramparts adding to the man-made hazards of the golf course. Where, perhaps, Celts once dodged the slingshots of invaders, walkers on the Cotswold Way must now be equally wary of mishit golf balls.

try that was to make the area both rich and famous. They fished salmon and eels from the Severn and built the county's first water mills. If the Romans laid the foundations of a road network that remained unchanged for almost two millennia, it was the Saxons who created a landscape that was still discernible at the start of the Industrial Revolution.

Though the major tree clearing of the Cotswolds and Severn Vale probably occurred before the Roman invasion, the use of the *leah* suffix on many Gloucestershire place-names implies that there were still substantial areas of woodland. *Leah* means a woodland clearing and has produced innumerable county names ending in '-ley' – Alderley, Coberley, Horsley, and so on.

Woodland was a critical resource for the Saxons – not only were their houses made of wood, but it was their only fuel. Large areas of old woodland still existed – Kingswood in the south of the county and Wychwood on the Oxfordshire border – and these were protected by local lords. The Forest of Dean was also still largely uncleared, great oaks from the wood being used in many major construction projects.

Division of Land

Land was divided into plots called 'hides'. A hide was nominally sufficient to provide a living for a single family. There is some suggestion that it might have been related to the area that could

MOOT POINTS

One aspect of Saxon life that has bequeathed us a phrase is the use of moot stones or points. These natural or erected stones where the locals would gather to discuss issues of concern or to hear proclamations were the original moot points – meeting places for discussion, argument or debate. One such point is the Kiftsgate Stone, close to the road near Dover's Hill. 'Gate' was the Saxon word for a track, so this stone stood on the 'chief's track', a reasonable place for a meeting point. Another moot point is the Tibblestone at the Teddington Hands crossroads, the junction of the A435 and A438 to the east of Tewkesbury. The name here derives from Theobald, an early landowner.

The Tibblestone.

be ploughed by an ox team in a day, but it does not seem to have been that precise. The land needed to satisfy a family's needs depended on its fertility and usefulness – a large expanse of swamp was of less value than an acre of fertile soil. However, the average area of a hide seems to have been about 15–50ha (30–125 acres).

All land was leased from the king, rents payable in farm produce and service in his army. A family usually held *folkland*, which could only be passed to a child; while a more important member of society might have *bookland*, which was held by charter and could be disposed of in any way approved by the king. Buckland, a spring-line village at the foot of the Cotswold Edge in the north of the county, was once bookland. Leases suggest that the king frequently collected rent in ale, and vast quantities of it at that.

The land occupied by one hundred families – a nominal rather than an exact number – was called a 'hundred' and was the main sub-division of a shire, a Saxon term. When the Normans invaded they brought their own word – *counte* (county). The two were synonymous for almost a thousand years until the reorganisation of county boundaries in 1974 created shire and metropolitan counties.

Gloucestershire folk enjoyed the benefit of access to the River Severn. The Severn was one of England's major fisheries, fish being caught by basket-traps (butts) or nets and wattle-fences, systems that survived into the nineteenth century.

The Hwicce and the Rise of Christianity

In AD628 there was another critical battle in Gloucestershire when the armies of the two Kings of Wessex, Cwichelm and Cynegils, were defeated by Penda, King of Mercia at Cirencester. Penda was to become ruler not only of Mercia, but also of Northumbria, a kingdom that encompassed England from the Thames to Hadrian's Wall. Under him there were minor ruling houses, one of which was called the Hwicce. The Hwicce controlled Worcestershire, south-western Warwickshire and Gloucestershire (apart from the Forest of Dean). The Wychwood villages just over the eastern county border in Oxfordshire take their names from the Hwicce, as does the surrounding area of Hwicce Wood.

According to Bede's *Ecclesiastical History of the English People*, published in the eighth century, by the time of the Battle of Cirencester, the kings of Kent, Essex and East Anglia had already been converted to Christianity. The growth of Christianity was attributed by Bede to the work of the missionaries sent to Britain by Pope Gregory under St Augustine. However, Bede's version of events does not allow for the likely survival of Christianity among the Celts. It is worth remembering that though the Saxons ruled the land, they represented only about 10 per cent of the population at first, and although many Celts moved west, some stayed and were assimilated into Saxon society. Despite the battles for supremacy between rival Celtic and Saxon lords, the 'ordinary' folk of both races probably lived in relative harmony. Therefore, it is likely that the Saxon conversion to Christianity was as much to do with the influence of the Celts as any later Roman missionaries.

The survival of Christianity is attested to by Bede who notes that St Augustine met with bishops from the 'nearest British province' at 'Augustine's Oak on the border between the Hwicce and the West Saxons'. This place has not been positively identified, some experts believe it to have been Aust, beside the Severn, while others favour Down Ampney. The British bishops would have come from the still-Celtic kingdoms west of the Severn where Christianity flourished. The kingdoms had become a home to many religious hermits – the early Celtic saints had established hermitages or monastic cells called *llans* from where they preached. These early Christian establishments are the reason why so many Welsh villages have the 'Llan' prefix and is also the derivation of Lancaut where St Cewydd had his cell. The church at Oldbury-on-Severn, though built by the Normans and rebuilt by the Victorians, is not only dedicated to a Saxon

saint, St Arilda, but almost certainly stands on the site of a Celtic church as the Celts favoured hilltop situations. Many other places throughout the kingdoms, including St Briavels, were named after early Celtic saints. The absence of Saxon burial or ritual sites indicates the early conversion of any Saxon incomers to these Christian communities.

Once converted, the Saxons embraced Christianity with enthusiasm. At first the form of Christianity was that of the Celtic saints, but following the Synod of Whitby in AD663 and the Council of Hertford in AD672, the English church became Roman.

Minster Churches

The Christian kings of the Hwicce built a number of monastic houses or churches, known as minsters, within their kingdom. The minsters tended to be headed by members of the ruling classes, both males and females being eligible for the position. Occasionally, if both a son and a daughter needed to be accommodated, a double minster would be built, two houses close together. In Gloucestershire there were double minsters at Gloucester and Withington.

A minster would have a religious teacher who was priest to all those who lived within his parish. The parishes were large – they roughly corresponded to hundreds (*see* page 58) – and at first there were only the minster churches, so the priest had to tour his parish and carry out his duties at specific points where the locals would gather. Such places would be identified by a cross, known as a preaching cross. Lypiatt Cross, on a minor road linking Bisley with Stroud, is the only preaching cross remaining in Gloucestershire. Only the shaft remains, its carved biblical figures barely discernible, eroded away by the 1,200 years since it was first erected. The cross almost certainly first stood at the crossroads a little way north-east and may also have been the hundred's moot point. It now marks a boundary of Bisley parish, which explains the 'BP' that has, sadly, been carved on it.

The Lypiatt Cross.

chapels and another storey, the porch becoming a tower. The rough nature of the building work – coarse stone mixed with areas of herringbone work, adds to the appeal of this marvellous building. The tenth-century, triangular-headed windows in the tower that overlooks the nave date from this enlargement and are believed to be the finest late-Saxon windows in any British church. The ninth-century Saxon font, rediscovered in the nineteenth century after serving time as a horse trough, is similarly acclaimed. The wonderfully aggressive animal heads on either side of the nave-side of the inner porch door, and another fine beast, much weathered, above the outside of the outer door are all Saxon works. The eighth-century relief of the Virgin with Child above the inner porch door seems almost contemporary in its abstract portrayal, but it is likely that the sculpture was originally painted. Another sculpture, also a relief, is more difficult to see as it sits high on an outside wall, past the apse foundations, close to Priory House that adjoins the church. The *Deerhurst Angel* is much weathered, but the wings and staring eyes are still visible. The eyes, in particular, suggest a Celtic influence.

Little survives of the first minsters, the best example being one at Deerhurst. This is first mentioned in AD804 when Aethelric, an *ealdorman* (local nobleman and magistrate) of the Hwicce bequeathed land to it. But this was not a bequest to build – a church must have existed already as Aethelmund, Aethelric's father, who was killed in battle at Kempsford in AD802, is said to have been buried there.

The original church was a simple stone oblong with a porch at the west end. The eastern end apse was added later. The church was enlarged (perhaps as part of a restoration following damage in a Viking raid) by adding side

---

ST ALPHEGE AND DEERHURST MINSTER

St Alphege was a monk, possibly the Abbot of Deerhurst. In AD970, he left to become Abbot of Bath because he found the regime at Deerhurst insufficiently strict. In 1012, having been made Archbishop of Canterbury, he was captured by Viking raiders and ransomed for £3,000 – a vast, almost unimaginable sum. Alphege refused to allow the ransom to be paid and was martyred by the Vikings giving vent to their drunken rage over his decision. One version of his death has him being struck down by hurled ox-bones.

Despite Alphege's apparent disgust with Deerhurst, it continued to be influential until the reign of Edward the Confessor when its importance waned and it was gradually overshadowed by other local monasteries. It later became a cell of Tewkesbury Abbey.

The farmhouse beside the church was probably a part of the original monastery and contains some work that has been dated to the eleventh century. It was extensively rebuilt in the fourteenth century and then remodelled in Tudor times.

Of other minster churches there are remains in Gloucester, and at Bitton in the extreme south of the old county, close to the border with Somerset. At Bitton the Saxon minster was built on a Roman site and only the long nave and the old doorway survive. The feet of a crucifix also remain, the rest having been lost when the church was remodelled in Norman times. The church is also worth visiting for its later architecture, having one of the finest towers in the Perpendicular style (late fourteenth century) in the area.

By the mid-eleventh century, just before the Conquest, the minster churches had been supplemented by many parish churches as most of Gloucestershire's medieval parishes – more than 300 of them – had been created. Several of these churches were on ancient sites, including some on the foundations of Roman villas, but they would usually be built close to the manor houses of the Saxon *thegns* (squires) even if that meant they were some distance from the village they were supposed to serve.

In one famous case, this led to the refusal of a bishop to consecrate the church. St Wulfstan of Worcester declined to perform the ceremony because the church at Longney was overshadowed by a nut tree close to the house of the local *thegn*, Ailsi, who used it to shade summer games and picnics. Such frivolity did not sit well with

Deerhurst Church.

The superb Saxon Virgin above the inner doorway of Deerhurst Church. The carving, in fine limestone, is fascinating both for its form and the fact that it depicts the Christ Child within the womb rather than in the Virgin's arms. The panel, which is believed to date from the late seventh or early eighth centuries, is considered to be one of the finest Saxon works of its type in the country.

This fine beast is one of a pair which now reside on either side of the inner door of Deerhurst Church. The heads were originally mounted on either side of the outer door. At some stage they were covered in plaster and only revealed as magnificently fierce Saxon beast heads many centuries later. They were moved to their present position during nineteenth-century restoration work.

Wulfstan who demanded the tree be felled before continuing. Ailsi refused. Wulfstan cursed the tree and departed. Soon, it is said, the tree died for no apparent reason. (The present thirteenth-century church at Longney houses a beautiful fourteenth-century font.)

No intact late-Saxon churches have survived (which makes the two Deerhurst buildings even more remarkable), but several county churches have architectural features from the period, and many more have sculpture fragments or grave slabs. One of the more interesting examples is at Leonard Stanley, where the Saxon church was superseded by a new Norman building and eventually became part of a farm complex. It now serves as a barn, a section of Saxon arch in the north wall indicating where a side chapel once stood.

The superb double-headed windows of Deerhurst Church are thought by many to be the finest Saxon windows in Britain. The upright stones of the windows are Roman in origin.

ODDA'S CHAPEL

About 200m (650ft) south-west of Deerhurst Church stands the equally excellent Odda's Chapel. Built 300 years later than the minster church, the chapel is unique (in Britain) in having an exact date of dedication that pre-dates the Norman Conquest. It is also remarkable for having lain not only undiscovered, but unsuspected for centuries. In 1675, a tree fell in the adjacent apple orchard and a stone with a Latin inscription was found embedded in its roots. Translated, it noted the building of a chapel by Earl Odda in honour of his dead brother Aelfric, and its dedication by Bishop Ealdred on 'the second of the Ides of April in the fourteenth year of the reign of King Edward of the English'. Aelfric died in 1053, the dedication took place on 12 April 1056. Odda died on 31 August 1056, just four months after the consecration.

It was assumed that the chapel of the inscription was Deerhurst Church, but in 1885 when repairs were being carried out on the 'ordinary' half-timbered house beside the orchard, the true nature of the house's kitchen was revealed by the discovery of an ancient window beneath later plaster. Extracted from the building that had incorporated it, the chapel now stands as a complete late-Saxon building, a remarkable survival.

St Andrew's at Coln Rogers has an intact nave and chancel. Features of the Saxon church at Daglingworth have survived a comprehensive nineteenth-century 'restoration' – look for three relief sculptures and, particularly, the sundial. The Saxons divided the day into eight three-hour *tides* and these are marked, together with half-tide lines and a particular line for 7.30am, probably to mark the start of Mass. Originally both the sundial (of course) and the doorway below it would have been on the outer wall of the church. The sculptures show a crucifixion, St Peter with the key to Heaven and Christ in Majesty, all very simple, but moving. Close to Daglingworth, at Duntisbourne Rouse, the Normans refurbished a late Saxon church. At Somerford Keynes, a village transferred from Wiltshire to Gloucestershire in 1897, the north doorway of All Saints Church is thought by some to be eighth century, though many experts believe it

was founded some 200 years later. Holy Rood Church at Ampney Crucis also has a Saxon doorway, again in the north wall.

Saxon Towns

The Saxons were not town dwellers. Their barter economy was best suited to small villages and scattered farms, so although the early Saxon settlers made use of the existing Roman towns, they did not have the need or technology to maintain them. Indeed, it is likely that vast towns such as Cirencester (which may have had a population of 20,000 in Roman times) and Bath with their elegant buildings and decoration may have seemed of supernatural foundation. Ultimately the Saxons realised the limits of

Odda's Chapel. The chapel forms the west end of the half-timbered farmhouse from which it was 'excavated'.

barter and a money-based, trading economy evolved, one in which towns played a natural part. Gloucester maintained its importance in the county, but Cirencester declined in favour of Winchcombe and, initially, Berkeley. When coinage was eventually minted there were mints at those three towns and also at Bristol.

As well as refounding Roman towns and building their own, the Saxons extended the Roman road system, making a new pattern of tracks that linked their settlements and farms. This pattern is very much what we see today. Of particular note are the white or salt ways, tracks built by the Saxons along which salt was carried by pack-horse. The white way that lies to the north of Chedworth Woods can still be followed. Salt also gave the name to several places and features in the county. The Saxon word for a track was 'gate', explaining its appearance in

some modern place-names. They also used 'street' for a road, particularly the Roman roads. Akeman Street is Saxon, from their word for Bath (Acemanes).

Gloucester

Osric, one of the co-rulers of the Hwicce, founded the minster church at Gloucester in AD681. It was a double minster, Osric's sister, Kynebirg, being the first abbess. Under Cnut the monastery became a Benedictine house. It was rebuilt in 1058 after fire had destroyed it, then again as the Norman St Peter's Abbey in 1089. St Peter's was to become Gloucester Cathedral.

Saxon St Peter's was not the only church in Gloucester. In AD909 Aethelflaed, wife of Aethelred the ruler of Mercia, which at that time was under the control of Wessex, brought the

A replica of the original dedication stone is now mounted inside Odda's Chapel. It is not an exact replica, some Latin contractions having been altered to assist modern readers. The original stone is in Oxford's Ashmolean Museum.

bones of St Oswald to Gloucester. St Oswald had been the Christian king of Northumbria but was killed in AD642 by Penda, Mercia's pagan king. Aethelflaed was a powerful woman, the daughter of Alfred the Great and sister of Edward the Elder, Alfred's successor. She effectively ran Mercia, as Aethelred was an old, ailing man. After his death in AD911, Aethelflaed ruled Mercia in her own right until her own death in AD918. A priory was built to house a shrine to St Oswald, the site chosen being an old Roman tileworks and the stone used salvaged from Roman Glevum. The priory was one of very few churches built during the time of the Viking raids, and the north wall of the nave, rebuilt during Norman times, can still be seen close to the junction of Pitt Street and Archdeacon Street.

Saxon St Mary de Lode (St Mary of the River Crossing) was built on the site of a Roman cemetery, near to the remains of St Oswald's Priory and close to a ferry across the Severn – hence the name.

Winchcombe

Offa, King of Mercia, founded a monastery at Winchcombe in AD787 and the town grew up around it. Kenulf, a later king, died in AD819 and was succeeded by his son Kenelm. We know that Kenelm was young at the time of his murder, though exactly how young is disputed. He

Most churches are built on level ground, but at Duntisbourne Rouse the Saxons chose not only sloping, but steeply sloping, ground. The Normans added to the small Saxon church, but the tower was not completed until 1587, over 500 years after the first stones were laid.

could have been anything between seven and twenty-four years old.

Kenelm had a sister, Quendryth or Quendreda, an ambitious and unscrupulous girl whose lover was Ascobert, the boy's tutor. Quendryth persuaded Ascobert to kill her brother and, with this end in view, Ascobert took Kenelm for a day's hunting. The boy knew what Ascobert intended. At one point, waking from a short sleep in the forest to find Ascobert digging a grave, he told him that this was not the place for the deed. To prove his point, he pushed an ash twig into the ground: it immediately burst into full leaf and flower. Despite this sign, Ascobert cut off Kenelm's head with a long knife. At the moment of decapitation, a white

dove flew from Kenelm's head with a scroll in its beak. The dove flew to Rome and deposited it at the feet of the Pope. The scroll bore a message in Saxon which, when translated, read:

> In Clent cow-pasture under a thorn
> Of head bereft lies Kenelm, king-born.

Monks were sent from Winchcombe to recover the body from the thorn tree under which it was buried, together with Ascobert's knife. Two legends describe how the appropriate tree was miraculously identified: in the first, a shaft of light shone from heaven to illuminate it; in the second, a white cow guided the monks to the spot. As the body was taken from the grave to be reburied by the side of Kenulf in Winchcombe Abbey, a spring welled up from the grave. Further springs gushed out wherever the body was laid down on the way to Winchcombe, one of which became known as St Kenelm's Well. As the body was being taken to its final resting-place, the procession passed Kenulf's palace. Quendryth came to the window and, as the body passed, her eyes fell out of their sockets to signify her guilt.

As with most legends, there may be an element of truth in the story of Kenelm. In 1815, excavations of the foundations of the abbey church revealed two stone coffins – one containing the bones of a grown man, the other those of a child and a large knife. They are on view in Winchcombe Church. Nothing is known of the subsequent fate of Ascobert. Quendryth became Abbess of Southminster, but history does not record whether or not she was blind.

So important did Winchcombe become – not least because of the miracles said to take place at Kenelm's tomb – that when the Saxons created administrative areas to cover the lands of the Hwicce, two 'shires' were formed, centred on Gloucester and Winchcombe.

Bristol

Although there were Iron-Age hill forts on Kings Weston Hill and the Blaise Castle Estate, and a Roman villa has been excavated on the northern edge of Shirehampton, there is little evidence for a settlement at Bristol before Saxon times. There is little evidence of the Saxon settlement either, but the name *Brig Stow* (bridge town) is Saxon and presumably refers to the first bridge over the River Avon, probably at the point where Bristol Bridge now stands. One incontrovertible Saxon find is the 'Harrowing of Hell', a large relief sculpture of Christ trampling the Devil, which was uncovered beneath the chapter house floor of the cathedral in the 1830s. It is often claimed that this panel is not only the finest Saxon work in Britain, but in Europe. The panel, which is now in the cathedral's south transept, is dated to the mid-eleventh century and is clear evidence of a Saxon church.

Conflict: Celts and Vikings

Until the early eighth century the southern part of the Forest of Dean was held by the Welsh, the natural border of the River Wye not being established until that time. Later in the eighth century, the most remarkable of England's Saxon monuments was constructed – the great dyke that formed the border between England and Wales, built by Offa, King of Mercia.

Offa, a descendant of a brother of Penda, was initially king of the Hwicce. Later, as king of Mercia, he effectively ended the kingdom of the Hwicce, which became part of Mercia – there are no references to the Hwicce after AD794. The reason for the construction of the dyke remains a mystery. Whether it was a defensive barrier against marauding Celts or a negotiated political or trade boundary is unclear. Whatever the truth, it was never completed – the final section to Prestatyn in north Wales being abandoned when Offa was killed in a battle with the Celts. At the southern end, the dyke finished at Sedbury cliffs above the River Severn. In places the dyke is difficult to see, but in Gloucestershire there is an outstanding section through the woodland above the ruins of Tintern Abbey. The earthwork is now the basis for a National Trail, that most modern of recreational activities. Walkers on the Trail can explore a breathtakingly beautiful section of Gloucestershire while following in the footsteps of the men who defined the county.

Though there were battles with the Celts, the main threat to Saxon England came not from the west but the east – the Vikings. In the last years of Offa's reign – he died in AD797 – Norse raids had begun on the east coast of England. In the wake of Offa's death, Mercian power declined and Wessex emerged as the most powerful Saxon kingdom, first under Ethelwulf, who defeated the Mercians, and then under his sons. One son, Ethelbert, defeated the Vikings at Reading in AD871, but died soon after and was succeeded by Alfred, his younger brother.

Seizing the moment, the Vikings took control of eastern Mercia and attacked Alfred in AD878,

Offa's Dyke above Shorn Cliff.

forcing him to retreat to the Somerset Levels where, according to legend, he incurred the wrath of his host's wife by burning the cakes. In the meantime, the Vikings had headed north to occupy Gloucester. After their defeatby Alfred at Edington, on the edge of Salisbury Plain, the Vikings retreated to Chippenham where Alfred besieged them. Guthrum, the Viking leader, surrendered and was forced to convert to Christianity. His army then retreated to Cirencester where it stayed for the winter before moving to East Anglia.

In the wake of his victory at Edington, Alfred created a series of *burhs* (fortified towns), located a day's march, about 32km (20 miles) apart. Garrisoned by folk from the town and thereabouts, these *burhs* were the front-line defence against the Vikings and were successful in rebuffing raids in AD885 and AD886. This paved

the way for a treaty between Alfred and Guthrum that divided England into Saxon and Viking kingdoms. Gloucestershire lay in the Saxon kingdom, and although no county towns were specifically defended, the importance of both Gloucester and Winchcombe increased at this time. The success of the *burh* system in the county is indicated by the defeat of a Viking attack along the Severn in AD914, the invaders being counter-attacked by an army collected from Gloucester, Hereford and neighbouring towns.

Alfred was succeeded by Edward the Elder, brother of Ethelfled, who was in turn succeeded by his son Athelstan. Athelstan was a frequent visitor to Gloucester from where he campaigned against the Welsh and succeeded in forcing them to pay an annual tribute, which, a Welsh epic verse maintains, was paid at Cirencester. When

THE BIRTH OF GLOUCESTERSHIRE

In the time of Edmund Ironside and Cnut, the *ealdorman* (local nobleman and magistrate) of Mercia was Eadric. Eadric sided with Cnut, marching with him through Cirencester and Stow as he sought to impose himself on Mercia. Later Eadric changed sides, supporting Edmund and persuading him to meet Cnut at Deerhurst. Later still, Eadric changed allegiance again, moving back to Cnut's side. Cnut rewarded Eadric with the earlship of Mercia when he (Cnut) became king, but was – perhaps not surprisingly – suspicious of Eadric and later had him murdered.

Eadric would be forgettable were it not for one thing. In 1017 he joined the shires centred on Gloucester and Winchcombe into one. With minor modifications, Eadric's new county – Gloucestershire – was to survive for over 800 years.

Athelstan died in AD939, his brother Edmund became king of Wessex. However, he was killed in AD939 at Pucklechurch in south Gloucestershire when he attempted to protect his manservant from attack. After a short reign by Edmund's brother Eadred, and then Edmund's eldest son Eadwig, the crown passed to Edgar, the younger son, who, twenty-five years later, was crowned in a coronation at Bath in AD973.

Edgar had two sons by two different wives. The eldest son, Edward, was murdered, probably by the mother of the younger son, Aethelred. Aethelred has gone down in history as the 'unready', though the correct translation of *unraed*, which was attached to his name during his lifetime, is 'ill council' as he was poorly advised. The nickname came from Aethelred's doomed attempts to come to terms with the Norse kingdom to the east. Aethelred neither fought nor adequately bribed the Vikings and when he died in 1016, his son, Edmund Ironside, was faced with an overwhelming threat. Edmund met Cnut, the Viking king, at Alney Island, the location of which has never been

clearly identified – was it a real island in the river close to Deerhurst or watermeadows closer to Gloucester? The two agreed to share the kingdom of England, but Edmund died shortly after, probably murdered, and Cnut became the sole king.

Cnut created four earldoms – Wessex, Mercia, Northumbria and East Anglia. Wessex, ruled by Earl Godwin, became the most important of these. Cnut had married Emma, Aethelred's widow, and their son Hardacnut succeeded his father. But Hardacnut died two years later and was succeeded by Edward the Confessor, the son of Aethelred and Emma. Edward was a much tougher ruler than he is sometimes pictured. When Earl Godwin overreached himself by refusing a royal order, Edward raised an army at Gloucester and marched to confront him. Godwin, who seems to have been determined to usurp the throne, gathered an army, which included his son Harold, at Tetbury. Legend has it that this army then marched north to Painswick Hill where it camped at Castle Godwyn, though most sources seem to place the confrontation at Beverston. Godwin backed down and Harold left England, taking a ship from Bristol to Ireland. Shortly after, a second confrontation occurred – this time Edward backed down and restored Godwin's earldom. Earl Godwin died in 1053 and Harold became the new Earl of Wessex. On Edward's behalf, Harold pursued Gruffydd ap Llywelyn, who had united the Welsh to form a real threat to the Saxons. Harold pursued Gruffydd, killed him and married his widow who thus had the unenviable fate of becoming widowed by battle twice in three years.

In 1066, Edward the Confessor died without an heir. Harold seized the throne, and raised an army to defend his claims against Harald Hadrada's Norse army when it landed in Yorkshire. Harold defeated Hadrada at Stamford Bridge on 25 September 1066, but as his army rested after the battle, he heard that another claimant to the English throne had landed at Pevensey.

5. THE NORMANS

The First Years

It is said that during the feast that followed the defeat of Harald Hadrada at Stamford Bridge, Harold heard that William, Duke of Normandy, had landed in Kent. Perhaps emboldened by his victory over the awesome Norse army, Harold rushed south to face the new invader with an army which, experts believe, was too small and hastily thrown together. Had Harold paused for a day or two, and he had that time, the history of England – and Gloucestershire – would have been much different. But he did not, and the battle of 14 October 1066 went the way of the invaders, two Gloucestershire *thegns* (squires), Rotlese of Beckford and Toribidenesei of Barrington, dying with Harold.

Despite his victory at Hastings, William was not immediately the master of England: it was to be several years before he had command of his new realm. In West Mercia, which included the north-west of Gloucestershire, there was resistance to Norman rule in 1067–68, and a more determined uprising in 1069–70. But Harold's death had left the Saxons leaderless, and gradually the Normans assumed control.

One weapon in the Norman arsenal that was particularly effective in maintaining control was the castle, and by the late 1070s one of the first of these had been built at Gloucester. The town's first castle was built in the area now bordered by Ladybellgate Street, Commercial Road and Blackfriars and would have been a 'motte and bailey'. The motte was an artificially created mound topped by a wooden palisade. The bailey was an area at the base of the mound enclosed by a second palisade. Such structures, a few metres across, could be built remarkably quickly. It is said that the Normans could build a very effective basic structure in just eight days and then, behind its defences, improve the castle at a more leisurely pace.

Castles were a very effective means of controlling the local population. If the imposing aspect was not enough, the heavily armed soldiers who could erupt from within at any moment ensured that those not chastened by the castle's appearance would generally be intimidated by the threat or actuality of violence. Seventeen castles are known to have been built in Gloucestershire between the Conquest and the mid-twelfth century, but only those at Berkeley, Bristol and Gloucester were built during the reign of the Conqueror. Of the others, three were built in Dean at Littledean, Lydney and St Briavels to protect the royal forest, the rest were mainly in the Cotswolds. Much still remains of St Briavels Castle, while remnants of the other Dean castles, as well as those at Brimpsfield and Miserden can still be seen.

The Saxons eventually accepted the reality of Norman rule. In part this was because of the continued absence of a Saxon leader, in part the brooding presence of the Norman castles. It was also due to the introduction of the feudal system of land management. Feudalism was a pyramid structure. The king, at the pinnacle, owned most of the land. Below him were a group of major noblemen who were given substantial holdings. Another rung down were minor noblemen with smaller holdings, and at the bottom were tenant farmers, the serfs of the system. Each layer of the pyramid supported the one above by payment in produce or service, which may have included military service. The system worked as long as England remained an agricultural society, but the growth of towns eventually destroyed it, as the craftsmen and traders of the towns could not be easily accommodated within the structure. Interestingly, feudalism lives on in the language.

Gloucester Cathedral.

KINGSHOLM

King's Holm (king's palace) is named after the palace of the Saxon kings that was built close to Gloucester, probably on the site of the original Roman fort. The 'palace' was unlikely to have been palatial in the modern sense of the word: more likely it would have been a defended, mainly wooden building whose main feature was a great hall where the kings of the Hwicce, and later, of the Mercians, held court. Then, and for many centuries after, the king and his entourage moved around the kingdom. This procession showed the ruler to his subjects and so reinforced the power of the throne – it also allowed the court to reduce its expenditure by letting the king's host pick up the tab for the visit. When Edward the Confessor was king he began a tradition of spending the major Christian festivals at England's three most important towns – Winchester (Easter), Westminster (Whitsun) and Gloucester (Christmas).

The Saxons spoke English, the Normans spoke French. The Saxons kept the animals – sheep, cows, fowls and ducks, while the Normans ate them – mutton, beef, poultry: the differing words reflecting the difference between production and consumption.

The Doomsday Book

Following the tradition established by Edward the Confessor, William spent Christmas 1085 at Gloucester, where after 'much thought and very deep discussion about this country, how it was occupied or with sort of people' he decided to commission a census of England. The information contained in the document would be beyond dispute, just like that presented at the Final Judgement. In keeping with this apocalyptic line of thought, the document was named the Doomsday Book (now more often written 'Domesday' to which the spelling was changed in late medieval times for no very good reason).

Commissioners were sent all over England to gather from each settlement information relating to the name of the place; who held it before 1066 and who the present holder was; the number of villagers, cottagers and slaves; extent of woodland, meadow and pasture; and the number of mills and fishponds. So detailed was the inventory that the *Anglo-Saxon Chronicle* records that 'so very thoroughly did he have the inquiry carried out that there was not a single hide... not even – it is shameful to record it, but it did not seem shameful to him to do – not even one ox, nor one cow, nor one pig which escaped his notice.'

This information was gathered into two volumes. The complete information for Norfolk, Suffolk and Essex made up one volume, and a shortened version of the information for the rest of England made up the second. There were omissions – Northumberland, Durham and several towns were not included, neither were Cumberland and Westmoreland as they did not yet form part of William's kingdom – and inaccuracies, but nevertheless the book is an invaluable snap-shot of late eleventh-century England and of the king himself.

The king held about a quarter of the land in Gloucestershire. Rents were high and paid in cash or kind, sometimes a curious mixture of the two – a tenant might pay in money, pigs, honey and loaves of bread. What the king was interested in was obtaining his due, a fact that led the writer of the *Anglo-Saxon Chronicle* to note:

The King and the leading men were fond, yea, too fond, of avarice: they coveted gold and silver, and did not care how sinfully it was obtained, as long as it came to them. The king granted his land on the hardest terms, and at the highest possible price. If another buyer came and offered more than the first had given, the king would let it go to the man who offered him more. He did not care at all how very wrongfully the reeves got possession of it from wretched men, nor how many illegal acts they did.

Doomsday shows that within a generation the Normans had completed the transfer of England

DOOMSDAY GLOUCESTERSHIRE

Gloucestershire's entry lists seventy-eight land-holders. King William himself is first on the list, followed by twenty-five abbeys, churches and churchmen. The rest are, with one or two notable exceptions, the new Norman lords. Some of the landholders are curious – why is Hugh Donkey so named and who was the Gerwy whose wife held land? In Gloucester, Roger of Berkeley, the first of the great Berkeley family, held one house and one fishery that had formerly belonged to Baldwin, a now-displaced Saxon. William the Scribe held a residence valued at 51d (less than 25p), while William the Bald's residence was valued only at 12d (about 5p). Was this discrimination against the tonsorially challenged?

Hugh Donkey held Bagendon, having taken it from Wulfward. Hugh had 'three hides which pay tax', 'five villagers with three ploughs', 'six slaves', 'a mill at 10s' and 'a meadow of eight acres'. In total the value of his holding was £4, which seems a very reasonable recompense for having such a comical name.

excluded from the volume of the Doomsday Book relating to Gloucestershire, we have no record of how many sheep were kept at this time. Arable farming mainly used the two-field system, each peasant farmer holding strips that were $16\frac{1}{2}$ft wide and one furrow long. Such measurements are the basis of the curious Imperial system, now phased out in favour of metric values. Four strips = sixty-six feet = twenty-two yards = one chain wide, and one furrow long = one furlong, which was ten times the four strip width of 220 yards. A villein worked his own land and the land of his lord. He might, by way of rent, be required to carry a certain quantity of brushwood or take a cart to Gloucester (or another market town) several times each year. He might also own stock that would graze on the common land, and pigs that would feed in the woods. With modifications, this system thrived until the enclosures of the eighteenth century, by which time it was at least 2,000 years old, perhaps older.

Monasteries and Cathedrals

While the piety of the founders of the Saxon monastic houses is beyond question, entry to monastic life was not always a matter of religious vocation alone. Saxon chiefs with several children needed employment for those who would not inherit leader duties, and being the head of a religious house had the advantages of a quiet, comfortable life that did not involve great labour. The Normans may have held similar views as many a nobleman's son entered the church, but there is also another possibility.

In the thirteenth century, the great abbeys were of extreme importance to the surrounding communities. The major function and responsibility of the monks within such houses was the maintenance of prayer. To this end, the day of the monks was punctuated by attendance at Mass. Even their sleep was broken for the prayers of the night office. In theory, the monks lived the harshest of lives, having taken vows of poverty and celibacy, and living apart from their fellow men. They gave the peasant, who had to

to their own hands. But it also shows that much of the land had been given to the church, some in England but some too in Normandy. Much of the English land was given to new monastic foundations or to refounded Saxon monasteries. The church held so much land in the county that it is believed that the expression 'as sure as God is in Gloucestershire' dates from this early medieval period. It could, of course, also refer to the productivity of the county: the sheep on the Cotswolds and the fertile soil of the Severn Vale demonstrating that God had taken a special interest in the area.

Land Usage

Land usage in Gloucestershire during the early medieval period remained much the same as in Saxon times. Dean was forest, the Severn Vale was arable farming, and the Cotswolds a mixture of arable farming and woodland, with sheep kept chiefly for milk and wool. As animals were work too hard to spend all his day praying, hope for salvation through their suffering. The monks also looked after the saintly relics enshrined in the house, to which the peasant could make pilgrimage to gain personal absolution. On the face of it, the system worked well and to the profit of all. The peasants gained the promise of eternal salvation for the price of the upkeep of a few holy men, the monks had the freedom to follow their vocations without fear of starvation, and the gentry were satisfied that the peasants had something to keep their minds off the injustices of life.

The great Gloucestershire houses were those at Hailes, Winchcombe, Gloucester, Tewkesbury and Cirencester, but there were also a large number of smaller houses such as St Augustine's Abbey at Bristol.

Hailes Abbey

Hailes was one of the last great Cistercian abbeys to be founded. The Cistercian order was a branch of the Benedictines whose lifestyle was based on hard work, leaving little time for leisure and idleness. Seven hours each day were devoted to religious exercises, with the rest of the time spent at work, chiefly agricultural.

Hailes was founded in 1245 by Richard, Earl of Cornwall, brother of Henry III. Richard had been returning to England from a crusade in the Holy Land when a storm threatened to wreck his ship off the Scillies. He vowed that if his life were spared he would build an abbey. Hailes was dedicated on 9 November 1251 at a ceremony attended by Henry III, Queen Eleanor and an array of bishops.

Hailes Abbey.

The abbey became the most frequented pilgrimage site, not only in the county but in south-west England. When Richard died in 1272, his body was buried at Hailes, next to that of his wife (though his heart was buried at Beaulieu Abbey). Before his death, the relic that was to bring Hailes almost 300 years of fame and prosperity, a phial of Christ's blood, was presented to the abbey. The 'holy blood' was a well-authenticated relic and its possession made Hailes one of England's greatest centres for pilgrims. In the *Canterbury Tales*, Chaucer has a pardoner swear 'by the blode of Christ that is in Hayles'.

Tewkesbury Abbey

It is said that a Saxon monastery was founded at Tewkesbury in AD751, but there is little supporting evidence. The first confirmed abbey was founded by Robert Fitzhamen in 1087. Fitzhamen did not live to see the abbey completed, dying after being wounded in battle in 1107, but he was buried in the chapter house. The building was completed by Robert Fitzroy, Earl of Gloucester, an illegitimate son of Henry I. The Norman building was consecrated in 1121 and remains one of the masterpieces of the period. The west font with its vast, recessed arch is by common consent the finest survival in Britain of the early Norman period. The arch was originally of seven orders, though only six remain after later alterations. The tower, 14m (46ft) wide and 40m (132ft) tall, is the largest surviving Norman tower in the world. The inverted 'V' on each face marks the position of the original roof, which was lowered in 1614.

Inside, the choir and transepts are thought to have been the first four-storeyed building in Europe. The nave roof is supported by fourteen massive columns, each 9m (30ft) high and 2m (6½ft) in diameter. The original ceiling and roof would have been made of timber, but in the fourteenth century both the nave and choir were vaulted. The vaulting is superb, particularly the lierne vaulting at the tower crossing, but many have questioned whether it is too sharp a contrast with the austerity of the plain columns. The south aisle holds the tombs of some early abbots. Near the choir is that of Abbot Alau who died in 1202. As Prior of Canterbury, Alau witnessed the death of St Thomas Becket and it is his account that is the basis of our knowledge of the murder. Abbot Alau's tomb is plain and unadorned. In sharp contrast is that of Edward Dispenser, who died in 1375, which is topped by his life-size kneeling effigy, painted and gilded, and in full armour.

The abbey is larger than sixteen English cathedrals and has more medieval tombs and monuments than any English church except Westminster Abbey (which is the only English church – as opposed to cathedral – to rival Tewkesbury in size and splendour).

The abbey church was used by both the monks and the townspeople – a screen crossing the nave (at the shallow step now ascended by a ramp) and separating the church into two parts. At the Dissolution, the town was anxious to obtain the whole church as building a new one would be so expensive. Henry VIII was therefore asked to sell it to Tewkesbury rather than a private individual, as was usually the case. The king agreed, charging the town the value of the roof lead and bell metal, a vast total of £543, which was raised, against the odds, in two years. Most of the remaining abbey buildings were sold for their stone, leaving the abbey to stand in splendid isolation.

Gloucester Abbey

Gloucester's monastic house has a longer history than Tewkesbury – indeed, one of the longest in the country. First founded by Osric in the late seventh century, the monastery became Benedictine in the early eleventh century. Though there was some rebuilding, the monastery was in decline by the time of the Norman Conquest. When the first Norman abbot, Serlo, took over in 1072, there were just two monks and a few novices. The Saxon church was destroyed in a fire that ravaged much of the town in 1087, and Serlo laid the foundation

Tewkesbury Abbey.

stone for a new abbey church in 1089. Much of that church survives.

Serlo's choir was remodelled in the early fourteenth century in what is generally considered to be the first building in the Perpendicular style in England. The Lady Chapel and cloisters were added, also in the Perpendicular style – in each the vaulting is magnificent. The stained-glass windows of the Lady Chapel were by Christopher Whall, an artist of the Arts and Crafts movement and date from the early twentieth century. The cloisters, while not unique, are one of the few surviving examples in Britain. Monastery cloisters were where the monks could walk and meditate, and perhaps also study or teach. In general, they were open arcades and so were usually placed on the southern side of the church. At Gloucester, unusually, they are on the north side and more enclosed. With their fan-vaulted ceilings, the cloisters are quite beautiful and include a lavatorium where the monks washed.

Leading off the eastern walk of the cloisters is the chapter house in which Robert, the eldest son of William the Conqueror, is buried. On William's death, Normandy was bequeathed to Robert; England to his second son, William Rufus; and 5,000 pounds of silver to his youngest son Henry. On William Rufus' death in 1100 – apparently shot dead by an arrow in the New Forest – Henry seized the throne and was crowned Henry I. In the same year, Robert, who had been on a crusade, returned to Normandy and then invaded England and forced Henry to pay an annual tribute of £2,000. Henry paid and brooded for six years, he then invaded

The lavatorium at Gloucester Cathedral is one of the finest examples in Britain.

Normandy, defeated Robert and imprisoned him for twenty-eight years. Robert died in Cardiff Castle in 1134, but was brought to Gloucester for burial.

Gloucester Abbey was also the burial place of Edward II after his murder at Berkeley Castle. His tomb with its delicate stonework and effigy of the king is on the north side of the presbytery. Close by is the east window, one of the glories of the abbey. Constructed in the 1350s in memory of Edward III's French campaign of 1345–47, it is 22m (72ft) high and 12m (38ft) wide, the largest in any English cathedral.

Gloucester Abbey was dissolved in January 1540, but rather than being sold and possibly destroyed, it was made the seat of a new diocese and became a cathedral in 1541, a transformation that ensured the survival of the cloisters and the chapter house.

Tewkesbury and Gloucester are the great survivals of the county's Norman monasteries, and the ruins of Hailes a reminder of former glories. They are, therefore, a sharp contrast to the houses of Winchcombe and Cirencester of which nothing remains.

Winchcombe Abbey

Winchcombe seems to have prospered initially, aided not only by the presence of the shrine of St Kenelm, but also by the commercial astuteness of the abbots. The end came for Winchcombe on 23 December 1539 'on a cold and windy night' when the abbot, Richard Anselm Mounslow, and the remaining monks surrendered the abbey and left. As usual, the plate went to the king; the abbey, ultimately, to Lord Seymour of Sudeley. The roofs were stripped of their lead and most of the buildings were destroyed. Of the little that remained, the elements and local townsfolk searching for building stone took their toll. By 1714 the site was levelled, and nothing of the abbey could be seen. Today the site is still unexcavated – it lies on private ground, a cross marking the position of the high altar. It is said that the ghostly chanting of monks can still be heard from the old site on still nights. Evidence of the

---

TOWN VERSUS ABBEY

It is clear that throughout its history, or at least from 1150 onwards, the town of Winchcombe had a somewhat ambivalent attitude towards the abbey. The house was a source of wealth: pilgrims needed to be fed and accommodated, and also provided a market for the sale of trinkets and suchlike.

But the abbey was also a grasping landlord. Under Abbot Thomas, the town vicar, Henry de Campden, vented the communal spleen by ringing the church bells loudly at times most guaranteed to disturb the monks in their observance of the canonical hours. The abbot reported the vicar's provocative behaviour to the Pope, Gregory IX, but although a commission was set up in 1231 to investigate the problem, no action was taken. The abbey remained unpopular, and in 1346 a band of townspeople broke in, assaulting the monks and stealing some valuables. The provocative bell-ringing was repeated in 1399, and this time the Pope issued a decree that there was to be no bell-ringing at night.

---

use of stone from the abbey for other buildings can occasionally be seen in the town – in Court Lane, for instance, which was close to the site, some of the old stones are marked with a 'W', the quarry-mark for Winchcombe Abbey.

Cirencester Abbey

Cirencester Abbey, the largest of the five Augustinian houses founded by Henry I, was begun in 1117. It stood in what is now Abbey Grounds, the lake having probably been the abbot's fishpond. The site chosen was that previously occupied by the Saxon minster, and work on what is now the town church began at around the same time. Though there does not seem to have been a bell-ringing incident between abbey and town in the manner of Winchcombe, there was conflict. The abbey took market tolls and profits from the town fair, which caused great anger. One abbot erected his own gallows and claimed the possessions of those unfortunate enough to die on it. He

The Spital Gate, Cirencester.

The slabs that mark the position of Cirencester abbey church in Abbey Grounds.

allowed his fellow abbots and local lords to use the gallows – at a fee – and became very annoyed when the squire at Brimpsfield erected his own. He also built a gaol and pocketed fines from the incarcerated.

When the abbey was dissolved on 31 December 1539, it was the wealthiest Augustinian house in England. The last abbot, John Blake, retired to Fairford on an annual pension of £200, a tidy sum that allowed him to live in comfort. No-one in Cirencester seems to have been too displeased at the closure. As elsewhere, the lead was stripped from the roof and the inevitable decay of the abbey's fabric that followed was hastened by the occasional sale of stonework for building. All that now remains are a section of the old precinct wall near

Gosditch and Dollar Streets, and Spital Gate (or Norman Arch) at the northern end of Abbey Grounds. Spital Gate is a gatehouse with a superb three-ordered arch, probably dating from the late twelfth century. In Abbey Grounds, the site of the abbey church is now marked with paving slabs.

Bristol Abbey

In 1140, Robert Fitzharding founded an Augustinian abbey at Bristol. He chose a site to the west of the River Frome, a spot that was said to have been visited by St Augustine himself during his journey of AD603 to meet British Christians, and where one of his travelling companions, St Jordan, was buried. As at Gloucester,

The Chapter House, Bristol Cathedral.

when the abbey was dissolved the church became a cathedral – it is a magnificent building, a masterpiece of soaring elegance. The Early English work of the older Lady Chapel, the later Lady Chapel and choir are superb. Best of all is the chapter house, which many consider to be the finest Norman building of its age (mid-twelfth century) in existence. Close to the chapter house are what remains of the cloisters, built in the fifteenth century. Much of what remained of the abbey after the Dissolution was later incorporated into Bristol Cathedral School, beside the cathedral. Close to the Cathedral, Abbey Gateway is the original abbey entrance. Dating from the sixteenth century, it is now joined to the city's Central Library.

Other Monastic Remains

Little remains of the other monastic foundations in the county. The church at Leonard Stanley was that of an Augustinian priory founded by Roger de Berkeley in 1131, while at Kingswood, near Wotton-under-Edge, the sixteenth-century gatehouse to a Cistercian abbey is a survival of what was probably the last phase of monastic building in England. The Cistercian abbey at Flaxley, one of only two houses west of the Severn, was founded by the son of the Earl of Hereford in the 1150s. It was placed on the site of the death of the Earl in a hunting accident on Christmas Eve, 1143. Parts of the original abbey have been incorporated into the present 'abbey', which passed into private ownership at the Dissolution.

There were priories at Brimpsfield, Horsley, Newent and Paulton but virtually nothing remains of these, or of the preceptory of the Knights Templar that gave its name to Temple Guiting. The other group of medieval charitable knights, the Knights Hospitallers, had a preceptory at Quenington, parts of which were incorporated into the present church.

Finally, there are the remains in Gloucester of a Welsh abbey and of the houses of the Dominican and Franciscan Friars, called Blackfriars and Greyfriars respectively because of the colour of their robes and hoods. Those of the Blackfriars include an early thirteenth-century arcade from the friary's infirmary and the thirteenth-century scissor-braced roof. Only three Blackfriars churches have survived in England (the others are at Newcastle and Norwich) and this roof is the finest survival of all. It owes its existence to the church having been converted into a house – Bell's Place – by Sir Thomas Bell, a local clothmaker. Bell used the other buildings of the monastery as a cloth factory. In contrast, Greyfriars is now a heavily stabilised shell, set, incongruously, close to the modern college and market buildings.

The Welsh abbey is Llanthony Priory, transferred to Gloucester as Llanthony Secunda after the original abbey, Llanthony Prima, in the Vale of Ewyas near Abergavenny, was abandoned when hostile Welsh locals threatened the monks. Little remains of the Gloucester priory except for remnants of the house that incorporated the church on Dissolution, and parts of the vast tithe barn.

The monastic system reached its peak in 1300. After that time, the population of monks and nuns declined, owing, in part, to a falling off in the numbers of those offering themselves to the life, and in part to the Black Death, which had decimated monks and laymen alike. By 1536 the great abbeys were declining both in importance and in their population of monks, some being more than half empty. There were, however, still almost 1,000 monasteries and nunneries in England and Wales, where some 17,000 men and women lived in holy orders at the time of the Dissolution of the Monasteries.

Hospitals

In Cirencester's Spitalgate Lane, close to the Spital Gate, are the remains of St John's Hospital, which comprise the delicate arcades of the hospital's 'nave'. The foundation date of this hospital for the sick and destitute of the town is not known with certainty as it was the subject of one of the conflicts between the town and the abbey. The town claimed foundation by Henry I

St John's Hospital, Cirencester.

in 1133, but the abbey claimed it was Henry II in 1168 and therefore the land and titles that the hospital enjoyed formed part of the abbey's holding. The Pope agreed with the abbot and granted St John's to the abbey in 1222, but arguments continued. In 1343 the townspeople were still protesting, but in 1348 Edward III confirmed the abbey's claim.

In addition to St John's Cirencester there were hospitals at Lechlade, Gloucester and Stow-on-the-Wold. At Lechlade, the hospital stood beside St John's Bridge. The bridge itself is of interest because it is thought to have been only the second bridge to be built over the River Thames. The present bridge dates from the nineteenth century, but is on the original foundations. Of the hospital nothing remains. After the hospital's founding, a priory was built nearby, but nothing

of that or of the hospital at Stow remains. By contrast, the chapel of St Mary's hospital at Wotton (Gloucester) still stands, though it was partially demolished in 1861. Built as a leper hospital in 1150, the chapel houses a fine recumbent effigy of a lady dating from the late thirteenth century.

Churches

The Normans built churches as well as monastic houses, one in every parish – it was the custom for the new landowner to replace the existing church or to provide one. So many were built that it would be impossible to provide a comprehensive guide to the county's Norman churches here, but there are some that should not be missed.

The typanum, Elkstone Church.

The buildings at Duntisbourne Rouse and Winstone represent the first Norman churches to comprise just nave and chancel, and were, in essence, no more than a stylistic modification of the Saxon design. Winstone is rare in having no east window. There are only five such churches in Gloucestershire (the others are at Aston Blank, Baunton, Brimpsfield and Notgrove) and it has been suggested that they may be a survival of a Celtic influence on the original Saxon churches on the sites.

The first visible Norman change was the introduction of a central tower. The churches at Elkstone, Hampnett and Staunton (near Coleford) are the best surviving examples. Elkstone is the highest (above sea level) Cotswold church and has some of the finest surviving fourteenth-century carvings. These appear on the tympanum (the semi-circular slab above a doorway) of the south doorway, which has a Christ in Majesty together with the symbols of the Evangelists below an arch of carved beakheads – monsters, birds and two human heads. The church also has a very rare columbarium (pigeon loft) above the chancel, a reminder of the time when pigeons and pigeon eggs were an important food source. Elkstone is also one of the few county churches to have a Norman stone-vaulted chancel. As an aside, though the beakhead work at Elkstone is superb, the best example in the county is around the south doorway at Windrush.

An equally fine tympanum from about the same period can be seen at Ruarden in the Forest of Dean. This interesting church, one of the series, few in number, which stand at the forest

Upleadon Church.

geometry. Perhaps the most unusual of all towers is that at Upleadon where a half-timbered tower was added in the sixteenth century. Upleadon also has a very good tympanum depicting an Agnus Dei between two mythical beasts.

Most early churches had straight-ended chancels, but there may have been exceptions. Temple Guiting seems to have had an apse, while there are suggestions that Dymock Church may have had a five-sided apse. If so, it would have been the only known example in England. St Briavels, like Dymock, on the west side of the Severn, retains its Norman arcade.

The Norman fonts at Rendcomb and Southrop are some of the finest in England. The Rendcomb font, with carvings of the Apostles, the space indicating where Judas Iscariot's image has been left blank, was rescued from its position as a garden ornament in the nineteenth century. The St Briavels' font is unique in having a stone frill.

Finally, a visit should be made to Newland, which houses the Free Miners brass. Newland Church is often called the 'Cathedral of the Forest' because of its size. It is a superb building, the beautiful stained-glass windows showering light into the spacious interior complementing the cathedral-like qualities of the exterior. In addition to the famous brass there are several fine tombs with stone effigies.

Of the thirteenth-century Early English churches, the best is that at Cowley, if only because it has survived later 'restoration' in the most complete fashion. Other good examples are Bibury and Eastleach Turville. There are also three outstanding examples below the Cotswolds: Teddington has a tower arch and window from Hailes Abbey (itself the prize example of the period); Slimbridge, whose spire is a landmark of the Severn Vale, has superb arcades; while nearby Berkeley shows the influence of its ownership by Bristol's Augustinian abbey.

Stow-on-the-Wold and Wotton-under-Edge have excellent thirteenth-century arcades, while Boxwell and West Littleton have fine examples

edge, has a tympanum of St George and the dragon. The sculpture shows a distinct continental influence and it is thought that the local squire, Oliver de Merlimond, took a sculptor with him when he took a pilgrimage to Santiago de Compostella. Another interesting tympanum, probably early twelfth century, is that above the north door at Quenington. It depicts the Harrowing of Hell with God represented as the sun's disc with a face.

Later churches had west, rather than central towers, North Cerney and Chedworth being good early examples. The churches at Ozleworth and Swindon have hexagonal towers, a very rare change from the usual square

Light streaming through the stained-glass windows of Newland Church creates colour patterns on an arcade pillar.

Rendcomb font.

THE SOUTHROP FONT

The font has relief carved panels beneath arches. One shows Moses with the Tablets of Stone, the others showing the Virtues trampling their respective Vices. The names of the Virtues are inscribed on the arches, those of the Vices are written backwards on the panels. The font, which dates from the mid-twelfth century, was discovered by John Keble, the founder of the Oxford Movement, who was born at Fairford in 1792. He was curate at Southrop from 1823–25. It was here that he wrote much of *The Christian Year*.

Southrop font.

of thirteenth-century bellcotes – a particular feature of Cotswold churches of the period.

Todenham is the only Gloucestershire church in pure Decorated (early fourteenth century) style, though Eastleach Turville and Southrop both show examples of the period.

Of the later, Perpendicular style there are numerous examples, consistent with the fifteenth and early sixteenth centuries being Gloucestershire's most prosperous era. This was the time of the building of the great wool churches (*see* page 105), though other, less elaborate, examples also exist, for instance at Stanton and Coberley.

Coberley is also interesting for several other features. It includes a heart burial (of Sir Giles Berkeley), the only one in the Cotswolds. The body of Sir Giles lies at Little Malvern. Such separate interments (occasionally involving more than two 'pieces' of the deceased) were common at the time, when the Norman knights held estates in different parts of the country. Even rarer than the heart burial is that of Sir Giles' favourite horse, Lombard, in the churchyard. It is believed that Lombard lies under the mound to the north of the church rather than below the new memorial tablet on the other side of the wall from the heart burial. Also in the church is the tomb of Sir Thomas Berkeley who lies in effi-

Berkeley Church. The high ground of the cemetery formed part of the defences of Berkeley Castle. Consequently the church tower was built away from the church so that, if it was captured, it could not be used to attack the castle.

gy on it, together with his wife. Under Edward III, Sir Thomas was responsible for the recruitment of archers. Those he found, including some from Gloucestershire, helped win the Battle of Crecy in 1346, where Sir Thomas also fought. Following Sir Thomas' death in around 1355, his wife Joan married Sir William Whittington. Their son, Richard, is still known to this day as the pantomime character Dick Whittington.

The Rise of the Wool Trade

It is appropriate to have spent so much time early in this chapter describing the foundation and history of Gloucestershire's monastic houses for two reasons. The first is the most obvious – that Tewkesbury Abbey and Gloucester Cathedral, survivals of those monasteries, are the finest churches in the county. The second is less immediately apparent. All over England the great monastic houses, as landowners, led a revolution in agriculture, increasing the number of sheep and altering the crops on arable land. The changes were not always to the advantage of the peasant farmers as many villages, sometimes in their entirety, were moved to make way for sheep pasture. But the rearing of sheep for wool rather than meat brought with it a massive increase in prosperity, and nowhere more so than on the Cotswolds.

The heart burial of Sir Giles Berkeley in Coberley church.

A 'Cotswold Lion'.

The long-faced Cotswold sheep, known as 'Cotswold lions', fared well on the grass of the high wolds. At first the local industry had been the production of raw wool, but a clothing industry grew up using the skills of craftsmen from the Low Countries, the abundance of water-power in the streams draining down to the Severn Vale and the deep layers of Fuller's Earth in the Southwolds. Soon the Cotswolds became the centre of the English clothing trade. In the mid-fourteenth century, England exported about 4,500 cloths per annum. Two hundred years later, this figure exceeded 120,000. The wool trade was vitally important to England's prosperity and more than half the exports were manufactured in the Cotswold area. It is estimated that at its height the Cotswolds held half a mil-

lion sheep, and that the wool trade employed half of all the area's workers. The importance of the wool trade has passed into our folklore. The Lord Chancellor sits on a woolsack, a memorial to the industry, and until metrication Britain still used a weight system based on a 14lb stone. The farmer held the 'stone', an actual stone that was tested against true weights carried by the buyers. When found to be accurate, the two weights were used to weigh out the fleeces weighing 28 pounds, or two stones.

The wool trade created the Cotswolds as we see them today. Many of the towns contain houses built by the rich wool merchants, who were also great benefactors of the church, in

The near-perfect Cotswold village of Stanton. The village owes much of its present state to the efforts of Philip Stott, an Oldham-born architect who, between 1906 and his death in 1937, restored many of the cottages.

some instances giving money for the building of the magnificent new 'wool' churches.

Ironically, it was the eventual decline of the wool trade that bequeathed to the nation the Cotswold villages that are such a beloved feature of both Gloucestershire and England today. Spared the later development of other county towns and villages, places such as Chipping Campden, Blockley, Stanton, Stanway, Bibury, the Swells and the Slaughters have become time capsules of an earlier age. The colour of the Cotswold stone used to build the dwellings, and the unspoilt nature of these towns and villages has made them notable tourist attractions. The indisputable beauty of the villages where the cottages and houses now change hands for fortunes,

belie their original purpose and the nature of life when they were first constructed.

Chipping Campden has what many consider to be the finest array of houses built by wool merchants. William Grevel, whose memorial brass in Chipping Campden Church is the largest and one of the oldest in Gloucestershire, built Grevel House in 1380. Grevel was a contemporary of Chaucer and was mentioned by him in the *Canterbury Tales*. Opposite Grevel House is Woolstaplers Hall, the only other intact – though in this case altered – fourteenth-century domestic building in Campden. The name now given to the building derives from its use as a meeting and buying place for the merchants of the wool staple, the staple being the raw fleece.

Woolstaplers Hall, Chipping Campden.

Blockley seen from the Heart of England Way. This long-distance trail starts at Bourton-on-the-Water and passes through Blockley and Chipping Campden before heading north to finish below Cannock Chase.

When the trade in wool rather than cloth was at its height, traders came from as far as Tuscany to buy Cotswold fleeces.

Buildings of a quite different type can be seen at Bibury, which William Morris claimed was the most beautiful village in England. Arlington

LOW-COUNTRY WEAVERS

Before the expansion of the cloth trade, Cotswold wool was exported to Holland where it was made into superb cloth and sent back to England. It was not long before it was realised that this made poor economic sense. Consequently, an agent managed to convince some of the Dutch under-masters that they would be better off as masters in England. The Dutch craftsmen were promised fat beef and mutton, profits, good beds and better bed-fellows. The latter offer implied that the rich English, with an eye to the main chance, would encourage their daughters to marry the

Dutch. The daughters concerned being of such beauty 'that the most envious foreigners could not but commend them'. Whichever of the offers – meat, money or daughters – was the most persuasive, the effect was a migration of Dutch and other Low Country craftsmen to England. In order to prevent any malcontent from persuading the others to go back home, they were widely spread. Some certainly settled in the Cotswolds where it is believed that the names of the villages of Dunkirk and Petty France (*petit France*) derive from the influx.

Arlington Row, Bibury.

Arlington Row, Bibury.

Row, a perfect terrace of seventeenth-century weavers' cottages is built in Cotswold stone. Thankfully, an attempt by Henry Ford to buy the cottages and have them shipped to the USA failed. The weavers would have washed their cloth in the mill leat (a diverted stream) that fed Arlington Mill before returning to the Coln. From the cottages a tiny bridge crosses to Rack Isle, between the leat and the river. Here, the cloth was 'racked' for drying.

Stephen and Matilda

William the Conqueror was succeeded by his second son, William Rufus who was killed by an arrow in the New Forest. Legend has it that on the Sunday before Rufus' death the Abbot of Shrewsbury had preached at Gloucester Abbey. During his sermon he noted that 'the bow from on high is bent against the wicked and the arrow is drawn from the quiver'. On Rufus' death, the Conqueror's youngest son Henry, who was a member of the New Forest hunting party, rode immediately to Winchester without even attending to the removal of his brother's body. Three days later he was crowned Henry I.

Despite having at least twenty illegitimate children, Henry had only two legitimate heirs: William, who died in a shipwreck; and Matilda, who was married to Geoffrey of Anjou.

On Henry's death (said to have been caused by eating too many lampreys, an eel-like fish that was one product of the Severn fisheries) there was civil war between the followers of Matilda and those of Stephen, a nephew of William the Conqueror. The war was fought mainly in and around Gloucestershire because two of Matilda's staunchest allies had castles in the county. One was Miles of Gloucester who Matilda made Earl of Hereford, the other was Robert, Earl of Gloucester, one of Henry I's illegitimate children (and therefore Matilda's half-brother). Both Miles and Robert were formidable warriors. At first things went well for Matilda, especially when Robert captured Stephen and imprisoned him in Bristol, where Matilda and her son Henry lived under Robert's protection at one time during the conflict. However, Matilda's arrogance alienated both her allies and the people of the county (and country) and she lost ground. Robert was captured and exchanged for Stephen, who promptly captured most of Gloucestershire's castles and then won the Battle of Faringdon, near Lechlade. Stephen became undisputed king of England. Matilda and her husband Geoffrey retired to their French lands, though they returned several years later to sign an agreement at Wallingford in Oxfordshire that their son Henry would succeed Stephen.

6. Medieval Gloucestershire

The Plantagenet Kings

Henry II succeeded to the throne in 1154, becoming the first Plantagenet ruler (named after the sprig of broom, *genet* in French, worn by Geoffrey of Anjou in his helmet). Henry's successor, Richard I (the Lionheart) increased the privileges of Gloucester and these were confirmed by his successor John. Richard spent many years of his reign away on crusades, his absence and the unpleasantness of John leading to the legend of Robin Hood. Sadly, there was no similar outlaw-hero in the Forest of Dean at the same time.

John's reign is famous for Magna Carta, forced on him by barons appalled by his excesses. The charter is often seen as a bill of rights for subjects of the king but it really concerned itself with the privileges of the nobility, the common folk continuing much as before. Article 10 noted that 'No one shall hence forth lose life or members for the sake of our venison', a restriction of the king's right to mutilate or execute transgressors of forest law in the royal forests, though such extreme punishments do not seem to have been applied often, if at all in the Forest of Dean. Though he had little impact on the county, John must be mentioned if only to recall the comment of Roger of Wendover who, on John's death maintained that 'foul as it is, hell itself would be defiled by the fouler presence of John'. John died in 1216 and was buried in Worcester Cathedral, the first Norman king to be buried outside France.

The barons who had opposed John offered the succession to Prince Louis of France, so those who supported John's nine-year-old son Henry could waste no time in declaring him king. Henry was in Gloucester with his mother Isabella on 18 October when news arrived of John's death. On 28 October, the boy was crowned in Gloucester Abbey by the Bishop of Winchester, who performed the ceremony using Isabella's bracelet as a makeshift crown. Though Henry was later crowned again, the Gloucester coronation was official and is the only one ever not to have been performed in Westminster Abbey.

Henry was intelligent and pious, but a politically naïve king. His piety resulted in the construction of fine cathedrals such as Salisbury, and a new Westminster Abbey. His reign saw the growth of the universities at Oxford and Cambridge, but his naïvety led to renewed conflict with England's powerful barons. In 1263, followers of the barons took Gloucester Castle, having disguised themselves as wool sellers to gain entry. Prince Edward, Henry's son, attacked the castle but was repulsed and retreated to Tewkesbury where he fought a short but vicious battle for control of the castle. Edward won and as a warning to the barons' sympathisers, hung the man who had let the disguised barons into Gloucester Castle from Tewkesbury's West Gate, imprisoned the town councillors who had supported the barons' cause and razed the town. The barons' leader was Simon de Montfort. Later in the year he captured both Henry and Edward, imprisoning them at Gloucester. Edward escaped, attacked the town and forced the barons to surrender, though the dispute was not finally resolved until 1265 when de Montfort was killed in the Battle of Evesham and Henry's position as monarch was secure.

Prince Edward effectively ruled England for the last years of his father's life, becoming Edward I on Henry's death in 1272. He campaigned against the Welsh (building the great 'ring of stone' castles) and the Scots, but had lit-

A 'Winchcombe Worthy', one of the gargoyles on Winchcombe Church.

tle direct impact on Gloucestershire or the other counties of a subdued England.

His son, however, was to be intimately connected with the county forever as a result of his gruesome death. Edward II became king in 1307 at the age of twenty-three. He was as different from his father as it was possible to be. Edward I was a physically imposing, decisive, bullying soldier – a man's man in the context of early fourteenth-century England. His son was no soldier and was homosexual, though he also had a wife and son. The barons were appalled by Edward's love for Piers Gaveston and eventually had Gaveston murdered. In 1314, the Scots under Robert Bruce routed an English army at Bannockburn, further lowering Edward's standing in the eyes of the nobility. Though Edward survived the immediate crisis there was an upris-

ing in 1322 when his army was attacked by a barons' army at Boroughbridge. Edward was victorious and ruled a sullen nobility for three more years until his wife, Isabella, and son Edward also turned against him. Isabella had become the lover of the powerful Roger Mortimer and he, together with Prince Edward who was just fourteen years old, gathered an army and forced Edward to renounce the crown in favour of the young prince.

Edward II was taken to Berkeley Castle where he was installed in what is now called the King's Gallery. In 1327 it would have been a smaller room, set over a deep well. Rotting carcasses thrown into this well created a stench in the room that had been successfully used before to asphyxiate prisoners held there. But despite his perceived lack of manliness, Edward declined to

Berkeley. The castle is to the right, with the church and its displaced tower to the left.

Edward II's tomb in Gloucester Cathedral.

die conveniently and was eventually dispatched by having a red-hot poker pushed into his insides through his back passage. It is said – and who would doubt it – that Edward's screams could be heard in the nearby village. The apparent reason for such a barbaric method was that no wound should be visible on the king's body – the poker cauterising the bleeding as it was thrust deep. However, it is difficult to avoid the thought that the murderers saw poetic justice in this method of disposing of a homosexual king. Edward was buried in Gloucester Cathedral in December 1327. His tomb – of local limestone, topped by an alabaster effigy with angels gently holding the king's head, the whole encased in delicate stone tracery – rapidly became a place of pilgrimage, a fact which says much about the views of the common folk, far removed from the machinations of the nobles, on kingship.

Edward III's long reign saw the beginning of the Hundred Years War with France, the Battle of Crecy and the catastrophe of the Black Death. It also saw a rise in the power of parliament. The reign of his successor, Richard II (Edward's grandson), was even more turbulent, including the Peasants' Revolt and battles between the king and his nobles that ended with Henry Bolingbroke's invasion of England and Richard's capture. Richard died in Pontefract (probably murdered) and Bolingbroke was crowned Henry IV, his reign dominated by the Welsh uprising under Owain Glyndwr, the Lollard heresy and civil unrest. The Welsh, united under Glyndwr, invaded England. They reached Woodbury Hill near Worcester, which must have spread alarm throughout Gloucestershire, but then retreated and were never again a threat.

The Wars of the Roses

The reign of Bolingbroke's successor, Henry V, was glorious – the great victory of Agincourt would later inspire some of Shakespeare's most stirring words. But his death when his son, Henry VI, was just one year old led to the Wars of the Roses, a conflict that ended with the Battle of Tewkesbury.

The Wars of the Roses began after a bout of insanity afflicted Henry VI in 1453. Richard, Duke of York, ruled in his place but was unwilling to give up power when the king's sanity returned in 1455. He waged war against Margaret, Henry's queen, and the legitimate heir to the throne, their son Edward (the Lancastrian, red rose claimant). In 1460 Richard was killed at the Battle of Wakefield, but his son – confusingly also called Edward (the Yorkist, white rose claimant) – fought on. He was crowned Edward IV in 1461, so England then had two kings, as Henry VI lived on until 1471 when he was executed by the victorious Edward.

In April 1471 Edward IV had defeated and killed the Earl of Warwick – Warwick the Kingmaker who had changed allegiance and become an ally of Margaret – at Barnet. Margaret and Prince Edward had landed at Portland intent on linking up with Warwick and a Welsh army to create what would have been a formidable, probably a winning force. With Warwick dead it was imperative that the Lancastrians should link up with the Welsh, so Margaret marched towards Gloucester and its bridge over the Severn. On 2 May she reached Berkeley with Edward IV in pursuit having reached Old Sodbury. The next day she reached Gloucester, but Edward had ensured that its gates remained closed to her. The Lancastrians therefore had to continue towards Upton and its bridge. They reached Tewkesbury, utterly spent after two long days of marching. Later that day Edward reached Tredington by way of Stroud and Cheltenham, and prepared for battle the next day, before the Lancastrians could cross Upton bridge and link up with the Welsh army.

The Battle of Tewkesbury

On 4 May, the Lancastrians took up a position straddling the present route of the A38 south of the town. Their right flank was commanded by the Duke of Somerset, the left by the Duke of Devonshire. The centre was nominally commanded by Prince Edward, but actually controlled by Lord Wenlock. Wenlock was an odd

Tewkesbury Abbey.

choice. He had fought for the Lancastrians at St Albans, then changed sides and fought for the Yorkists at Towton. Now he had changed sides again. Opposing the 6,000 Lancastrians were about the same number of Yorkists. Their centre was commanded by Edward IV with his brother Richard, Duke of Gloucester (later Richard III) to his left, and Lord Hastings and George, Duke of Clarence (Edward's other brother) to his right.

Somerset began the battle by advancing through woodland on his right to try to surprise Gloucester's left flank. The plan was for Wenlock to charge when he saw Somerset attack Gloucester. But Edward IV was a canny soldier and had placed spearmen in the wood. They attacked Somerset and Gloucester also turned on

---

FIGHTING IN THE ABBEY

It is said that some Lancastrians sought sanctuary in the abbey where Abbot Strensham was celebrating Mass. Still holding the Sacrament, he hurried to the west door and ordered the fighting to stop. The abbot was only partially successful – the killing in the church stopped but the Lancastrians were hauled outside for summary execution. Prince Edward was one of those who died, though whether on the field or afterwards as a captive is a matter of debate. He was buried in the abbey's choir. Later, the monks toured the battlefield collecting pieces of armour, which were cut into strips and used to reinforce the inner side of the door of the sacristy.

him. Now was the time for Wenlock to advance – but he stayed still. Somerset's men were forced to retreat and were then routed. Many were chopped down in the aptly named Bloody Meadow beside the Avon, many more drowned trying to cross the river in heavy armour.

Somerset rode back to Wenlock and cursed him, calling him a traitor. He then took his axe and struck him dead. Whether Wenlock was actually a traitor has been debated ever since. Certainly his refusal to move was suspicious, but blame also lies with Prince Edward – had he charged, the men of Wenlock's command would almost certainly have followed. Now those men, demoralised by Wenlock's murder and Somerset's rout, turned and fled. They were pursued by the triumphant Yorkists and cut down as they sought refuge in Tewkesbury.

Margaret escaped to Malvern, but was captured and spent five years as a prisoner before returning to France. Anne, the young widow of Prince Edward, married Richard of Gloucester and became a queen after all. The Duke of Clarence, disliked by his brothers, became an inconvenience and was executed – not drowned in a butt of Malmsey wine, as is claimed in a more colourful but less accurate version of his death. He and his wife lie in a vault below Tewkesbury Abbey's high altar.

Edward IV reigned until 1483. When he died, the crown should have passed to his twelve-year-old son Edward V, but he and his younger brother disappeared. History, and in particular Shakespeare, sees the deaths of the 'Princes in the Tower' as the work of their uncle, Richard of Gloucester, who became Richard III. The debate over whether Richard was an evil, murdering hunchback or the victim of a propaganda campaign still rages, but an interesting sidelight on the deaths of the princes is the local story that it was from Gloucester that Richard sent the instructions for the killings.

The Black Death

Though the self-sufficient farming community of Gloucestershire's medieval period may represent a rural idyll to some, in reality it was a hard, cruel life. Hunger was frequent, especially in winter, and starvation was only a flood or period of bad weather away. Incapacitating injuries could be death sentences, as were many of the diseases that medical advances and improved hygiene have now eliminated. One such was bubonic plague, the Black Death, which broke out in June 1348 at Melcombe Regis in Dorset when infected black rats came ashore from a ship. As the plague advanced, terrified folk tried to stem the spread: anyone from Bristol, for example, was banned from entering Gloucester. But in the absence of an understanding of the mechanism of infection such measures were useless. The nursery rhyme 'Ring-a-ring of roses' for all its apparent innocence, speaks of the disease. The ring of roses refers to the discoloured swellings that affected the groin and armpits of sufferers. The 'pocketful of posies' was the flowers held to ward off the disease, which was thought to be carried by bad smells. 'Atishoo, atishoo' is the sneezing of the sufferers before 'we all fall down' – dead. Death usually occurred within five painful days. By 1349 the plague had affected all of Britain and about half the population of approximately five million was dead or dying. By 1350 the worst was over. Ironically, the inevitable labour shortage that followed led to increased wages (despite an attempt by the king to stop the rise) and a general improvement in living standards and prosperity. The population, now reduced by half, remained at this level into the sixteenth century.

Country and Town

The Black Death put a strain on the feudal system because the labourers who benefited from the wage increase were at the bottom of the social pyramid. Villeins (feudal tenants who worked, in part, for the lord) did not benefit, but had to pay increased wages to their labourers. Worse was to come when Richard II, short of cash, introduced a poll tax. This was collected in 1377 and 1379, but there was widespread evasion when it was applied again in 1380. In 1381,

Coleford, the Dean town which received a charter in the seventeenth century.

a determined effort to enforce the tax led to the Peasants' Revolt led by Wat Tyler (a revolt which was echoed 600 years later when a new Poll Tax was introduced).

The villein paid rent to his lord, in cash or kind, and his lord did likewise, the king being at the top of the pyramid. Some knights paid the king their tax in military service, but from the time of Henry I they could pay *scutage* (cash) in lieu. This was better for the king as a knight's service might only last a few weeks, too short a period for a campaign, particularly if it was in France. The king could then use the cash to pay local mercenaries for such campaigns and so also reduce transportation costs.

The church was also a zealous collector of taxes. As the centuries passed, the church became less a spiritual haven than an agency of civil authority, as much concerned with wealth and power as the nobility – a fact that was particularly true of the abbeys.

The feudal system was also under pressure from the expansion and growth in importance of towns, particularly those that had been granted charters to hold markets and fairs. In medieval Gloucestershire, most of the towns of the modern-day county were already in existence. In the Forest of Dean, the towns of Alvington, Beachley, Dymock, Lydney, Mitcheldean, Newnham and St Briavels had all received charters by the fourteenth century: indeed, all but Mitcheldean and St Briavels had received them some hundred years previously. Coleford received its charter in 1661, but this may have been a restatement as it is known that there was a market hall in 1643 that was destroyed during the Civil War. In the Vale, the towns of Berkeley, Gloucester, Tewkesbury and Thornbury were early (eleventh century) chartered towns, joined by Dursley in the twelfth century; Almondsbury, Bitton, Chipping Sodbury, Frampton, Pucklechurch, Tockington and Wickwar in the thirteenth century; and Alkerton, Deerhurst, Leonard Stanley, Newport, Tortworth and Winterbourne in the fourteenth century. In the Cotswolds, Winchcombe was an early chartered town, with Chipping Campden and Stow receiving charters in the twelfth century; Blockley, Cheltenham, Fairford, Hawkesbury, Kempsford, Kings Stanley, Lechlade, Minchinhampton, Marshfield, Moreton-in-Marsh, Northleach, Painswick, Prestbury, Tormarton and Wotton-under-Edge received charters in the town explosion of the thirteenth century; and Brimpsfield, Guiting and Horsley received theirs in the fourteenth century. The number of towns reflects both their importance and the slow pace of travel in medieval Gloucestershire: towns being established at, roughly, intervals of a day's cart movement.

The architecture of some of the towns reflects their origins. Of these, one of the best examples is Chipping Sodbury, which was created as a market town and has both the usual wide street and the name, 'chipping' being the old name for a market.

The fairs of Stow-on-the-Wold, held annually on 12 May and 24 October since Edward IV's grant of a charter in 1476, included the sale of tens of thousands of sheep. Accommodating, feeding and satisfying the thirst of the sellers and buyers made the town prosperous, while the taxes levied on those who sold their goods at market, and on the merchants and craftsmen who sold to the market-goers allowed councils to modernise their towns, adding to the enthusiasm of people to live in them. However, many of the merchants who came to English towns in the early medieval period were Norman, adding to the resentment felt by the Saxons for their new lords. As towns increased in importance they became clear symbols of wealth, authority and control, which must also have fuelled the resent-

ment of the almost exclusively Saxon farm labour force that kept the whole system operating.

The development of a town depended not only on having a charter but also on who actually owned it. Cirencester, owned by the abbey which took the market tolls, and Berkeley, a possession of the castle-owners, were prevented from developing in a similar way to Gloucester, which was free of such stifling ownership.

Because most town buildings were built of wood, fire was a constant threat and a regular feature of life in county towns throughout the medieval period. Fires devastated Gloucester in 1101 and again in 1122. Though it is often, and rightly, claimed that the Great Fire of London allowed the rebuilding of a previously disease-ridden, unhygienic town – and the same case could be made for other English towns – such arguments would have been of little comfort to those whose property and lives were at risk.

By the time of the Norman Conquest, Bristol was a notable sea-port, but not a site of strategic importance and was completely overshadowed by Gloucester. Norman Bristol, protected by the Avon and Frome rivers, was small and almost completely enclosed. However, it became the site of a castle, built by Geoffrey of Mowbray, the first Norman lord of Bristol. The castle was sited to the east of the town, filling the space between the two rivers and so completing the defensive ring. A town wall was also built, the rivers effectively forming a moat beyond it. Of the medieval gates through the town wall only St John's Gate survives. The figures that stand above it are Brennus and Belinus, legendary founders of the city. The groove for the gate's portcullis can still be seen. There is also a bastion from the thirteenth-century wall in the courtyard of the St Nicholas Almshouses in King Street.

Castles

Stone was at first reserved for the town walls and castles though it was later the building material of choice for the nobility and rich merchants. In Gloucester, the Normans strengthened

St Briavels Castle, now one of Britain's most popular Youth Hostels.

Sudeley Castle. The picturesque ruins of the fifteenth-century castle stand beside the more complete, later buildings.

the town walls, demolished the Roman East Gate (leaving one wall intact) and rebuilt it, and built a new stone castle to the north-west of the motte and bailey structure. They also built a bridge over the Severn. It was this castle and bridge that were to play such an important role in the build up to the battle of Tewkesbury. Nothing now remains of Gloucester Castle, but the county still has remnants of Berkeley, another Norman castle.

Berkeley Castle was built in the years following the Norman Conquest – first as a motte and bailey and then as a shell-keep. The latter dates from 1153 and surrounds the truncated motte of the original. Of this rebuilding, details remain,

though the present building is largely fourteenth century with later modifications. Inside it has some superb features. Historically, the King's Gallery where Edward II met his dreadful death is the most interesting. Architecturally, the Great Hall is the centrepiece: it has a magnificent roof and a very interesting screen, originally built in Pembrokeshire. The roof of the hexagonal kitchen is also delightful, a spider's-web of cross-beams. The grand stairs, the morning rooms and the drawing rooms complete the architectural treasures.

St Briavels Castle dates from the late thirteenth century. The most striking part of the surviving buildings, and the only one which is in any way complete, is the gatehouse, often called a keep-gatehouse as it could be closed off at both the front and rear to form a contained, fortified unit. The castle was the home of the Constable of the Forest of Dean: a pit under one of the porter's lodges in the gatehouse being assumed to be the prison for those who had transgressed forest law. St Briavels Castle is now owned by the Youth Hostels Association.

The other castle remains in the county, notably Sudeley and Thornbury, also date from the later medieval period and consequently are country houses rather than war engines – the change from symbols of control to palatial residences mirrored the change from Saxon and Norman to English. Of these new 'palaces' Berkeley is a good example, but one in which the original purpose of the building was modified. Sudeley Castle, built by Ralph Boteler in the mid-fifteenth century, is another. The first castle

was built as a mansion, but with embattled towers and gatehouses. Three towers and the gatehouse survive, as do the remains of the slightly later banqueting hall. Of the latter only an elegant wall and an associated octagonal tower remain, but the Gatehouse, Garderobe, Portmore and Dungeon towers are still almost complete. The Dungeon tower sounds formidable but was actually living rather than prison accommodation despite the name. The remainder of Sudeley dates from the late sixteenth/early seventeenth centuries and is very elegant in style. The whole now stands in beautiful formal gardens, the work of the Dent family who acquired Sudeley in the early nineteenth century.

Though the first Thornbury Castle was built in the early twelfth century, the present building dates from the early sixteenth century. Much of the Tudor building remains, despite the building having been deserted and roofless for almost three centuries. It was partially restored in 1720, but not fully refurbished until the early nineteenth century.

Great Houses

As the centuries passed and the differences between Saxon and Norman became blurred, nobles felt able to build unfortified houses. Of the houses from this period, the best are at Horton, Little Sodbury, Owlpen and Pauntley.

Horton was built in the first half of the twelfth century and has a claim to being the oldest continuously occupied house in the land. Being both domestic and unfortified, it is one of the earliest of the type in Britain, though some parts have been replaced: the roof, for instance, is fourteenth century.

Little Sodbury Manor dates from the late fifteenth century. It was once owned by Sir John Walsh, twice High Sheriff of Gloucestershire, who acted as King's Champion at the coronation of Henry VIII in 1509. Later, he was host to Henry and Anne Boleyn who stayed for a few days, probably in the Oriel room, the name given to the room overlooking the Severn Vale that contains an oriel window. Owlpen Manor,

---

THE BATTLE OF NIBLEY GREEN

In March 1470, the last pitched battle fought on British soil between private armies took place on Nibley Green in the Cotswold village of North Nibley. A thousand men loyal to William, Lord Berkeley, faced the same number drawn up in support of Thomas Talbot, Lord Lisle. The argument was over the succession to the castle and great estate of the Berkeley family. Lord Thomas Berkeley and his beloved wife Margaret had only one child, a daughter called Elizabeth. When Margaret died tragically young, Thomas refused to remarry and died without a male heir. (The memorial brasses of Thomas and Margaret can be seen in Wotton-under-Edge Church – they are among the very best in the county.) The succession passed to his nephew. Half a century after Thomas' death this succession was contested by the young Lord Lisle, a grandson of Elizabeth, who challenged Lord Berkeley, a descendant of Thomas' nephew, to a battle to settle the issue.

The battle was swift. Lisle's men charged but were defeated, and 150 lives were lost including that of Lisle himself.

Horton Court. The earliest house, standing beside the church, is one of the oldest domestic houses in Britain. It was later the home of Dr William Knight, Henry VIII's chief secretary, who added to the building in Gothic style and was responsible for the ambulatory, complete with medallions of Roman emperors, which stands beside it.

one of the most beautiful and romantically positioned houses in the Cotswolds, dates from the mid-fifteenth century, though it was enlarged in the eighteenth century. It was abandoned in about 1850 and rediscovered by Norman Jewson, an Arts and Crafts movement architect. The manor has a superb Great Hall.

Other houses of the period include Ashleworth and Brockworth Courts; Bishop's Cleeve and Buckland Rectories – among the most authentic medieval rectories in Britain; Daneway House, which was later to be associated with the Arts and Crafts movement; Down Ampney House; and Forthampton Court, the country house of the Abbots of Tewkesbury, the last of whom, John Wakeman, used it before becoming Gloucester's first bishop.

Wool Churches

The most significant buildings from the county's medieval period are the superb 'wool churches', so-called because they were endowed by rich wool merchants. By common consent, the finest of these churches are those at Chipping Campden, Northleach and Cirencester, but other churches are also worth noting.

Chipping Campden – both the town and the church – owed much to the generosity of Sir Baptist Hicks, a mercer and financier from

Owlpen Manor, the finest of all the county's small manor houses.

London with Gloucestershire antecedents. He was incredibly rich even by the standards of the day and had been made Contractor for the Crown Lands by James I who borrowed immense sums from him on various occasions. He lived in London, having built the first country house in the village of Kensington on land he won at cards. This house was named after Campden and stood on the site of the present Campden Hill Square.

The fine Jacobean pulpit and brass falcon lectern in the church were gifts from him, but the most notable gift was the South Chapel, which was given to the church in the early 1600s to house the remains of the Hicks family and their successors. The chapel is a treasury of fine, monumental masonry or a demonstration of an overwhelming self-indulgence – depending on the visitor's point of view. It includes the canopied tomb of Sir Baptist Hicks and his wife Elizabeth, the couple depicted in full-size alabaster effigies representing them in their coronation robes and, most bizarrely, effigies of Sir Edward Noel and his wife Juliana, the eldest daughter of Sir Baptist and Lady Hicks, as larger than life-size figures dressed in shrouds in the act of resurrection on the Day of Judgement. Close to the church are all that remains of the house Sir Baptist built for himself at a cost of £29,000, with internal decorations costing an extra £15,000 – the market hall, which he bequeathed to the town, was built at a cost of £90. The house, which, not surprisingly, upset many of the locals at the time by its ostentatious splendour, was burned down during the Civil War.

While the nobility lived in superb stone houses the ordinary folk of medieval Gloucestershire had to make do with much simpler constructions. For many years the standard building method was the use of a cruck frame with infill panels, as illustrated in this house at Didbrook.

DICK WHITTINGTON

Another fine house from Gloucestershire's medieval period is Pauntley Court. The present house is mainly an eighteenth-century refurbishment of an older building, which was the birthplace of Richard Whittington in 1350. As the third son of William Whittington (and being very much younger than his elder brothers), Richard had little hope of a significant inheritance. Aged about thirteen, he was sent to London as an apprentice to John Fitzwarren, a mercer. He married Fitzwarren's daughter, which was probably the basis of his own initial success as a merchant.

Richard rapidly became one of London's foremost importers of silks, brocades and damasks, and actually imported the material for the wedding dresses of Henry IV's daughters. He was elected Sheriff of London in 1393 and was Lord Mayor four times between 1397 and 1420. His wealth allowed him to lend money to the king and also to finance building works. He was responsible for work at Gloucester Cathedral, St Bartholomew's Hospital, London, and also for the rebuilding of Newgate Prison (a more charitable work than it might seem,

as the original was a squalid disgrace – not that the new one was a great improvement). Richard died in 1423, but his tomb in St Michael de Paternoster was lost when the church was destroyed in the Great Fire of 1666.

The pantomime version of his life derives from a practice, common during that time, where merchants such Fitzwarren would allow their employees to put one item on a trading ship and keep the profit it made. Legend has it that Dick put his cat (his only possession, bought to keep rats and mice down in his room) on the ship. When it reached Africa's Barbary Coast, a local Moorish lord used the cat to deal with a plague of rats and was so impressed by it that he paid the ship's captain a fortune to keep it – and that is the basis of the famous tale. In the pantomime, Dick and the cat are leaving London when he hears a peal of bells telling him to turn again as he will become Lord Mayor. Quite how the cat story arose is still debated, the most likely explanation being that Dick's fortune was founded on *achat* (trading) and that this sounded like *a chat* and so became a cat.

The exterior of Northleach Church is magnificent, its soaring pinnacles and windows all pointing to heaven, but the real treasures are inside. The Northleach memorial brasses are the finest collection in Britain, almost all of them to wool merchants, many of the merchants with their feet on woolsacks. The earliest brass is from about 1400, the finest being that of 1458 to John Fortey who was largely responsible for the rebuilding of the church. This huge brass is over 1.5m (5ft) high and shows Fortey in a gown with collar and cuffs, fastened with a belt. Elsewhere in the church, one particularly interesting item appears in the memorial to John Taylour, his wife and fifteen children, in the south aisle. At the base of the brass there is a woolsack, a sheep, a shepherd's crook and a pair of wool shears, a comprehensive list of the items that brought Taylour his wealth.

Cirencester is a church of superlatives – the tallest tower in Gloucestershire at just over 49m

(162ft), the oldest twelve-bell peal in England, the largest porch of any English church. The south porch was built in 1490 on land that belonged to the abbey rather than the town. It served as offices for the abbey, being used for meeting people who did not need to enter the abbey itself. After the Dissolution it was the town hall and was only given to the church in the seventeenth century. It is now the finest church porch in England and stands three storeys high and three bays wide and deep, with a superb open stonework parapet and ground-floor ceiling vaulting.

Inside the church there is one of the few pre-Reformation wineglass pulpits in the country, a fine stone piece with good tracery. There are also some remarkable brass memorials; excellent wall paintings in St Catherine's Chapel, which date from the late fifteenth century; and the Boleyn Cup, a gilded silver cup hallmarked 1535 and bearing the crest of the family of Anne Boleyn.

The alabaster effigy of Lady Elizabeth Hicks in St James' Church, Chipping Campden. This formidable looking woman was the wife of Sir Baptist Hicks, a major benefactor of the church and town.

Of other churches that benefited from wool money, Winchcombe is worth visiting for its gargoyles. Magnificent in their ugliness, the 'Winchcombe Worthies' are said to depict either local personages whom the stonemasons disliked or unpopular monks – plausible, given the conflict between town and abbey. The church tower is topped by a superb weathercock, by far the finest in the Cotswolds and one of the best in Britain.

Fairford Church, a miniature cathedral in appearance, was built by the wool merchant John Tame in the late fifteenth century. It is

famed for its windows, the only complete set of medieval glass of any parish church in Britain, although repairs were required to the west windows after a severe storm in 1703. The original work was carried out under the direction of Barnard Flower, Henry VIII's Master Glass Painter. The windows portray the life of Christ, scenes from the Old Testament, the Evangelists, Apostles and Prophets. Though ageing has affected some of the detail of the figures, the bold use of colour on the glass can still be appreciated.

Finally, Lechlade Church must be mentioned as it is entirely Perpendicular in style, which has led many to assert that it is one of the half-dozen finest in Gloucestershire. The soaring elegance of the spire was described by Leland, the Elizabethan traveller as a 'pratie pyramid of stone'. The single style owes much to the generosity of local wool merchants whose gifts allowed the church to be built very quickly. Inside there are some good medieval brasses and a sixteenth-century carved figure of St Agatha. Though a little crude, the figure is a powerful emblem: St Agatha, a third-century martyr, was tortured to death, the torture including mutilation of her breasts which is unsparingly depicted. (She has become a symbol of women undergoing mastectomy as a result.)

The woolsack, sheep, crook and shears at the base of the memorial brass to John Taylour in Northleach Church.

Northleach, one of the three great Wool Churches of the Cotswolds.

Resurrection Morning, one of the painted glass windows in the Corpus Christi Chapel of St Mary's Church, Fairford. The windows of Fairford Church date from the late fifteenth/early sixteenth centuries and are the most complete set of medieval glass in any British parish church.

Medieval Dean

It is likely that in Dean, as elsewhere in Gloucestershire, the process of forest clearance began in prehistoric times. This nibbling at the edge of the forest continued in Saxon times, as the number of hamlets that end in 'ton' (settlement), particularly on the southern fringe, indicates. But in Saxon times the use of the forest as a hunting ground for kings and noblemen was well established. Bath Abbey, which owned the manor of Tidenham, had to repulse several attempts to incorporate the holding into the royal hunting forest. The abbey continued to hold the area after the Conquest, but finally lost it in the thirteenth century.

It was with the Normans that the name Forest of Dean became established. At the time of the Doomsday Book the forest had no name, but the

strip of country stretching east–west across the north of the area, centred on Mitcheldean, was known as Dene. Mitcheldean itself means 'great valley' in Saxon, so Dene must have been applied originally to the northern base of the raised plateau. In Norman times St Briavels was the administrative centre of the forest, the castle there having probably been built by Milo of Hereford. By the fourteenth century the forest was occasionally called St Briavels, sometimes Dean, and it was the latter that became the more common, and then the accepted, name.

The forest was a favourite hunting ground of the Norman kings. The position, close to Gloucester, one of the three royal centres of Saxon and early Norman England, made it readily accessible. It is said that William the Conqueror was hunting in the forest when he was told of the Danish invasion of 1069. The animals the Norman kings hunted were deer and wild boar: King John is said to have been particularly fond of Dean boar. The chief deer of the forest was the fallow, introduced to England by the Romans. Although the early medieval forest also held small numbers of red and roe deer, they eventually disappeared, the fallow now being the only Dean deer. For much of the medieval period the reduction in animal numbers was attributed to poaching, but it is clear that the real cause was over-hunting by the king and his noblemen guests. It is recorded that at Christmas 1254, Henry III had 100 Dene boar at his feast. Such killing was unsustainable: by 1267 boar were scarce and by the end of the thirteenth century they were probably extinct.

A complex system of officials and courts was set up to control the Forest of Dean. At the top of this pyramid of officialdom was the king, below him there were two Justices of the Forest, one controlling the forests north of the River Trent, the other those to the south. Below these chief justices were itinerant justices who visited the forest sites to hear cases. The Forest of Dean was policed by the Constable of St Briavels Castle. Below him were nine or ten Foresters-of-Fee, each of whom policed a portion of the forest. There were also eight to twelve Sergeants-of-

---

SHEEP IN THE FOREST OF DEAN

Although pigs were allowed to roam the royal forest, rooting out nuts and fungi, sheep were banned for the improbable reason that they made the woodland grass inedible to deer. It is more likely that the sheep, nibbling very close to the ground, were preventing the growth of new shoots. In all areas with a large population of sheep, the regrowth of forest is halted.

Despite this ban, sheep did eventually become a feature of the forest. Their owners, known as 'sheep badgers', kept the animals to supplement the low wages paid by mining. It is likely that the forest sheep date from the late medieval period when hunting was less of a preoccupation with royalty and the forest laws were less strictly applied. However, contemporary sheep badgers dispute this, claiming a more ancient right and opposing attempts to fence the forest and so restrict the movement of their animals. Wandering sheep are seen by many as a nuisance and there is, at the time of writing, another debate over the rights of the sheep badgers, this time generated by the Foot and Mouth Disease outbreak of 2001 and the decision to allow sheep to re-enter the forest.

Autumn (above) and winter (below) in the Forest of Dean.

Speech House.

Fee who held a roving brief across the entire forest. Both Foresters-of-Fee and Sergeants-of-Fee had foresters and woodwards who actually carried out such planting and clearing work as was required. This system concerned itself with both 'venison' and 'vert', the former being anything related to the animals of the forest, the latter relating to the greenery – the trees and undergrowth, everything that provided food and shelter for the animals.

There was a second system that came below the Sheriff of the county. This consisted of four verderers and twelve regarders. The regarders made regular inspections of the forest and reported their findings to the itinerant justices. The verderers were a first line of justice. They held Courts of Attachment at which minor offences against vert could be tried. No vert case which might result in a fine of more than 4d could be tried at a Court of Attachment, and the court had no jurisdiction over venison cases, though it could commit an accused person to gaol pending a case before an itinerant court. The Court of Attachment in Dean became known as the Speech Court and was held at the Speech House in the centre of the forest. The present Speech House was built in 1680, replacing Kensley House, on the same site, which had been used since at least 1335. Speech Court is still held there, though Speech House is now a hotel, and the forest still has four verderers, though their duties are now largely symbolic.

The overall effect of forest law has been debated for many years. The outlawing of poaching is often claimed to have helped sustain the numbers of deer, but, as noted previously, royal over-hunting was almost certainly the major reason for the decline in numbers, poaching probably being a secondary effect. What is certainly true is that restrictions on activities in the forest and on forest clearing allowed the forest to survive. More significantly, had forest law not applied, it is likely that Dean would now be much as the Cotswolds are, small pockets of woodland surrounded by larger areas of farmland.

THE ENCHANTED GLADE

According to one of the most charming legends of the Forest of Dean, in medieval times there was an enchanted glade at the heart of the forest. If a hunter entered it and said 'I am thirsty' a boy dressed in green would appear carrying a golden horn of mead. One day a visiting knight was hunting with a local noble and was taken to the glade. Seeing the golden horn the knight's eyes lit up and, after ensuring he was the last to leave the clearing, he concealed the horn under his cloak. As he was riding back to his host's lodgings, his cloak was thrown back by the wind, revealing the horn. Realising he had been found out, the knight rode off. He was hunted down by the noble's men and taken to Gloucester where he was tried and hanged. The horn was taken back to the forest and placed in the centre of the glade, but the boy never returned to claim it and was never seen again.

Autumn in the Forest of Dean

7. THE TUDORS

Henry VII

On 22 August 1485, Richard III became the only English king other than Harold to die in battle. The victor at Bosworth Field was Henry Tudor, a man with a tenuous claim to the throne. He became Henry VII and married Elizabeth of York, Edward IV's daughter, amalgamating the red and white roses of the Lancastrians and Yorkists to form the Tudor Rose. Henry's enthusiasm for accruing wealth made the tax-collecting activities of his predecessors seem positively philanthropic, though with the prosperity of England increasing, the burden of extra taxes could be tolerated without significant unrest. Henry also placed an embargo on the export of unfinished woollen cloth, which was not only economically astute (as the import of finished product meant a net outflow of wealth), but also tax efficient as he could put a higher tax on finished cloth.

The Port of Bristol

In the fourteenth century, Bristol expanded beyond its enclosing rivers as its importance both as a clothmaking town and a port grew – ships sailed up the Avon to the heart of the city with trading goods from Europe. Welsh Back, near Bristol Bridge, is part of the medieval port from which the trading ships sailed. Fishing fleets also sailed from the port to the cod-filled waters of the Atlantic. The decree of the Catholic Church that only 'cold' food could be eaten on Fridays had made fishing highly lucrative – fish being considered cold as they lived in the cold sea. Cod, which when salted lasted a long time before spoiling, was a particularly prized catch. The fisherman of Bristol grew wealthy on cod, at first catching it close to Iceland and then from a new fishery much further away. Of particular interest to historians are reports that Bristol's fishing fleets would return to port with the catch already salted. This may shed light on the discovery of the New World, as salting was a process that required a land base. Locally, it is said that before his westward journey, Columbus visited the city and spoke to the fishermen who told him of their finds. It is also said that Bristolian merchants wrote to Columbus after his voyage complaining that he was taking credit for discovering what was already known. Had the Bristolian fishermen already discovered America when fishing the cod-filled waters off the New England coast? That would certainly explain why John Cabot came to Bristol to seek sponsorship for his search for the North-West Passage.

The Bristolian merchants of Cabot's time had elegant houses within reach of the port. One merchant, William Canynges, owned a fleet of ships and employed almost 1,000 men. Canynges was wealthy enough to entertain royalty at his house (Edward IV stayed there) and was chiefly responsible for the rebuilding of St Mary Redcliffe, Bristol's most famous and beautiful church. Built on the scale and lavishness of a cathedral, St Mary Redcliffe was described by Elizabeth I as 'the fairest, goodliest and most famous parish church in England'. With its soaring lines, exquisite vaulting and numerous treasures, St Mary Redcliffe even outshines the great Cotswold wool churches.

Henry VIII

Henry VII's eldest son Arthur – a link with Henry Tudor's own Celtic background – was married to Catherine of Aragon when he was fifteen. Sadly, Arthur died just five months later. Fearing the loss of the dowry he had received for Catherine, Henry wanted to marry her to his

Catherine Parr's Tomb, St Mary's Chapel, Sudeley Castle.

JOHN CABOT

Under the terms of the Treaty of Tordesillas in 1494, the Pope granted the western hemisphere to the Spanish and the eastern hemisphere to the Portuguese, a situation intolerable to the English, French and Dutch as it made them the buyers of the spices and other treasures of the east not the merchants. Shortly after the signing of the treaty, a man arrived in Bristol offering to lead an expedition to Cathay. The man was Giovanni Caboto, now the honorary Englishman John Cabot.

Cabot was given letters patent by Henry VII to explore for new lands and a passage to Cathay. Cabot's licence stipulated that he was to give 20 per cent of all profits from the voyage to the king and that no-one was to disembark on any land discovered without Crown permission. Cabot left Bristol on 20 May 1497 in the *Mathew* (probably named after his wife, Mathye, rather than the Disciple) with a crew of eighteen. On 24 June he landed in Newfoundland, just a short distance from L'Anse aux Meadows. Finding evidence of inhabitants and fearing confrontation, Cabot took on water and left, exploring the local coast before returning to Bristol. On the next voyage Cabot (now the Grand Admiral Cabot, England's answer to Admiral of the Ocean Columbus) sailed with five ships, one of which soon returned after being damaged in a gale. The fate of the rest is a mystery. Sebastian Cabot, John's son, claimed to have been on this trip and gave a plausible account of crossing the Arctic Circle, encountering 'monstrous heaps of ice swimming in the sea', days eighteen hours long and the entrance to a gulf heading west where many men died of cold. Kind historians wonder if he had sailed into Davis Strait and found Hudson Strait. Less generous folk claim that as Sebastian was a known storyteller he may not even have been on the expedition. Certainly he sheds no light on the fate of his father.

Cabot is commemorated in the tower on Bristol's Brandon Hill, which was erected in 1897.

younger son, Henry. The Catholic church forbade such a marriage, but Henry sought and received permission from the Pope, which was to have unforeseen implications. Henry also had a daughter, Margaret, whose marriage to James IV of Scotland was to give rise to the Stuart dynasty of English kings.

Henry VII died in 1509 and was succeeded by Henry VIII. There was no indication during the early years of Henry's reign that he was on a collision course with the Catholic Church. In the late fourteenth century, John Wycliffe had preached against what he saw as the errors of the church, and his followers, the Lollards, had continued his teachings, but the movement had few followers and was relatively short-lived. When, in 1517, Martin Luther nailed his ninety-five theses to the door of Wittenburg Cathedral, a pamphlet denouncing his views was published in England. Officially, the author was King Henry and he was awarded the title *Fidei Defensor* (Defender of the Faith) by a grateful Pope, though most experts believe the actual author was Sir Thomas More.

By now Henry was at odds with the Pope over his refusal to annul his marriage to Catherine of Aragon. Henry wanted a son: Catherine had given birth to five children, all of whom died, and then to a healthy girl, Mary. There followed a series of miscarriages. By the early 1530s, Catherine was nearing fifty and beyond childbearing age, and Henry was in love with Anne Boleyn. To clear the way for marriage to Anne and, he hoped, for the birth of the legitimate son he dreamed of, Henry needed a divorce from Catherine. But only the Pope could grant an annulment of their marriage, and he was a virtual prisoner of Charles V of Spain. Charles was the nephew of Catherine and Spain was no friend of England. Papal authorisation was not forthcoming: its absence cost Thomas Wolsey his life and brought Henry into direct conflict with Papal authority.

One of the men Henry sent to the Pope was Dr William Knight, resident at Horton Court. Knight is an interesting figure who rose from lowly beginnings to high distinction under Henry. He held a doctorate in law and was an

St Mary Redcliffe Church

After the death of his wife, William Canynges, a wealthy merchant, gave away his wealth and became a priest, celebrating his first Mass at St Mary Redcliffe at Whitsuntide 1467. Each Whit Sunday since 1493 a special service has been held to commemorate this. For the service, the floor of the church is strewn with fresh rushes and herbs, a memory of the time when herbs and flower posies were believed to ward off plague and other diseases. Today, the service is one of Bristol's leading ceremonies, attended by the Lord Mayor and the City Council.

Within the church, the Chatterton Room is named after Thomas Chatterton (1752–80) who, aged fifteen, wrote poems on parchment he found there and then claimed they were by a medieval priest called Rowley, chaplain to William Canynges. The true source was discovered, but rather than being hailed as a poetic genius, Chatterton was ostracised, and he committed suicide aged seventeen. Today Chatterton's work is claimed to have played a major part in the 'Romantic Revolution' of early/mid-nineteenth century poetry. It is fitting therefore that two of the Lakeland poets associated with the movement, Samuel Taylor Coleridge and the Bristolian Robert Southey were married in the church to the sisters Sarah and Elizabeth Fricker in 1795.

St Mary Redcliffe Church seen from Bristol's Floating Harbour.

eminent churchman, having held positions in the cathedrals of Lincoln, Bangor and Salisbury. He was also, for a time, Henry's chief secretary. At Horton, Knight added the Tudor gothic court to the original Norman hall in about 1520. Knight also built the loggia, with its four Roman emperors' medallions in the garden. But, brilliant diplomat though he was, Knight could not change the Pope's mind.

In taking on the Catholic Church, Henry risked a potential confrontation with his English subjects, but the population was ripe for change. Many abbots and bishops had vast incomes and lived as well as, often better than, the nobility. They also had great power over the ordinary folk and were not reluctant to exercise it. This caused resentment among the people, which was fuelled by the ignorance of many of the clergy who often held positions of influence without always offering much in exchange. Even after the Dissolution, one bishop who interviewed his clergy found that almost two-thirds could not quote the Ten Commandments, some who could not recite the Lord's Prayer and even more who did not know who the author had been. Many of these complaints found their way to Henry in Simon Fish's *Supplication of the Beggars* in 1529. Fish, who did much to distribute Tyndale's English *New Testament*, had collected examples of greed and bad practice from across England in his pamphlet, which Henry is said to have carried with him for a long time.

WILLIAM TYNDALE

William Tyndale was born in Gloucestershire, though exactly where is a matter of debate, current scholarship favouring the Forest of Dean over the Severn Vale. Equally uncertain is the actual year of his birth, but it is thought to have been between 1490 and 1495, these dates being arrived at by working backwards from 1515 when he received his MA at Oxford and was ordained.

He moved to Little Sodbury Manor in 1521 to join Sir John Walsh's household, where he probably acted as tutor to the children, secretary to Sir John and chaplain to the household. Tyndale's time at Little Sodbury was crucial to his life's work. By then he had seen that the typical clergyman of the day was more interested in his social position than in teaching the Christian ethic. He observed the condition of the local peasants: for the most part they were hardworking, but underfed and desperately poor. They were also superstitious, which Tyndale believed to be due to a lack of positive guidance.

It was at a dinner in the manor house that he made his famous remark to a visiting high dignitary, who in an enraged attempt to silence the scripture-quoting upstart shouted 'We were better be without God's law than the Pope's', to which Tyndale replied 'I defy the Pope and all his laws. If God shall spare my life, ere many years I will cause the boy that follows the plough to know more of the Bible than thou doest'. Remarks like this one, coupled with an intimate knowledge of the Scriptures with which to back his arguments, made Tyndale many enemies and his presence at the manor house became an embarrassment to Walsh. Finally, in 1523 he left to go to London.

While at the manor house he had already translated some of the works of Erasmus. It seems he quickly became disillusioned with London and went to Hamburg in 1524, where he continued his translation work. In 1526, his English *New Testament* was printed at Worms. Only two copies now exist of this printing, one in the library of St Paul's, London, the other at the Baptist College in Bristol. Tyndale, now working in Antwerp, then began a translation of the *Old Testament* in 1530, assisted by Miles Coverdale. Although the religious climate was changing, it was not changing quickly enough to prevent the imprisonment of Tyndale, who was charged with heresy, tried and found guilty. On 6 October 1536 his body was burnt at the stake in the courtyard of the Castle of Vilvorde after he had been executed by strangulation.

Within two years the change in England was complete. In 1538, Henry VIII decreed that every church in England should have an English Bible. He gave permission for two translations, one by Miles Coverdale, the other by John Rogers (under the name of Thomas Matthew). Although Tyndale's name is in neither, most of both of the translations are his work.

Henry made a royal addition to this general antipathy when Anne Boleyn gave him a copy of William Tyndale's *Obedience of a Christian Man*. This argued that a king was responsible for both the physical and spiritual welfare of his subjects. To Henry this was an argument in favour of allowing his divorce, as it meant that while English clergy might owe the Pope spiritual allegiance, they owed the king an allegiance that superseded the spiritual and that he must not be denied moral authority. When the Pope disagreed, Parliament passed a law giving the Archbishop of Canterbury precedence over the Pope in ecclesiastical matters. Archbishop Thomas Cranmer then annulled Henry's marriage to Catherine on 23 May 1533 and Anne Boleyn (who had married Henry secretly in January) was crowned on 1 June. In September 1533 the royal couple's first child was born. To Henry's great disappointment it was a girl, christened Elizabeth. In December an Act of Parliament declared the king 'next under Christ the Supreme Head of this Church of England'. It became a criminal offence to refer to the Pope: he was to be referred to as the Bishop of Rome. Another Act required all Englishman to take an oath accepting the king as Supreme Head or to be guilty of treason. It was this that led to the execution of Sir Thomas More and others.

The Tyndale Monument, North Nibley.

The Dissolution of the Monasteries

In 1536 Parliament passed the Suppression Act, which saw the closure of small monastic houses (those with annual incomes below £200 or less than twelve monks) in order to reduce their numbers. Evidence was presented of immorality in the smaller houses, royal visitors reporting on the 'manifest sin, vicious, carnal and abominable living... used and committed amongst the little and small abbeys'. This first round of the Dissolution led to the Pilgrimage of Grace in northern England, but was generally met with little more than grumbling or soon-diluted anger in the south (and in Gloucestershire).

In 1537, the Dissolution of the major houses began, a process accelerated by a second Act of Parliament in 1539 which stated that the remaining monastic houses 'of their own free will... without constraint, coercion or compulsion' would hand their property and possessions to the Crown. Whether Henry proceeded with the Dissolution because he feared that the houses would become centres of Catholic dissent or whether he merely coveted their wealth is still debated.

St Augustine's Abbey in Bristol and St Peter's Abbey in Gloucester were both suppressed in 1539, Tewkesbury Abbey in January 1540 but in each case the abbey church survived, becoming the cathedrals of Bristol and Gloucester and the great parish church of Tewkesbury. John Wakeman, the last Abbot of Tewkesbury became the first Bishop of Gloucester.

But these were exceptions. For the most part, the abbey buildings were sold off, having first been stripped of plate, bells and the lead from the roofs. Deprived of their roofs, the abbey buildings rapidly fell into decay – a fate accelerated by the wholesale looting of the stone for farm buildings and walls. Often only the shells now remain, as at Hailes Abbey, while nothing at all remains above ground of others.

The Tudors and Sudeley Castle

Anne Boleyn's failure to produce a male heir led to her eventual execution. Henry then married Jane Seymour. Henry's love for Jane meant riches for her family, her brother Thomas being made Lord Sudeley. Jane produced the longed-for son and heir, Edward, but died soon after the birth. For political reasons Henry married again – to Anne of Cleves whom he called his 'Flanders Mare' – a marriage which was never consummated and quickly ended. Anne had been the choice of Thomas Cromwell, whose Catholic rivals persuaded Henry to accept Catherine Howard, daughter of the Duke of Norfolk, a confirmed Catholic, as his fifth wife. She was a poor choice, with a history of affairs before the marriage and a continuance of similar behaviour afterwards for which she was beheaded. Henry's last wife was Catherine Parr.

THE HOLY BLOOD OF HAILES ABBEY

The end of Hailes Abbey came late in the Dissolution, Abbot Sagar and the twenty-one monks who were all that remained of the community, surrendering the abbey on Christmas Eve, 1539. The previous October, the suppression of shrines had resulted in the confiscation of the Holy Blood by Richard Tracy, who was in the family line of the founder of nearby Stanway House. The relic was taken to London for examination. In the words of Bishop Latimer of Worcester, the examiners:

> ...thought, deemed and judged [that] the substance and matter of the supposed relic [was] an unctuous gum coloured, which, being in the glass [the Holy Blood was enclosed in a round beryl, garnished with silver], appeared to be a glistering red, resembling partly the colour of blood; and after we did take out part of the said substance and matter out of the glass, then it was apparent glistering yellow colour, like amber or base gold and doth cleave to, as gum or bird-lime.

On 24 November, Bishop Hilsey of Rochester preached publicly at St Paul's Cross and displayed the relic. He declared that it was 'honey clarified and coloured with saffron, as has been evidently proved before the King and his council'. The relic was then destroyed.

It was claimed that the relic's container had formed part of an elaborate hoax to deprive penitents of their funds. The monks, it was said, contended that a man in mortal sin could not see the Holy Blood. The glass vessel had one side thicker than the other, which rendered it opaque. At first, the penitent was shown this opaque side, and only when he had paid a sufficient sum was the container turned so that the Holy Blood came into view.

Catherine Parr had received a proposal of marriage from Thomas Seymour at about the same time as Henry's. She accepted Henry's of course, but shortly after the king's death she married Seymour who had become the Lord High Admiral of England. Seymour was an ambitious, ruthless man. His marriage to Catherine was one of convenience – she was, after all, Henry VIII's widow – and he spent some of his time at Catherine's Chelsea home attempting to seduce the young Princess Elizabeth who he may even have wanted to marry. According to a piece of local folklore, the young Elizabeth came to stay at Sudeley and died there, the scheming Seymour replacing her with a boy from a local village (this was later used an explanation for her spinsterhood and masculine habits). But although the young princess did not in fact die, Catherine Parr did, of puerperal fever, a week after the birth of Seymour's daughter Mary.

Not content with being married to the king's widow and attempting to get the king's youngest daughter into bed, Seymour also tried to marry his niece, Lady Jane Grey, to Edward VI, Henry's only son who had succeeded to the throne when he was just nine years old. Thomas Seymour's brother, Edward, Duke of Somerset, was Lord

---

CATHERINE PARR'S TOMB

Catherine Parr gave birth to Seymour's daughter at Sudeley Castle and died there. Henry VIII had requested that Catherine be buried beside him but she wished to be buried at Sudeley and her wishes were respected. Catherine was interred at St Mary's Chapel beside the castle. After the Civil War the castle was 'slighted' (rendered useless for military purposes) and fell into disrepair, first being used as an inn, then by tenant farmers. In 1782, one of these farmers discovered Catherine Parr's coffin and opened it. To everyone's amazement the body was in a near-perfect state of preservation. Over the succeeding years it was often opened and some of the contents, including a large chunk of hair, were stolen for personal collections. Eventually, in 1817, the body was reburied. Shortly after this, the Dent brothers bought Sudeley Castle. They restored both the castle and chapel and erected a marble tomb for the remains of Queen Catherine.

Protector of the young king and, on hearing of the plot to marry Lady Jane to the boy, had Thomas arrested, tried and executed.

At Catherine Parr's funeral, Lady Jane Grey was the chief mourner, her presence ensuring Sudeley Castle of a place in history – it had been visited by no less than five Tudor queens. Catherine of Aragon and Anne Boleyn had been at the castle with Henry VIII, Catherine Parr had lived and died there, Elizabeth I was to visit later and Lady Jane Grey was there before her unfortunate nine-day reign.

Sir Anthony Kingston of Painswick

The Dissolution of the Monasteries was, at least in part, prompted by Protestants in Henry's court, yet Henry's own feelings towards Protestantism were at best ambivalent, at worst hostile. Henry had Thomas Cromwell, the Protestant architect of the Dissolution (but also the architect of the Anne of Cleves disaster) executed, and put to death more Protestants than Catholics in the last years of his reign.

While in the Tower awaiting his execution, Thomas Cromwell negotiated the sale of Painswick Manor, which he had acquired years earlier, with Sir William Kingston. The deal did not go ahead because Cromwell's lands were confiscated. However, Kingston, a favourite of Henry VIII, was granted the manor without paying.

On Sir William's death the manor passed to his son Sir Anthony, a man for whom the infliction of suffering seems to have been a delight, a man with an appetite for cruelty that was unusual even by the standards of the day. He learnt to exercise this talent when he led a force of Gloucestershire men to help suppress the Pilgrimage of Grace.

By 1549 he was Provost-Marshal of the king's army that suppressed the western rebellion in Cornwall. The Mayor of Bodmin had sided with the rebels but, following their defeat, pleaded that he had acted under duress and was in reality a loyal servant of the Crown. His pleadings

appeared to have won the day, and he was much relieved when Kingston suggested they should dine together, believing it to be a demonstration of friendship. Consequently the mayor prepared an excellent feast and welcomed Kingston with open arms. Before the meal, Kingston called the mayor aside and told him that if there were rebels in Bodmin, there must be deaths also. He asked that the mayor should have a gallows erected in the town with haste, to be ready by the end of the meal. The mayor, eager to comply with the wishes of such an important man, gave the order straight away, and host and guest sat down to eat. At the end of the meal, Kingston asked to be taken to the gallows and, on seeing it, queried whether it was strong enough. The mayor assured him that it was. Kingston then revealed that the gallows was provided for the mayor, who was thereupon hanged.

Kingston's enthusiasm for harsh treatment was also felt in Painswick. He opened a prison there and had a gallows erected on nearby Sheepscombe Green, installing two men in a nearby house to act as executioners.

Kingston met an appropriately violent death. He was involved in a plot to overthrow Queen Mary in favour of Princess Elizabeth, captured and taken to Coberley Court for trial. He was drowned on the way, while crossing the Thames at Lechlade, though whether it was suicide or a failed escape bid has never been established.

Religious Conflict

Edward Seymour, Duke of Somerset, Lord Protector of Edward VI was a Protestant. He ensured that the Latin Mass was abolished and that Thomas Cranmer's *Book of Common Prayer* was compulsory in all churches. This led to a rebellion in Cornwall and Somerset's own downfall. His rival for the Protectorship, John Dudley, Duke of Northumberland, crushed the rebellion and had Somerset executed. Northumberland then married the young Lady Jane Grey to his son Guildford Dudley and persuaded Edward VI on his deathbed – he died in

Bishop John Hooper looks towards the cathedral from his monument in St Mary's Square. The monument, by Edward Thornhill, was erected in 1862 and stands on the site of Hooper's martyrdom.

The execution of Bishop John Hooper. An engraving from John Foxe's Acts and Monuments. *This book, commonly known as* The Book of Martyrs, *was originally published in Strasbourg in 1554 (while Foxe was living in exile) and dealt with the persecution of Christians by the Romans. Foxe expanded the work to include the English martyrs, the book being published in England in 1563 and revised in 1570. Foxe's book runs to 4 million words, five times the length of the Bible, the longest book ever written by a single author. Its effect was profound. By law a chained copy was placed in every English cathedral beside the Bible. As a consequence, despite the horror of Hooper's death, which had appalled many of the spectators, Foxe's passionate account of the persecution of English martyrs fuelled suspicion and outright hostility to Catholicism which lasted several hundred years.*

1553 aged just sixteen – to accept Lady Jane as his heir, to ensure a Protestant succession. Lady Jane's reign lasted nine days before Mary Tudor, the rightful heir, became queen. Northumberland, Guildford Dudley and the unfortunate Lady Jane Grey were executed and England became Catholic once more. The Latin Mass was reintroduced and devout Protestant clerics and other folk who would not renounce the new faith were condemned as heretics.

In Gloucestershire, eleven people were burnt at the stake for their failure to embrace Catholicism. The most famous victim was Bishop John Hooper. Hooper had spent much of

Bishop Hooper's Lodgings, Gloucester. Tradition has it that Hooper spent the night before his execution in this house. Though the building was almost certainly in existence at the time of his death it is more likely that he actually stayed in the New Inn. The building now houses the Gloucester Folk Museum.

his youth in Switzerland where Luther's ideas had a large following, and had returned to England a committed Protestant. Appointed Bishop of Gloucester in 1550, Hooper was sent to Fleet Prison before taking up his office after complaining that the bishop's vestments he would be required to wear were too rich and, therefore, 'popish'. He was released only after agreeing to wear them on formal occasions. With the accession of Mary Tudor, Hooper was required to recant his Protestantism. He declined and was charged with treason. His condemnation was inevitable and he was taken back to Gloucester for execution. Impressed by his gentleness, his guards declined to place him in the

city's prison, but exactly where he was lodged is a matter of debate. Tradition maintains that he lodged in Bishop Hooper's Lodgings, now the county Folk Museum, in Westgate Street, but records of the time suggest the New Inn, at the junction of Eastgate and Northgate streets. During the evening a local blind youth, Thomas Drowry, was brought to him. Drowry had also refused to recant and would later suffer the same fate as Hooper. That night the bishop comforted the boy, telling him that God had deprived him of his sight, but had enabled him to see the light of the Gospel.

On Saturday 9 February 1555, before a crowd of 7,000 – rather more than the popula-

THE TRACYS OF STANWAY HOUSE

Stanway House is a superb mansion, bought by the Tracy family when Tewkesbury Abbey was dissolved. The house probably incorporated parts of the earlier building, but was rebuilt in 1620 in fine Renaissance style. The Tracy family had a long history – one of their ancestors was in the band of knights who murdered St Thomas Becket, and it was Richard Tracy who delivered the Holy Blood of Hailes to London for analysis.

But most interesting was Richard's father, Sir William Tracy of Toddington who died in 1530. He was a Protestant when the country was still Catholic and left a will that was so markedly Protestant that it was deemed heretical by the Archbishop of Canterbury. As the perpetrator of the heresy was dead, he ruled that the body be exhumed and reburied away from consecrated ground. He then changed his mind and ordered that the body be tied to a stake and burnt. Sir William therefore became the first religious martyr in Gloucestershire, if such a term can be applied to a corpse.

tion of the city at the time, suggesting imperfect accounting or a substantial crowd from the local area – Hooper was led to the stake in St Mary's Square, where his memorial now stands. He was refused permission to make a last statement. The city council, in an effort to save cash had scrimped on the faggots for the burning and bought cheaper, green wood. There was a strong wind blowing and the combination meant that the fire went out after Hooper's legs had been burnt off and had to be relit. Hooper stood on his stumps praying, taking forty-five minutes to die. Chained to the stake – using ropes might allow a victim to escape the stake as they burned through – Hooper spoke until his blackened and charred lips could no longer move, and beat his breast with his arms until one arm was burnt through and fell off, the other becoming welded to the red-hot chain that bound him to the stake.

The horrors of the execution appalled many, but not the authorities. In May 1556, blind Thomas Drowry went to the stake together with Thomas Croker, a bricklayer.

The gateway of Stanway House, standing close to the village church.

The Elizabethan Age

Mary Tudor was thirty-seven and unmarried when she succeeded to the throne. She married Philip, the son of Charles V of Spain, a match that cemented relations with Spain and sealed England's return to Catholicism, but failed to produce the heir Mary craved. Apparently she adored her husband, but he did not reciprocate her feelings and soon left to return to Spain. After a brief return, Mary was overjoyed to find herself pregnant – or so she thought. In reality her condition was more likely due to a tumour or disease and she died in 1558 aged forty-two.

Mary was succeeded by her half-sister Elizabeth I, who had spent the years of Mary's reign concerned for her own safety, as she was a Protestant. The Elizabethan age is still renowned as England's Renaissance: Shakespeare and Marlow wrote their plays; Spenser wrote *The Faerie Queene* (inspired by Elizabeth herself); Byrd and Gibbons revitalised

music; Hilliard continued with the courtly painting movement begun by Holbein. There were also advances in science and, most importantly, the rise of a new class of men whose positions were based on ability rather than family background. The Spanish Armada was defeated and England prospered, and above it all shone the light that was Elizabeth I. She was indeed a remarkable woman, intellectually formidable and politically astute. She could also swear like a docker, which doubtless helped in a man-dominated world. On religion she declared herself unwilling to 'make windows into men's souls' and seemed intent of following a middle way, an idea with modern resonance. In reality, Elizabeth's England returned to Protestantism, though the executions of recusants were halted in favour of fines or other, non-life threatening, penalties.

The Tudor Landscape

On the land little changed during the Tudor period, the new landowners often being as brutal, or more so, to their tenants as the abbots had been. The still-profitable wool trade persuaded some landlords to 'acquire' arable land for sheep pasture and to enclose areas of common land, each of which increased the pressure on the rising population of tenant farmers.

But while the conditions of the tenant farmer or farm labourer deteriorated, the prosperity of townspeople improved. The independence of towns from landowning lords helped them to grow and prosper and they were revitalised by the new ideas and practices of the Renaissance. There was also more trade: Bristol and the ports of the Severn, chiefly Gloucester, but also Newnham and Tewkesbury, were well placed to take advantage of the booming trade with Ireland.

Of course, many town dwellers were poor and their squalid living conditions were often as bad, if not worse, than those in the country. But the general enlightenment of the period did mean that such poverty now pricked the con-

SHAKESPEARE IN DURSLEY?

There is some evidence that Shakespeare lived in the town in 1585 when hiding from Sir Thomas Lucy, who wished to have words with him regarding certain poached deer. There were certainly Shakespeares in the area at the time, one of them having been buried at Bisley in 1570.

Conclusive evidence is lacking, but a line in *Henry IV*, Part Two, Act V, Scene I, refers to Woncot – the vernacular rendering even now of Woodmancote – and to men known to have lived in the area: Visor, the Dursley bailiff; and Clement Perkes who lived, as the line says, on the hill (Stinchcombe Hill). Another line, in *Richard II*, refers to the view of Berkeley Castle 'by yon tuft of trees', implying that the poet had seen the castle from the top of Stinchcombe Hill. Indeed, there is a walk in Hermitage Wood, on that part of the hill immediately south-west of the wood, still known as Shakespeare's Walk.

sciences of the wealthy, and a number of almshouses were constructed for the deserving poor. The Chandos Almshouses in Winchcombe date from 1573, while those of Sir Baptist Hicks in Chipping Campden and Hugh Perry in Wotton-under-Edge date from the early seventeenth century. The excellent almshouses that fill the street on the southern side of the churchyard at Newland date from 1615. In Bristol, the first almshouses were built in the thirteenth century. Known as St Bartholomew's Hospital, they were taken over by Bristol Grammar School when it was founded in 1532. Others include the Merchant Venturers' Almshouses in King Street, dating from the 1690s and still in use; and Foster's, built in the late fifteenth century by James Foster, a local Bristol merchant. Standing

close to the top of Christmas Steps, the almshouses were rebuilt in the nineteenth century. The chapel beside the almshouses is dedicated to the Three Kings of Cologne, a dedication which is unique in Britain: Foster is assumed to have seen the shrine of the Three Kings in Cologne Cathedral during a trading journey along the Rhine.

Such enlightenment did not always extend to the treatment of offenders. The gallows was a feature of many towns and even villages, the list of transgressions that could end with a felon mounting its steps being very long. The stocks, which can still be seen at Forthampton, Painswick, Stow and Winchcombe, were altogether different. The use of public humiliation rather than incarceration or fine, suggests an

Newnham. Today a picturesque small town on the Severn, but in Tudor times an important Irish trading port.

The Hicks' Almhouses in Chipping Campden. Beyond is St James' Church, one of the great wool churches of the Cotswolds.

The Perry Almshouses, Wotton-under-Edge.

attempt at rehabilitation as well as punishment. It is claimed that the reason the Winchcombe stocks have only seven holes is that one individual who suffered their indignity particularly frequently had only one arm. At Stow the holes are set so far apart that discomfort must have been added to humiliation. At Forthampton the old whipping post can also be seen.

Tudor Gloucestershire also saw an increase in civic building consistent with greater independence and prosperity. The market halls of Chipping Campden and Tetbury, the latter a marvellous structure, date from this time. So too does the Curfew Tower at Moreton-in-Marsh, the oldest building in the town. The bell, dated 1633, would be rung each night to remind townsfolk to cover their fires, fire being a major danger in medieval towns.

Great Houses

The Elizabethan period was also the time when many of the great houses of Gloucestershire were built. Chavenage with its 'E'-shaped plan is breathtaking. It was built with stones from Horsley Priory and its history includes two memorable episodes during the Civil War (*see* pages 144 and 149). The de la Bere mansion at Southam, the manor house at Upper Slaughter and Bibury Court have all been converted into hotels. In the Cotswolds, the great houses include the manors at Ablington, Aston-sub-Edge, Upper Dowdeswell and Upper Swell, Stowell Park and Whittington Court. It was at Whittington that Elizabeth I stayed the night of 9 September 1592 on her way to Sudeley Castle where three days of celebrations marked the

The Market Halls of Chipping Campden (above),
Tetbury (below) and Newent (right).

THE MORETON CURFEW BELL

Moreton-in-Marsh confuses many first-time visitors by being so-named rather than 'in-the-Marsh', which is what they would expect. It is unlikely that there has ever been a marsh hereabouts, the name deriving from the town's position on the *march* (a boundary of several ancient regions). These regions eventually became counties: the Four-Shires Stone, just a little way to the east, marking the spot where Gloucestershire, Worcestershire, Warwickshire and Oxfordshire once met.

The bell in the town's Curfew Tower, one of few such towers now surviving in Britain, was rung at every night to warn the townsfolk to cover their fires. After fire became less of a hazard, the bell continued to be rung until 1860. This followed a bequest made by Sir Robert Fry, who became lost on his way home one foggy night and followed the ringing bell to the town. He left money for the bell to be rung (and for the clock to be wound), but by 1860 the townsfolk had had enough and the curfew ceased.

fourth anniversary of the defeat of the Spanish Armada. In the southern part of the county are Cold Ashton Manor, Newark Park (built with stone from Kingswood Abbey) and Siston Court. To the west of the Severn are Elmore Court, beautifully positioned in a loop of the river, Highnam Court, and Naas House, Lydney, built in about 1580 by William Jones, a haberdashery merchant with connections in both Gloucester and Hamburg.

Looking rather more like the 'conventional' Tudor building, with its half-timbered walls and overhung floors, is Bishop Hooper's Lodging in Gloucester. Other half-timbered buildings include Parliament Room in Gloucester, the fine manorial house of Preston Court and Great House, Hasfield. There are also several superb half-timbered buildings in Tewkesbury: the whole of High Street had been constructed by the fourteenth/fifteenth century and, with some modifications, many of the houses date from that time. The Black Bear Inn is said to date from the early fourteenth century – there is even a claim that an inn had stood on the site since the twelfth century. Close to the junction with

SIR MATTHEW HALE

Matthew Hale was born in 1609 at Alderley Grange, a fine Elizabethan house that dates from the early seventeenth century. Widely respected as a man of honesty in corrupt times, he was knighted and served as Lord Chief Justice from 1671–76. Hale was extremely religious, once claiming not to have missed a church service for more than thirty years, and was reputedly kind and gentle. These qualities did not extend to the Bench, however, where he is known to have condemned a woman to death for witchcraft. He certainly believed in witches, claiming that they were proved by 'the Scriptures, laws of all nations and by the wisdom of Parliament'. He died in Alderley in 1676, two years before the publication of his work *Pleas for the Crown*, which he described as a 'brief and inaccurate digest of criminal law'. He is buried in Alderley's churchyard.

The late fifteenth-century Cross House in Church Street, Tewkesbury.

The House of the Golden Key, another of Tewkesbury's fine half-timbered houses. Not surprisingly, this building in High Street has also been called the 'House of the Nodding Gables'.

Barton Street virtually every building on the river side of High Street is worthy of attention. In Church Street, Abbey Lawn Terrace and Craik House opposite are exquisite, as is the nearby Lilley's Alley. Close to the leat cut from the River Avon to drive the abbey mill, Mill Bank Cottages are also superb.

On the Lighter Side

Finally, before leaving Tudor Gloucestershire for the more traumatic times of the Civil War and the austere Puritan period that followed, it is worth considering how the county folk spent their leisure time. It is likely that mystery plays, morris dancers and maypole dancing, as well as other types of entertainment had been part of country life for hundreds of years, but the Elizabethan era saw the first flourishing of a true leisure industry.

There had been inns as long as there had been villages (the Royalist Hotel, Stow is claimed to be the oldest inn in England, an inn having stood on the site since AD947), and there had certainly been a growth in the number of inns close to the great abbeys favoured by pilgrims. However, the demise of the abbeys and associated trade led some, notably the New Inn at Gloucester and the George at Winchcombe, to seek alternative clientele. The George had been a pilgrim hostelry, the initials RK above the door referring to Richard Kidderminster, Abbot of Winchcombe 1488–1527. The galleried courtyard here, and at the New Inn (itself a pilgrim hostelry for Gloucester Abbey) would have been used for plays, as were the market halls and places of many market towns.

Dover's Olympick Games

The most elaborate of the new leisure ventures was started by Robert Dover who lived, initially, at Saintbury and then at Chipping Campden. Dover practised law in London while living at Campden, and his clients included some of the more famous names of the day including the Shakespeares of Stratford and Richard Catesby, cousin of Robert Catesby of Gunpowder-Plot fame.

Dover's Hill, on the Cotswold Edge above Chipping Campden may have previously been the venue for some form of games, but the more organised events of Dover's 'Olympick' Games started around 1612.

In their day, the games were famous. Shakespeare, who died in 1616, may have visited the games: he certainly knew about them as he has Slender asking of Page in *The Merry Wives of Windsor* – 'How does your fallow greyhound, Sir? I heard he was out-run on Cotsall'. In 1636 Matthew Walbancke, a friend of Dover's and later printer to the Long Parliament, printed *Annalia Dubrensia – Upon the yearly celebration of Mr. Robert Dover's Olympick Games upon Cotswold Hills*. This was a slim volume containing thirty-four poems, thirty-three by friends of Dover saluting him and the games, and one by Dover himself, thanking those friends who had compiled the book. The contributors included Michael Drayton and Ben Jonson.

The Civil War put an end to the games, but after the Restoration they were revived. In the mid-eighteenth century they fell from general favour on account of the rowdy crowd they had begun to attract. About one hundred years later, when the Oxford, Worcester and Wolverhampton railway was being constructed nearby, the disorders got out of hand – the railway workers running riot not only at the games but also in Chipping Campden. In 1853, following an act of enclosure, the land on which the events were held was divided and fenced, and the games came to an end.

In 1928, the National Trust bought what is now known as Dover's Hill, including part of the land on which the games were held. In 1951, there was a revival with the formation of a Robert Dover's Games Society and games are now held annually on the eve of the Scuttlebrook Wake (the Saturday following the Spring Bank Holiday).

THE COTSWOLD OLYMPICK GAMES

The games were held on the Thursday and Friday after Whitsun and included wrestling, 'leaping', dancing, 'pitching the bar', 'handling the pike', leap-frog and walking on the hands, together with the peculiarly Cotswold pastimes of singlestick fighting and shin-kicking. In singlestick or backsword fighting, each man held a long stick in one hand and had the other tucked into his belt. The idea of the game was to 'break the other's head'. Shin-kicking needs little explanation. It is claimed that some contestants strengthened their shins before the event by having them beaten with a wooden plank or a hammer.

In addition to these games there were running races, hare-coursing, and horse-racing; while indoor games such as cards and chess were played in the tents. It appears these were introduced by Dover to bring a little refinement to the rough pastimes of the peasants. With an eye to Hellenistic tradition, he also had a man dressed as Homer, playing the harp.

A page from Annalia Dubrensia, *the 1636 volume of poems celebrating Robert Dover's Olympick Games.*

8. THE CIVIL WAR

Prelude to War

Elizabeth I died childless and James VI of Scotland, a great-great-grandson of Henry VII, became James I of England. The early years of his reign were plagued by religious fanaticism. Puritans, followers of an extreme form of Protestantism, stood on one side, while on the other were those who believed that James, his nobles and ministers should be assassinated and a Catholic England restored. However, James was an intelligent man and he managed to steer a reasonably successful course between the factions: in 1620 the *Mayflower* took the Pilgrim Fathers to the New World (one leading pilgrim was Stephen Hopkins of Wortley), and the desire for a Catholic revival lost some fanatical support.

A quite different voyage had taken place a few years earlier. In 1603, inspired by Richard Hakluyt, Bristol's prebendary and author of *Famous Voyages* (the Hakluyt Society, which republishes accounts of journeys of exploration is named after him), and financed by Bristolian merchants, Martin Pring sailed to explore the coast of Virginia. The journey was influential both in establishing the New England colonies and in cementing the link between Bristol and the New World that was to be the basis of the city's later prosperity.

James I was succeeded by his second son, Charles, his eldest son Henry having died suddenly at the age of eighteen. Within two months of his coronation, Charles I married the French Catholic Princess Henrietta Maria. A resolutely Protestant Parliament, deeply suspicious of this match, was further alienated by Charles' refusal to summon it in the years 1629–40, in part because direct rule allowed the imposition of taxes that might not have been otherwise sanctioned.

By the early 1640s the situation between Charles and Parliament was out of control and in 1642 the Civil War broke out. The exact reasons for the war are still debated. In reality there was no one single cause, more a collection of festering problems: the rise of a merchant class at odds with the hereditary nobility; general resentment about Charles' high-handed taxation policy and also his foreign policy; and continued religious confrontations, chiefly between the Puritans and the Church of England.

On 22 August 1642 Charles raised his standard at Nottingham and Parliament responded by forming an army to preserve 'the religion, laws, liberty and peace of the kingdom'. In October the two armies faced each other at Edge Hill.

Prince Rupert, commanding the Royalists, routed the Parliamentarian horse, and then chased them across country instead of turning on the infantry. By the time Rupert returned, the Roundhead infantry had beaten the Royalists. Most historians call the battle a draw, but the indecisive nature of Edge Hill led Charles to abandon an advance on London in favour of setting up a headquarters in Oxford. The proximity of Oxford to Gloucestershire, where the Severn formed an effective border with Royalist Wales, meant that the shire saw significant action during the Civil War.

War in the County

At the outbreak of the Civil War, much of the Forest of Dean and the north-east of the county were pro-Royalist, the south of the county and Bristol supported Parliament, while the rest was divided between the two. But in Gloucestershire as elsewhere, the situation was never that clear-cut: the Civil War set father against son, and brother against brother. The first action in the

Wintour's Leap.

THE RACE FOR CATHAY

In the early years of Charles I's reign, the merchants of Bristol learnt that London's merchants were financing an expedition to search for the North-West Passage. Such a route, if discovered, would offer rapid access to the riches of the Far East. The Bristolian merchants, naturally, did not want to miss out on the trading advantages this would bring.

So, in 1631, two almost identical ships, named after the monarchs, left London and Bristol in a race of discovery. The master of the *Charles*, the London ship, was Luke Foxe, a self-taught Yorkshireman, a career seaman with a high, but largely justified opinion of his worth. 'North-West' Foxe, as he called himself, had been trying for years to gain sponsorship for such a voyage. The captain of the *Henrietta Maria*, the Bristol ship, was Thomas James, a Welsh-born barrister with only limited experience of the sea and sailing, though he had once taken charge of a small fleet that sailed to clear the English Channel of pirates. To avoid a charge of favouritism, Charles gave each man an identical letter. The winner of the race was to deliver it to the Emperor of Japan. The letters were in English as it was reasoned that the Emperor, being both a king and a cultured man, would obviously speak the language.

Neither ship found the North-West Passage (which was not navigated for another 300 years), but James did discover James Bay, the indent at the southern end of Hudson Bay. He also had the distinction of almost killing his men by fire at a time when they were suffering the terrible cold of an Arctic winter. In an attempt to attract local Indians, he set the trees alight on the island where they were camping, the fire got out of control and his crew were lucky to escape alive.

county was probably at Stow-on-the-Wold where on 10 September 1642, a group of students from Oxford heading west to join the Royalist army was ambushed by an armed band of locals and taken prisoner.

Early in January of the following year, Prince Rupert attacked Cirencester but was repulsed. With Tewkesbury and the Forest of Dean holding up any advance of Royalists from Wales, and Gloucester and Bristol being pro-Parliament, the county was now critical to Charles' success and on 2 February, Prince Rupert attacked Cirencester again, this time taking it. The town lacked the defensive walls of Gloucester and so was more difficult to defend against a determined army of superior numbers. In the aftermath of victory the town was sacked and over 200 cartloads of looted items were hauled away. Over 1,000 soldiers were imprisoned in the church then force-marched to Oxford, chained, and dressed only in shirts. A chronicler wrote that the prisoners were 'driven... as you do swine to London... or as... the Spaniards... drive the Indians'. As an example of how not to win the hearts and minds of people it could hardly be bettered, and the action almost certainly stiffened the resolve of Gloucester for the attack that was now inevitable.

A few days after Cirencester fell, Lord Herbert of Raglan took his Royalists into Dean and defeated a Parliamentarian force under Lord John Berrow at Coleford. This secured the forest for the Royalists who held it for the rest of the war using its iron deposits to cast guns and shots. It is claimed that so much artillery and ammunition was made in the forest that stocks sometimes piled up because there were not enough draught horses to haul it out. Following the victory at Coleford, Lord Herbert headed north-east to Highnam Court where he took up residence within striking distance of Gloucester.

In the south of the county things were going badly for Parliament. Sir William Waller's Parliamentarians were forced to take up a position on Lansdown, close to Bath, and were then defeated at Roundway Down on 13 July. Two weeks later, Prince Rupert stormed and captured Bristol. As England's third city and a major Atlantic port it was clear to both the Royalists and Parliament that control of Bristol meant effective control of the west of England. The city was held for Parliament by Colonel Fiennes who attempted to strengthen its defences by building a series of earthworks on the northern perimeter: the last of these can still be seen on the western

Cirencester. The capture of the town was a major success for the Royalists in the early stages of the war.

side of Brandon Hill. The area of the earthworks saw heavy fighting and it was their breach by Colonel Henry Washington that led to the city being taken by Prince Rupert in July 1643. The city's loss was a major blow to Parliament's cause, but a huge boost to Royalist morale. Having secured it, the victorious Royalists turned north towards Gloucester, which was now the only Parliament stronghold between Cornwall and Lancashire.

The Siege of Gloucester

Many have speculated on the reasons for Gloucester's opposition to Charles. They must have been strong, for the city's siege was one of the major events of the Civil War, only the pitched battles being more important. Resentment at royal taxation certainly played a part – Gloucester passed so much revenue to the Crown that it was unable to assist its own poor. The imposition of the Ship Tax on Gloucester had caused particular aggravation. This tax had originally been imposed only on coastal towns to pay for naval protection, but was subsequently applied to inland towns as well.

One other issue was specific to Gloucester. In 1616, Charles appointed William Laud as Dean of the cathedral. Laud was a follower of Arminiamism, which stressed the ceremonial and sacramental aspects of the Mass rather than sermons and readings from the Bible. Without reference to Bishop Miles Smith, Laud began to refurbish the cathedral. In part this was neces-

Winter in the forest. Bitter fighting took place in the Forest of Dean during the early phase of the war.

SIR BEVIL GRANVILLE AT LANSDOWN

In early July 1643 a Royalist force advanced on Bath. Facing them was Sir William Waller, who had brought his army south to counter the Royalist threat. Waller did not want a siege of the city, neither did he want a battle on the flat lands to the west where his army would probably be wiped out by the superior Royalist army. He therefore took up a position on Lansdown, the steep ridge to the north of Bath. When the Royalists attacked up the hill, they sustained heavy casualties – the attack seemed doomed and the day lost, but Sir Bevil rallied his Cornishmen and led them in a charge. Riding back and forward across the hillside, oblivious to the gunfire, Granville inspired his men, urging them to keep attacking. Finally, the Cornishmen reached the scarp edge and Waller's men turned and fled, taking up a new position behind a stone wall. In the final moments of the charge, Granville was unhorsed and attacked as he lay on the ground. His men, exhausted by the battle and demoralised by their leader's injuries, did not pursue the Roundheads. Sir Bevil was taken to Cold Ashton Manor across the county border in Gloucestershire, where he died during the night.

Church had caused outrage as it implied that the clergy were separate from the congregation, which the Puritans found anathema. At Gloucester it is said that after Laud's changes Bishop Smith refused ever to go into the cathedral again. Charles then made Laud Archbishop of Canterbury, which further fuelled fears of a Catholic revival, especially when Laud fined the town for its support of the radical Puritan John Workman.

In charge of Gloucester's defences was Lieutenant-Colonel Edward Massey. Parliament was very fortunate to have him in command: as later events were to show, he was one of their finest commanders. Massey first ordered the withdrawal of small garrisons at Berkeley, Sudeley and Tewkesbury: these would have been swiftly over-run and the men were therefore better employed defending Gloucester, which Massey was determined to hold at all costs. Next, the water meadows on the north and west of the city were flooded to reinforce the meagre defences on those sides. Marshland and the Severn now protected the city's western perimeter. Charles arrived in August and took over Matson House.

The Royalists decided against a direct assault on the city. Prince Rupert had succeeded with that tactic at Bristol, but had lost many men and Charles obviously felt that a repeat was not justified at Gloucester. Instead, the city was to be taken by siege. All the houses outside the walls were burned and pulled down to give clear fire-paths for artillery and to avoid their use by the defenders in guerrilla attacks. Next, the water supply pipes were cut and the River Twyver was diverted. There were mills on the Twyver that could have been used to pump water from the Severn: now the defenders would have to bucket water from the river. The Royalists' artillery then began a prolonged assault on the city walls, the defenders filling in the breaches with earth as best they could.

Inside the city a woman discovered a bomb with its fuse still burning and 'with a payle of water, threw the water thereon, and extin-

sary as Smith, a scholar, had neglected the fabric of the cathedral in favour of time spent studying, but Laud's changes were more than just cosmetic. He moved the altar from the middle of the building to where it currently stands at the east end of the presbytery and he erected communion rails in front of it, nominally to stop dogs fouling the altar. (This was not as ludicrous an idea as it sounds – at the time many took their dogs to church and often the dogs were let loose: at Stanton Church the deep gouges in the pew ends made by the dog chains of the more considerate can still be seen.)

The changes seem innocuous today, but in the early seventeenth century they would have smacked of Catholicism in a town that leant towards Puritanism. Even the turning, rather than moving, of the altar table in Deerhurst

THE KING AT PAINSWICK

On his way to Gloucester, Charles I spent a night at Berkeley Castle and then another in Painswick, probably in the Court House. On August 10, he issued a proclamation from 'our court at Payneswicke'. The proclamation was to the effect that any soldier found guilty of stealing or looting from any property possessed by the army would be executed. Charles returned to Painswick on or around September 10. There is a local story that on this occasion, when one of the young royal princes asked his father when they were going home, the king replied that they had no home to go to, but this appears improbable, since the king's position at that time was by no means desperate.

Interestingly, close to Painswick, on the Cotswold Way trail there is a stone known locally as Cromwell's Stone, which was erected to commemorate the lifting of the siege of Gloucester. Quite why it stands on the Cotswold Edge is something of a mystery.

guished the phuse thereof, so that it did not break'. The unexploded bomb weighed 27kg (60lb), which says much both for the woman's courage and the power of the Royalist cannons. After a month of siege, a relief force arrived led by the Earl of Essex. When they reached Gloucester on September 5, they discovered that the city was down to its last three barrels of gunpowder. Amazingly, only about thirty-five people had died during the siege, this number including two children who had been killed when the East Gate was hit by a cannon ball. The cannon ball was discovered during later (archaeological) excavations of the site.

The Sieges of Beverston and Sudeley Castles

In 1644 the Royalists in Gloucestershire began to fragment, petty feuding between local commanders meaning that they began to concentrate on their own private fiefdoms rather than the war. The Royalist Colonel Oglethorpe withdrew to Beverston Castle, while on the west side of the river Sir John Wintour concentrated on protect-

ing his own enclave in Dean. This allowed Massey, still Governor of Gloucester, to go on the offensive and attack Beverston. Oglethorpe and his men put up a strong resistance and Massey, somewhat bruised, laid siege in the hope of forcing a surrender. Massey then discovered that a servant girl at Chavenage House was Oglethorpe's mistress and was passing information to him, Chavenage being staunchly for Parliament, as Nathaniel Stephens owned it. When the girl heard that there was to be no attack on the castle that night she would place a candle in a certain window of the house and Oglethorpe would make his way through Massey's lines for a night of passion. Massey watched for the candle, arrested Oglethorpe and offered safe conduct to the castle troop if they surrendered. Appalled by their officer's conduct and capture, the troop did surrender. They were allowed to go free and made their way eastwards to Malmesbury, where, a few days later, they were all captured again when Massey, having secured Beverston, attacked the town.

Beverston fell on 23 May. In June, Sir William Waller arrived in the county chasing the king's army through Cirencester and Stow-on-the-Wold to Evesham, pausing to capture Sudeley Castle, which surrendered after a three-hour bombardment. The castle's octagonal tower still shows the signs of this bombardment. Much of the rest of the castle was 'slighted' (made unfit as a defensive structure) by order of Parliament in 1648. Charles had stayed in the castle several times during the early stages of the war and he felt its loss keenly – Parliament must have realised its potency as a Royalist symbol.

The Capture of Bristol

Though there was more skirmishing in Gloucestershire in late 1644 and early 1645, two events in 1645 effectively ended the war in the county. The first occurred in May when Charles and Prince Rupert led their armies to Stow-on-the-Wold where they met Lord Astley and the Royalist infantry. In 1645 Oliver Cromwell's New Model Army had been deployed for the

Painswick Church, one of the most distinctive in the county. It is famous for its tombs – there is even a tomb trail – and for its yew trees. Legend has it that there can only be 99 and that if a 100th tree is planted one dies. A count of the trees seems to disprove the story.

first time. When the Royalists moved north they were defeated by it in June. A month later they lost again at Langport in Somerset. The second critical event occurred in September when Bristol was retaken.

In an effort to hold the city the Royalists had fired the villages (now suburbs) of Bedminster, Clifton and Westbury-on-Trym to stop them falling to Parliament, but the tide was turning against them and the city could not hold out against Parliament's siege. Though relatively short, the siege was terrible, with an estimated 3,000 people (20 per cent of the population) dying of disease before Sir Thomas Fairfax was finally successful in overwhelming the defences. So important was the taking of Bristol that when it was secure, Parliament ordered a day of national thanksgiving. Later, Cromwell ordered

---

WINTOUR'S LEAP

The high, steep cliff above the River Wye to the south of the Forest of Dean is named after Sir John Wintour, one of the county's staunchest Royalists. Wintour fortified his own mansion at Lydney, though he was away when a Roundhead army called. He need not have worried for his wife defended the house so strongly that the Parliamentarians wearily retreated.

Sir John was anxious that the cliffs near Beachley should be fortified, the Severn at that point being easily crossed by barge. He was about this business when his group was surprised by a contingent of Roundheads commanded by Colonel Massey. The Royalists were heavily defeated, some, including Wintour, scrambling down the Sedbury cliffs to the safety of boats. This incident is likely to have given rise to the story of Wintour's Leap where Sir John leaps down the shallow Beachley cliffs on horseback. A later action, near Lancaut, also saw Wintour involved in a last-minute retreat and it is was this event that gave rise to the naming of the cliffs – the horseback leap being transferred here in the popular imagination. It is, after all, unlikely that Sir John could have leapt down these cliffs, in one go or several, and survived.

---

that the castle should be destroyed so that Bristol could never again represent a threat to Parliament's power. A few foundations and the name – Castle Green – are all that now remain of the Norman building. Once Rupert had promised Charles that he would hold Bristol for four months, but he had not allowed for the antipathy of Bristolians to the king or the might of Fairfax's New Model Army. Charles was furious with Rupert claiming that the four promised months had not amounted to four days when Fairfax's assault came.

With the loss of Bristol the war in Gloucestershire effectively ended. Berkeley Castle was retaken by Parliament, some of those helping being miners from Dean who had fled the forest rather than work for the king when the area had been taken in 1643. There was also a bitter skirmish at Lechlade, but the Royalist cause was now lost.

The Battle of Stow

What is now considered the last battle of the first Civil War was fought in March 1646 when a Parliamentarian army under Colonel Thomas Morgan routed a Royalist force under Sir Jacob Astley. Charles had sent Astley to attempt to raise an army in Shropshire and Worcestershire. Despite the defeats inflicted by the New Model Army, the king was optimistic. With help from Ireland and France and Astley's recruits he might still turn the tide. But such was the Parliamentarian control of England that Astley could not go unnoticed. As he returned towards Oxford he encountered Colonel Morgan on the other bank of the Avon near Bidford. Each commander had a force of about 3,000. Astley marched his troops back and forward, trying to shake off Morgan and so find a safe place to cross the river, but the Parliamentarians countered his every move. Eventually, hoping to link up with other Parliament forces and to force Astley's hand, Morgan withdrew to Chipping Campden. The Roundhead reinforcements arrived, and on the evening of 20 March 1645 a

Stow-on-the-Wold. The site of a bloody battle is now a quiet town famous for its fairs and popular with tourists.

combined force of about 6,000 men moved against Astley's force, catching them in open country between Stow and Donnington. The Parliamentarians attacked just before dawn, overwhelming the Royalists, who were almost completely surrounded as they attempted to escape towards Stow.

It is said that Digbeth Street and some of tures leading from the Square ran red with blood (ture is the local name for an alley, cut narrow to prevent stock escaping on market day). There seems little doubt that this was true, but it is not clear how it came about. One story has the fleeing Royalists being caught and hacked down in the centre of town, but another has wounded soldiers being laid out in the street after the battle. It is known that fewer than 300 Royalists escaped and that as many as 1,700 prisoners were crammed into Stow Church. Despite the carnage, there is only one memorial to a victim of the battle – Hastings Keyt, a Royalist commander. On the memorial, an incised slate in the floor of the chancel, Keyt is shown in the Royalist 'uniform' of a lace-edged sash, with helmet, pike and gauntlets in two corners and skulls in the other two. After serving as a prison, the church was declared a ruin, but was restored in 1680.

SIR JACOB ASTLEY

Astley, the defeated commander at Stow, is most famous for his prayer before Edge Hill, the first battle of the Civil War:

> Lord I shall be verie busie this day
> I may forget Thee, but doe not Thou forget me

At his surrender after the last battle, Astley was a sorry sight: 'taken captive and wearyed in his fight, and being ancient – for old age's silver haires had quite covered over his head and beard... his soldiers brought him a Drum to sit and rest himselfe upon'. Astley told his captors to 'sit downe and play, for you have done all your worke' adding, prophetically 'if you fall not out among yourselves'.

The memorial to Hastings Keyt in St Edward's Church, Stow-on-the-Wold. In 1992 a memorial stone to the battle was erected in the churchyard.

The Commonwealth

After the defeat at Stow, Oxford surrendered in June and the war ended. Charles surrendered to the Scottish army in Nottinghamshire and was handed over to Parliament. In 1647 he escaped from Hampton Court to the Isle of Wight where he plotted a further Royalist uprising. In August 1648, Cromwell won an overwhelming victory at Preston in what is sometimes termed the second Civil War. The king now represented a threat to the security of England. He was tried and executed on 30 January 1649.

In 1645 Governor Massey of Gloucester was promoted to Major General in Fairfax's army, much to the sadness of the city dwellers who petitioned for him to remain in post. The Puritans of the city were so delighted with him that they made up the following rhyme:

> He that doth stand so well upon his guard
> I hope shall never miss a good reward.

which includes, in the last five words, an anagram of his name rendered as Edward Massie Governor. Despite the city's pleadings and the rhyme, Massey was replaced by Colonel Thomas Morgan, who, in 1648, was replaced by Sir William Constable – one of the judges at the king's trial and signatories to his death warrant.

During the years 1649–53, England was a Commonwealth. Oliver Cromwell campaigned in Ireland during 1649, his massacres in Drogheda and Wexford remaining the cause of bitterness some 350 years later. In 1650 Charles I's son and heir landed in Scotland, but the Royalist uprising was defeated by Cromwell at Dunbar. A more serious rebellion in 1651 resulted in Charles and a Scottish army marching into England. They were met and defeated at Worcester by Cromwell, Charles escaping and crossing the county boundary into

THE FUNERAL OF NATHANIEL STEPHENS

The best rooms in Chavenage House are those named after Oliver Cromwell and General Ireton. It is claimed that the pair stayed at the house while persuading the owner, Nathaniel Stephens MP, of the need to execute Charles I. Although Stephens had been a Parliamentarian officer, he was reluctant to support regicide, but eventually gave his support to the plan. Stephens died soon after the execution and reputable sources claimed that after he had been laid in his coffin, a hearse drew up outside. That was no surprise, but it was then noticed that the driver of the hearse had no head. Stephens' corpse then rose from the coffin, walked to the hearse, bowed to the driver and climbed aboard. As the hearse rode away the onlookers realised that the driver was King Charles.

Gloucestershire. He rode to Stow, then on to Cirencester, Beverston and Yate before staying at Abbots Leigh outside Bristol. From there he escaped to France.

Cromwell was made Lord Protector, a position he held until his death in 1658. Parliament decided to make Cromwell's son, Richard, Lord Protector, but Richard rapidly realised he had inherited none of his father's political skills. He resigned and left political life, but his departure left a vacuum that no-one seemed willing or able to fill.

Massey had become disillusioned with the Protectorate and had chosen to go into exile with Prince Charles. Seizing the moment, he returned to Gloucestershire in 1659 and attempted to organise an uprising. He received support from the men of Dean, and those from around Wotton-under-Edge, but was then arrested with two others. On 31 July as they were being taken along the Cotswold Edge on the way to Gloucester, a thunderstorm broke above them and Massey escaped by jumping from his horse and rolling headlong down the Edge at Nympsfield. Massey's intended rebellion ended before it began, but may have been an additional spur to General Monck's decision to march an army from Scotland to London to form a Parliament that invited Prince Charles to accept the throne as Charles II, which he did in 1660.

The Restoration

From the county's point of view, one of the major political advances made during the reign of Charles II was the Dean Forest (Reafforestation) Act of 1668. Despite the existence of forest law there had been a reduction in the Forest of Dean during the early medieval period, oaks often being granted to monastic houses for the construction of roofs. The timbers of Blackfriars roof in Gloucester are of Dean oak, seventy-one trees having been granted to the prior. When royal interest in the forest waned and forest law was no longer rigorously applied, the reduction in the size of the forest accelerated. There were several reasons – illegal clearance for farming, over-grazing (particularly by sheep) which prevented regrowth and, most significantly of all, charcoal burning which not only took huge quantities of wood, but also turf to cover the pile. Although coppicing had been encouraged as a way of generating wood for charcoal, demand exceeded the supply of coppiced timber, especially when charcoal-fired blast furnaces were built in the forest.

The charcoal burners cut wood into lengths of approximately 1.5m ($4\frac{1}{2}$ft) with a diameter of about 15cms (6in). This was then stacked into a dome or cone 2–3m (6–10ft) high with a hollow centre to act as a flue. The dome was usually about 5m (16ft) across. Bracken and undergrowth might be added to the pile to help with initial burning. The dome was then covered with turf and set alight. Charcoal, a form of carbon mid-way between wood and coal, was formed by the anaerobic 'burning' of wood. Its production was a highly skilled process; if the dome was uncovered too early the pile could burst into flames, the charcoal-burner then having nothing to show for his considerable efforts. The burners were itinerant, moving around the forest collecting wood and making piles – the modern forest is dotted with hundreds of still visible hearths.

THE CAMPDEN WONDER

On 16 August 1660 in Chipping Campden, William Harrison, steward to Lady Juliana Noel, the eldest daughter of Sir Baptist Hicks, went out to collect rents for Her Ladyship. He had been a faithful servant of the family for fifty years and at the time he was nearly seventy years old. When he did not return at his usual time, his wife sent John Perry, his servant, to look for him. Perry did not return either. The next morning Harrison's son Edward, leaving home to search, met John Perry returning to the house. Perry had an odd tale to tell: he had met several friends along the way but was afraid to continue searching because of the dark, and he had slept for an hour in a hen-roost. Then, overcoming his fear, he had continued the search, only to become lost in the mist so that he had to wait the night out under a hedge. Edward Harrison and Perry continued the search together and met an old woman who showed them a bloodstained comb and hat-band she had found. The men immediately identified them as Harrison's and a full-scale search was organised. No other sign of Harrison was found, but suspicion fell on John Perry. His story of meeting friends was checked and confirmed, but despite this he was detained and questioned, and during the questioning his story began to change, eventually becoming quite bizarre. First he said that a wandering tinker had waylaid Harrison, then that a gentleman's servant had killed him. Finally Perry said that his mother, Joan, and brother, Richard, had killed Harrison after robbing him. Later he admitted that he had been present when Richard strangled Harrison and had helped him to throw the body into a nearby mill-pond.

Joan and Richard were arrested; both protesting their innocence, and the pond was searched for the body. No body was found, but all three were sent for trial. In the absence of a body, the judge declined to try them for murder, but they were not released, and in the spring of 1661 they were brought before a more amenable judge. They were found guilty and sentenced to death. The executions were carried out on Broadway Hill and, as was usual at that time, crowds turned up for the event. Since there was a local belief that Joan Perry was a witch and had bewitched her sons, it was decided to hang her first to break the spell. Next was Richard, who implored John to tell the crowd of his innocence and save him. His pleas were to no avail and John watched, apparently unmoved, as his brother died. He then started to protest his own innocence, saying that the story was not yet over and that one day the crowd would know the truth. Following the executions, Joan and Richard Perry were buried beneath the gallows, while John's body was hung in chains to rot.

Two years later, William Harrison walked into his home. He claimed that, while out collecting rents, he had been attacked by three men, knocked down, tied up, robbed, and thrown into a pit. Later he was taken to Deal and put on to a ship, which after six weeks' voyage was attacked by two Turkish warships. He was taken prisoner and sold as a slave in Smyrna, but escaped and made his way on foot, through many perils, across Europe to Lisbon. There, an unknown man paid his passage to London from where he had walked to Campden.

This story is highly improbable, particularly in view of Harrison's advanced years. In a careful assessment of the evidence in 1959 by Sir George Clark, it was suggested that Harrison had been embezzling money from the Noels during the frenzied years of the Commonwealth and was afraid that the return of the rule of law would uncover the deed. He therefore contrived, with Perry's help, to fake a robbery and disappear for two years, during which time he lived on the embezzled funds.

An alternative story was that he was spirited away by the Noel family itself so that his knowledge of their supposed anti-Royalist behaviour would not cause embarrassment. Either story implies that Harrison allowed three people to die for a crime he knew they had not committed. It is apparently true that following his return, his wife hanged herself, but Harrison himself continued in the Noel employ until he died at the age of about eighty.

This signpost, on the main road south-west and above Chipping Campden, is reputedly set on the site of the gallows on which the Perrys were executed.

Chipping Campden. St James' Church and the entrance to Campden House, all that now remains of Sir Baptist Hicks' mansion. Chipping Campden is now an idyllic place, and justifiably extremely popular with Cotswold visitors, facts hard to reconcile with the events of the Campden Wonder.

There were attempts in Tudor times to regulate destruction of the forest because its value for the construction of warships was recognised. Indeed, there were rumours that one of the aims of the Spanish Armada was the destruction of the Forest of Dean, a story that still surfaces occasionally though there is little credible evidence to support it. But the story does point to an understanding of the forest's value, which makes it even stranger that Charles chose to grant almost the entire forest to Sir John Wintour. Wintour was a Lydney-based ironmaker (and also private secretary to Henrietta Maria, Charles I's queen, a position that would have done his prospects of ownership of the forest no harm at all) and he set about converting the forest to charcoal to feed his furnaces. It is likely that had the Civil War not disrupted his plans, the forest might have been completely destroyed. After the Restoration, Wintour twice tried to persuade Charles II to reinstate the grant, only to see wiser heads intervene.

The 1668 Act gave legal status to ideas that had already been put forward by Major John Wade on the need to preserve what remained and to create areas for regrowth. Wade had already created enclosures in which he was planting acorns and oak seedlings, but the locals resented this attempt to reduce the land available for their animals and had pulled them down. The Act recognised Wade's efforts and also re-established the Verderers' Court to protect the forest. The new Speech House was built and St Briavels Castle was renovated to act as a gaol for offenders against forest law. When the famous diarist Samuel Pepys, Secretary to the Navy, visited the forest in 1671 he reported that he saw little that led him 'to expect much thence for the support of the Navy in future ages'. But Pepys' view was too gloomy: in 1674 the king's ironworks in the forest were demolished, and Dean's future secured.

9. Decline and Rise

The Puritans

Parliament's victory in the Civil War allowed the Puritans to complete their work of removing idolatrous symbols from England's churches. Rood screens and lofts were removed, statues destroyed and wall paintings obliterated with whitewash. There are now very few rood screens in the county, the best surviving being at Ashcombe (Perpendicular in style, significantly restored but in excellent fashion); Cirencester (where there are four, across the chancel and three east chapels); Fairford and Rendcomb. The latter two are thought to be the work of the same carver, making them an even more remarkable survival. Both were the gift of Sir Edmund Tame, who died in 1534, and include the emblem of Catherine of Aragon.

Perhaps the most astonishing thing about wall paintings is that finds are still being made. In 2001, a painting of St Thomas Becket's martyrdom, with God receiving his soul in the form of a dove, was discovered in Cirencester Church after lying hidden for more than three centuries beneath an obliterating coat of whitewash. The Cirencester work is a remarkable find, but to see the best of the county's wall paintings it is necessary to travel to Hailes, Kempley or Stowell where the same whitewash that obscured yet protected the Cirencester painting has preserved superb works. The Hailes sequence includes a wonderfully fluid hunting scene in the nave, dogs advancing on a cowering hare, a rendering of St Catherine of Alexandria, and an exquisite short-eared owl (an often-seen symbol of darkness or evil). All of the works are thought to date from the early fourteenth century. The Kempley works include Christ sitting on a rainbow, a wonderful winged ox, beautiful figures of the Apostles (though all but two of the fences are gone, probably scraped away by the Puritans)

The Rococo Garden, Painswick.

and a Wheel of Life. The paintings are believed to date from the twelfth century. It is said by many experts that the Kempley series of paintings are the finest in England and are a particularly remarkable survival because of their age and completeness. At Stowell the paintings date from the early thirteenth century and include a fearsome Doom. An equally excellent survival is the painting of the Last Judgement, in oils on

A detail of the rood screen at St Peter's Church, Rendcomb.

St Mary's Church, Kempley. These paintings are on the north wall of the nave. The 'Wheel of Life' represents man's transient existence. To the left of the window is St Anthony of Padua, while to the right the Archangel Michael weighs the souls of the dead, the Virgin Mary pleading for their acceptance into Heaven.

wood, in Mitcheldean Church. The painting is believed to be fifteenth century.

Though the people of Gloucestershire would have greeted the end of hostilities with enthusiasm, and the restoration of Charles II was equally acclaimed, the situation of many soon worsened. While the king was enjoying the oranges and other favours of Eleanor (Nell) Gwynn (and also the favours of a less famous, but far more influential mistress named Louise de Keroualle) the wool trade was in crisis and would collapse by the end of his reign.

The Decline of Cloth Making

The Cotswold wool trade was essentially a cottage industry. The rough wool from the shearers was first sorted to remove burrs and other impurities, and then scoured to loosen the natural greases. This scouring was usually done by boiling, sometimes in water to which stale wine had been added. Following this, the wool was rinsed in clean water and dried. It was then teased out on the scribbling machines to give a more even and finer consistency, and was then carded. Then came spinning, a difficult job that required a high degree of skill from the wheel operators. Consistency was demanded and, if it was not achieved, the wool was chopped up, remixed and sent back to the spinner. It was usual for the spinner to be paid only for accepted wool.

The final processes were carried out at the mill. First there was the fulling mill where the wool, having first been beaten to make it more

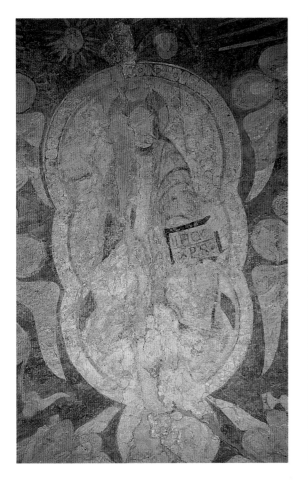

'Christ in Majesty' on the chancel vault of St Mary's Church, Kempley.

A delightful owl, one of the wall painting series in the church at Hailes.

compact, was cleaned with Fuller's Earth and then dressed up on the teasel frames. The teasels, set in drums, raised the nap of the wool. The next job was shearing, when the long, tasselled nap was hand-sheared to length. This job was extremely skilled and called also for great strength, as the shears were very heavy. Weaving was also done at the mill, by a master weaver with assistants to set up the loom. Dyeing, carried out either on the wool or on the cloth, was itself a skilled task. Uley was famed for its blue, while it was believed that the water in the Stroud area had a 'peculiar quality' which made possible the manufacture of an excellent scarlet cloth,

and it is certainly true that the 'thin red line' of the British army was clad in this scarlet.

Fortunes were made from wool in the Cotswolds, but such fortunes were not made by the workers. For them it was unremitting toil for fourteen hours a day, by candlelight in winter. The rewards were pitifully small and the housing, in general, poor. It was these folk who were hit hardest when the industry went into decline. There were several reasons for the decline, the main one being that following the religious turmoil in Europe, during which Britain's cloth industry had a virtual monopoly, cloth-making had begun again in France and Holland – Britain lost half its trade in just a few years. The government tried different ideas to boost the trade, the most obviously desperate being the 'Burial in Woollen' Act, which stated: 'from and after 1st August 1678... no corps of any person... to be buried in any stuffe or things other than what is made of sheep's wool only'. This and other measures were ineffective and the decline accelerated in the eighteenth century.

The rise in the use of water-power had concentrated the cloth industry in the valleys around Stroud, with virtually all production centred on Stroud itself, Dursley and Wotton-under-Edge – this in itself having already caused hardship in the northern Cotswolds. Now the effects were felt in the Stroud valley, particularly in the mid- to late eighteenth century with the introduction of mechanisation: the spinning jenny of Hargreaves in 1764, the power loom of Cartwright in 1785 and, following these, the general use of steam-powered mills. The Cotswold mill owners were slow to realise the potential of these machines and the workers quick to oppose them, and consequently there was a shift in the centre of the cloth trade to the north of England where, despite opposition, mechanisation went ahead.

This had an immediate effect on the local people, who were paid less for their work so that the profits could remain the same. The inequality of the rewards of mill owner and worker had long been a source of discontent, and a reduction in wages was not a new development. In 1756 the weavers complained that the wages had been reduced to such an extent that the men could not earn sixpence a week, even by working sixteen hours on all seven days. Not satisfied with the assurance of the owners, the men went on strike and there were riots in Stroud, some of the owners being temporarily imprisoned in a meeting they were holding. Since strikes were at that time illegal, the government had to act quickly and troops were despatched to the area. The soldiers, dressed in tunics of scarlet wool dyed in Stroud, faced the men who had made them. A young colonel gaining his first experience of full command, a man later to be a famous general – James Wolfe – led the troops.

The riots were suppressed, but the situation did not improve for the workers. To squeeze out the last of the available profits, the owners resorted to child labour, with nine-year-olds working a thirteen-hour day. In a remarkable linking of the slave trade with the cloth trade of Gloucestershire, during his speech moving the second reading of the Factories Regulation Act in 1832, Sadler said: 'You have limited the labour of a robust negro to nine hours, but when I propose that the labour of the young white slaves shall not exceed ten, the proposition is deemed extravagant'. In the Stroud area, the poverty was appalling. There had been an old saying in Painswick that the inhabitants were

A MAN OF DURSLEY

The cloth trade was not always carried on in the most ethical manner. Cloth could be folded so that it concealed a portion that was badly coloured or woven, or to conceal a short width. When this was made illegal by Act of Parliament, fraudsters would increase the yardage by stretching the cloth, a procedure that required the application of 'flock' powder to restore the thickness. The practice became so notorious that eventually Bishop Latimer himself was moved to condemn stretching and filling with 'devil's dust' in a sermon. By the fifteenth century, the activities of the cloth traders from Dursley, who were masters of these dishonest deeds, had entered the language – the expression 'a man of Dursley' was used as a term of abuse, not only for dodgy traders but also for anyone who offered a great deal, but delivered much less or nothing at all.

In 1603, the vicar of Berkeley used the term during a service, not to make any point but just dropping the phrase accidentally into his sermon. It provoked a near-riot in the congregation, as there were Dursley men present who took exception and non-Dursley men who retaliated by stating their own opinions on the truth of the phrase.

The most photographed mill in the Cotswolds is that at Lower Slaughter. It was not, however, a cloth mill having been built in the early nineteenth century to grind corn.

too poor to live, yet too healthy to die – but this was no longer true. Whole families died, and the only remedy was to leave. Some went to the mines of south Wales and the Forest of Dean, others to Australia and America.

Crises in Agriculture

There had been enclosures of fields and common land in the seventeenth century. During the Civil War there had been instances of locals taking the opportunity to tear down the fences erected by landowners. At Slimbridge, for example, the locals tore down enclosures of the Berkeley family several times during the war, and again in 1646 when it ended, even after Lord Berkeley had managed to obtain confirmation of the legality of the enclosures from Parliament. But throughout the early eighteenth century, the rate of enclosures increased, particularly after Parliament passed acts making it legal.

The effect of enclosure was to improve yields, as it resulted in greater acreage under production and more efficient farming. It also encouraged innovation in farming methods and led to increased use of fertilisers, which improved the soil and further increased yields. In 1700, Jethro Tull invented the seed drill. This resulted in greater crop yields because the seed was planted at the correct depth rather than being scattered on the surface, which resulted in haphazard germination. (For this innovative idea, which helped Britain out of the cycle of winter hungers that had become the norm, Jethro Tull is now mainly remembered as the name of a 1960s folk-rock band.) Other innovations led to better crop cycling and animal breeding. All these ideas improved quantity and quality, but led, inevitably, to further enclosures.

Higher yields meant greater surpluses for market, which led to increased demand for carts and horses, and for better roads. While enclosure brought prosperity, it also had disadvantages: it led to the impoverishment of peasant farmers who had depended upon the common land that was now enclosed; to the eviction of a very great number of farmers who had no obvious title to the land they worked; and a reduction in the number of labourers required to work the land. The poor left the land and migrated to the towns where, in these pre-industrial times, there was insufficient work for them, leading to an increase in the number of urban poor.

Tobacco

On the western edge of Winchcombe there is a street called Tobacco Close, an odd name for the Cotswolds but one that has its roots in a curious aspect of Cotswold farming. Tobacco first reached England in 1565 when John Hawkins brought it back from America. Smoking rapidly became popular, despite the astronomic price of tobacco – at first the leaves fetched their weight in silver – as it was claimed that it 'dissipates the humours of the brain'. When the first plants were brought back to England (probably by Walter Raleigh, though this claim, along with the claim that he also brought the first potatoes from the New World, is disputed), fields of tobacco were soon in cultivation, not least in the area from Cheltenham to Winchcombe.

Tobacco was first planted near Winchcombe by William Stratford and, when it proved successful, the fields from there to Cheltenham were rapidly taken over for its production. Indeed, there were isolated fields of tobacco as far south as Bristol, and it soon became an important cash crop. However, Parliament soon became fearful that this home-produced crop would harm the prosperity of the new colonies in America (especially Virginia), which were almost entirely dependent on their tobacco crop, and so made its cultivation illegal. The decision was not popular and a series of pro-tobacco propaganda pamphlets was issued. The best of these was *Henry Hangman's Horror, or Gloucestershire's request to the smokers and tobacconists of London*. This was a nice piece of black humour, for it claimed that the hangman's trade had declined locally since the lawful growing of tobacco had become widespread, and that the real aim of the ban was to produce a crime wave and hence an increase in executions.

The propaganda, however, was unsuccessful and illicit growing was stamped on hard. Riots were frequent as soldiers arrived to destroy crops. The locals were referred to as a 'rabble of men and women calling for blood for the tobacco', and blood they got when they attacked an army detachment, killing men and horses. Henry Hangman got his way and the growing ceased, although a large field near Bristol continued to grow the crop for a further fifty years.

One irony of the ban on tobacco was that it led to an increase in the wealth of Bristol, though not immediately. The Crown not only outlawed the growing of tobacco in England, but also gave a monopoly to London for importing tobacco from Virginia. This monopoly failed in the face of persistent smuggling, chiefly through coves along the coast of the Bristol Channel, the market finally being opened in 1639. Bristol immediately became a major tobacco port, its quick access to the Atlantic offering a head start over competing ports. Tobacco was a trade that flourished for several centuries; the local Wills family eventually opening cigarette factories in the city and becoming major benefactors of Bristol institutions.

Nonconformity

The poverty of many in a time of increasing prosperity was one reason for the rise in non-comformity, the established church being perceived as always siding with the landowners and businessmen. Another, perhaps equally potent, reason was a general weariness with the continuing battle between Catholic and Protestant and the somewhat joyless religious practices of the Puritans. Nonconformity was most prevalent in industrial/commercial areas, where the oldest chapels can be found. The Quakers (Society of Friends) were the most vocal of the early non-Anglican groups, their meetings leading to many confrontations during and immediately after the Civil War. Their Meeting Houses are among the

oldest to have survived: that in Broad Campden dates from 1663. A little later are those in Frenchay (1671, but rebuilt in the early nineteenth century), Cirencester (1673), Nailsworth (1689) and Painswick (1705). Cirencester's Gosditch Street chapel was built for Presbyterians in 1672, while the Congregational chapel in Upper Cam dates from 1702. In Hanham, now a suburb of Bristol, the Baptist chapel is one of the earliest of that movement, dating from 1721, though Baptists were active in the county before the Civil War.

Stroud's Wesleyan chapel, later taken over by the Salvation Army, dates from 1763 and is the

---

FAIRFORD'S FROGS

On being restored to the throne, Charles II, essentially a tolerant man, tried to promote harmony in Parliament and in the country as a whole. But his attempts at creating religious tolerance were dogged by the continuing bigotry of groups of extremists from all sects.

In June 1660, separatist congregations in Fairford were harassed by mobs, and the local squire, Andrew Barker, and Justice of the Peace William Oldsworth, did little to protect them. According to a pamphlet printed and distributed locally, the houses of Barker and Oldsworth were then invaded by a plague of frogs and toads. This was seized upon by other pamphleteers as proof that God had decided to punish the pair for not doing more to protect legitimate congregations. Such ideas were instantly countered both in pamphlets and the sermons of local Puritan vicars who claimed that the frog story was a lie, dreamed up to offer credibility to separatists who deserved no such credence or tolerance. The whole episode descended into such confusion that it soon became unclear exactly what, if anything, had happened. Historians sifting through the mass of claim and counterclaim have concluded that the Barker and Oldsworth houses were indeed invaded by frogs and toads, but far from being a sign of divine displeasure, such population explosions were a well-known, if infrequent, natural phenomenon.

oldest octagonal Methodist chapel in England. John Wesley preached here in 1765. From the same period are two interesting tabernacles from other aspects of the evangelical revival that flourished in the second half of the eighteenth century. Gloucester-born George Whitefield, a friend of the Wesley brothers, was responsible for the Rodborough Tabernacle (1750), while Rowland Hill's name is still associated with the tabernacle in Wotton-under-Edge (1773).

In Bristol the Unitarian chapel in Lewin's Mead was originally built in 1694, though rebuilt in 1791. It is claimed to be one of the best Nonconformist chapels in Britain. Bristol also has the oldest Methodist chapel in the world, built in Broadmead in 1739 by John Wesley.

The State of the County's Towns

The poor from the country – then as now – gravitated towards the towns, increasing the burden on over-stretched councils and creating a new urban poor. In the reign of Elizabeth I, a system of parish overseers had been created who used local taxation to relieve the poverty of the parish paupers, but in the towns this system was now becoming overwhelmed. Further legislation therefore allowed the building of 'houses of industry' – workhouses – where the poor could be collected together. The idea was that a combination of harsh conditions and long hours of tedious work would 'encourage' the poor to change their ways, become industrious and reduce the burden on taxpayers.

In Gloucester, the bell foundry still produced bells for many of England's churches, but a new industry of pin making had developed. Pins were not only supplied throughout England, but exported to Europe and, later, America. The pins were made in small 'factories' within larger houses (for example, Bishop Hooper's Lodgings) but were also made by the workhouse poor.

As the number of poor increased, the towns became increasingly concerned about the costs of maintaining relief programmes and sought ways to reduce the numbers. In Gloucester Robert Raikes and the Rev Thomas Stock were

ROBERT RAIKES

Robert Raikes was the owner of the *Gloucester Journal*, a newspaper that had been started by his father in 1722. Legend has it that while walking in St Catherine's Meadows (now the home of Gloucester RFC) one Sunday, he saw the ill-clad children of local pin-makers playing. He was moved by their plight and decided to set up a Sunday school. In reality, Raikes was building on work already begun by others. An Independent minister in Nailsworth, JM Moffat, had started a Sunday school some years earlier and his idea had been taken up by Thomas Stock, a vicar in Gloucester. Raikes did much to publicise the idea in his paper, which resulted in the rapid growth of the movement and led directly to the founding of the National Society in 1811 (by Andrew Bell, a one-time Cheltenham resident) and the British Society (for non-conformists) a little later. One of the first 'British' schools was opened in Tewkesbury.

convinced that Christian education of the young would prevent them from growing up to become criminals, criminality being linked with poverty, and so promoted the idea of Sunday schools.

Another idea prevalent at the time argued that the basic problem was the number of illegitimate births. Without a father to support them, such children would become an obvious burden on society. Unmarried mothers were therefore harshly treated, the intention being to discourage them from having further children and to act as a deterrent to others. In Gloucester unmarried mothers were whipped and imprisoned, while in the workhouses they were forced to eat separately from the more deserving poor and fed only on leftovers.

In the nineteenth century, the Poor Law amended the relief systems, creating 'Unions' within counties that administered the poor of an area. In Gloucestershire there were twenty-three unions. Each had a union workhouse, requiring, in some areas, the construction of new buildings. Of these, the best preserved is that in Cirencester which was opened in March 1837 to accommodate 300 poor. It is now the headquarters of

Cotswold District Council. Doubtless the irony of council officials now occupying the place would not be lost on the former inhabitants.

The County's Prisons

In 1777, John Howard toured English prisons and published his report *The State of Prisons*. He found conditions in Gloucester deplorable. At the time there were two local prisons, in the old East and North Gates, and the county gaol in the old castle keep. All were dreadful. There were few or no facilities for exercise; smallpox and typhus (then called 'gaol fever') were endemic; adults and children were kept together and corruption was rife. Matters were made worse following the demolition of East Gate in 1780, as it led to further overcrowding in North Gate gaol.

In that same year, Sir George Onesiphorus Paul became Sheriff of Gloucester. Sir George was a successful clothier and a very rich man. In his early years (he was born in 1746) he had spent a great deal of money on race-horses and high living, but he had also invented a machine for raising the nap on cloth, which had further increased his fortune.

As Sheriff, he visited the city gaols and was appalled. As a result he became a staunch supporter of Howard's reforms, arguing for the care and rehabilitation of offenders. On Sir George's initiative, the castle keep was demolished and a new county gaol built on the site. Four 'houses of correction' were also built in the county. Of these, Littledean (now owned by the Ecclesiastical Insurance Co) and Northleach (now a museum of rural history), still survive. Little remains of the House at Horsley, and nothing of that at Lawford's Gate in Bristol.

Though Sir George's reforms saw exercise yards, dormitories and sick bays added to prisons, and attempts made to reform offenders, the prisons were still harsh by modern standards. But at the time, Sir George's prisons were seen as the epitome of humane treatment, and they were used as models of good practice in prisons throughout Britain.

Dean: The Forest

The general peace of the eighteenth century led to a relaxation of the laws that had been strictly enacted in 1668. But with Napoleon's rise in Europe there was, once more, a need to strengthen Britain's 'wooden walls' and in 1803 Horatio Nelson visited the forest to assess its condition and value to the Navy. He was appalled. His report began optimistically – 'The Forest of

---

EDWARD JENNER

One discovery which did more than almost any other to improve the lot of the county folk, both rich and poor (and also the people of the entire world), was made in Berkeley in 1796.

Edward Jenner was born in Berkeley vicarage in 1749, the youngest surviving son of the town vicar. In 1754 both his parents died within just a few weeks of each other, leaving the young boy to be raised by his older siblings and an aunt. He went to school in Wotton-under-Edge and Cirencester, and then trained as a doctor at Chipping Sodbury. After qualifying, he returned to Berkeley, later living in the house that is now a museum to him.

In his experience as a rural doctor, he was able to observe at first-hand that cowmen who had caught cowpox never caught smallpox – a fact well-understood by country people. This led Jenner to believe that, if such was the case, immunisation with cowpox could provide similar protection against the scourge of smallpox, which routinely killed hundreds of people in widespread outbreaks.

In 1796, he extracted fluid from a cowpox pustule on the hand of Sarah Nelmes, a local milkmaid. He then injected it into the arm of eight-year old James Phipps. The boy caught cowpox. Next, Jenner injected the boy with real smallpox. Fortunately, the boy did not succumb to the disease.

Jenner has been called the 'greatest human benefactor of mankind' and memorials all over the world have been raised in his honour. But at the time, many of the locals saw only witchcraft behind this momentous discovery, and a rumour was started that the result of Jenner's injections would be local children turning into cows.

In a work, which is unique in Britain, a Free Miner is shown in a brass in Newland Church. The miner stands on a helmet and is shown with his mattock, used for excavating ore; his hod, used for hauling ore back to the surface; and a stick – usually of clay – clenched between his teeth, on the end of which is the candle that lit his work. It is thought that the miner stands on a knight's helmet to emphasise that Free Miners were above the normal laws of society. The brass is let into one commemorating Robert Gryndour, which dates from the mid-fifteenth century. The miner is a newer brass. Its exact age is not known, but the clothing and equipment suggest that it is probably sixteenth century.

Dean contains about 23,000 acres of the finest land in the kingdom'. He noted that the forest, if well-managed, could produce 9,200 cart loads of 'timber fit for building ships of the line every year'. But then came the bad news – he had noticed on his visit that there were barely 3,500 loads in the entire forest. He further noted 'shameful abuses, probably known to those high in power' and went on to suggest remedies. Given Nelson's standing in the country his report led to action, though it took until 1808 to pass a new act with similar provisions to that of 1668. Enclosures were rebuilt, reducing the number of trees lost annually to pit-prop production and almost five million trees were planted. In 1781, Weymouth pine, the first conifer in the forest, had been planted near Cannop. Now Scots pine (technically a re-introduction as it had thrived there in Neolithic times) and Norway spruce were added to the native species. But with the needs of the Navy paramount, four million of the five million trees were oak.

However, the forest was still not entirely secure. A plague of mice and voles in 1813 is thought to have destroyed at least 200,000 trees: 100,000 rodents were trapped and destroyed. In 1831, locals destroyed several hundred miles of enclosure fences and released their animals into the forest. Then in 1850, to reduce the activities of poachers who, the authorities claimed, were destroying young trees and so endangering the Navy, the forest's remaining fallow deer were exterminated. The killing was a clear over-reaction and it is impossible not to see exasperation with a few locals and the need to make a point as the real driving force.

The American Civil War sounded the knell for wooden warships and led to a gradual increase in the acreage of larch, a quick-growing tree excellent for pit-props. During the First World War, the need for pit-props increased rapidly. Timber was also required on the Western Front, and there was an increase in charcoal burning. The Forest of Dean, like Britain's other great forests, suffered badly, and in 1919 the Forestry Commission was set up to ensure their regeneration. Reorganisations and re-namings aside, the forest is still administered in the same way.

A Free Miner. The photograph is believed to have been taken at the Prosper Mine at Fetterhill some time before 1965.

Dean: The Iron Industry

The iron mining industry of the Forest of Dean is intertwined with the rights of the Free Miners, one of the most extraordinary groups not only in Gloucestershire, but in Britain. The rights of the Free Miners are ancient, so ancient that when they were first formalised in the Laws and Customs of the Miners in the Forest of Dean (usually known as the Book of Dennis) in 1687, they were referred to as having existed 'since tyme out of minde' at the time of 'the excellent and redoubted Prince, King Edward'. It is widely believed that the 'Edward' referred to was

Edward I and that he might have been legalising existing rights as a reward for Dean miners having undermined the defences of Berwick-upon-Tweed in 1296. However, it is equally likely that the rights date from the reign of Edward III, who is known to have granted similar rights to miners in Cornwall and Derbyshire. Whichever is correct, the book of 1687 makes it clear that even 400 years before, the rights of the Free Miners were already ancient.

A Free Miner has to have been born in the St Briavels Hundred to a Free father and to live within it, and he must have worked in a coal or iron mine for a year and a day. A Free Miner

FROM DEAN TO RENAISSANCE ITALY

One of the by-products of the iron deposits in the Forest of Dean is the production of ochre. Iron oxide is well known to almost everyone, even if they do not know its chemical name – it is rust. But the oxide can, when in the presence of other chemicals, create colours other than rust-red – yellows, browns, purples and many other shades of red. These colours are perfect paint pigments and were especially valuable before artificial dyes became available. In the late medieval period, the Free Miners of Dean exported ochre from the forest, some travelling all the way to Renaissance Italy where, it is believed, it was used in the paintings of masters such as Leonardo da Vinci, Michelangelo and Raphael. Ochre is still mined at Clearwell caves and used to produce natural paints for picture restorers and artists.

The Drummer Boy stone, which lies beside the forest road near Blackpool Bridge, is either an ancient smelting hearth stone or a mould stone, the hollows having given it its curious name.

was allowed to mine coal or iron without hindrance and to make such roads and take such timber as his work required. At first, the Free Miners could dig wherever they chose, but this resulted in a chaotic system of claim and counterclaim, and to be fair to all an official system was introduced. Mine Law was administered by the Constable of St Briavels Castle. The Constable's mining official was known as the gaveller. It was he who granted 'gales' (the land that could be mined) and was called when official sanction was required. To obtain a gale, a Free Miner had to take a deputy gaveller to his chosen spot. If the gale was deemed not to encroach or interfere with another, the deputy gaveller cut a turf on the site. He then cut two sticks, one straight, the other forked. He notched the straight stick twice, one notch for the Free Miner, one for the king (as the Free Miners were required to pay royalties on all extracted minerals). The deputy gaveller then placed the notched stick on the bare earth, held it in position with the forked stick and covered both with the turf. The Free Miner then paid the required fee (originally five shillings) and the gale was his.

Mining law was administered by a Court of Mine Law that met at the Speech House. By the 1770s the law that allowed Free Miners to dig for iron and coal was becoming increasingly inconvenient to 'foreigners' (as non-Free Miners were known) who had the capital to exploit the forest's riches, but not the right to do so. In August 1777, all the documents relating to the Court of Mine Law disappeared from the Speech House. Court officials denied all knowledge of the theft – and no-one was ever apprehended – but used the loss to stop the court's sessions,

Soudley Ironworks. The photograph is believed to have been taken in the immediate post World War II period. Today only the ruins of the building in the foreground remain, close to the Dean Heritage Centre.

freeing the way for foreigners to begin mining. Thirty years later, a meeting of all interested parties was held at the Speech House. Though the Court of Mine Law was not reinstated, despite the urgings of the Free Miners, it was agreed that regulation of mining was required and the Free Miners retained a significant role. When forest iron making became uneconomic, the foreigners moved on, leaving the Free Miners behind. Today there are still Free Miners in the forest, operating much as they have for at least 800 years. There is still a gaveller too, but his duties are now largely symbolic.

Iron making in the forest probably began in pre-Roman times with the mined ore being smelted in bloomeries (small furnaces heated by wood). The bloom was a small puddle, about fist-size, of molten iron that formed in the furnace. When charcoal and bellows allowed larger quantities of better quality metal to be produced, the molten iron was poured into mould stones. This process changed little for many centuries. It was an inefficient process, producing a relatively poor iron with many impurities, only some of which were removed when the iron was hammered into shape. At first the hammering was done by hand, but powered hammers in forges rapidly took over the task.

By the late twelfth century there were furnaces – or bloomeries – and forges in the forest. These were relatively small and portable, being moved when ore became scarce or difficult to

ROBERT FORESTER MUSHET AND STEEL-MAKING

The name of Sir Henry Bessemer is well known. It was he who patented the process of turning molten pig iron into steel by blowing air through it in a Bessemer converter. What is less well known is that without the input of Coleford-born Robert Forester Mushet, Bessemer's experiments might have ended in failure and humiliation. Mushet overcame a problem that Bessemer had failed to address – that of the over-oxidation (burning) of the metal inside the converter, a process that removed most of the vital carbon from the steel. He added his patented 'triple compound' (a high-carbon ferromanganese), and later he found another solution, adding spiegeleisen, an iron-manganese alloy.

It was only with Mushet's ideas that the Bessemer process became viable and a commercial success. But Mushet was not as commercially astute as Bessemer and failed to renew his patent, which therefore came into the public domain. Bessemer gave Mushet a small pension, but only much later and after years of ignoring Mushet's contribution to his own success. Mushet did eventually achieve some commercial success with his invention of the 'R Mushet Special' steel, a self-hardening tungsten-alloy steel that was used at Sheffield for the production of tool steel.

A tribute to the miners who defined the Forest of Dean. The sculpture, by Antony Dufort, was installed in Cinderford in 2000.

work. By the thirteenth century, Dean iron was well known as a quality metal and an arms industry had developed at St Briavels. Forest iron was brought there to be fashioned, particularly into cross-bow bolts that were exported to Europe (and occasionally finished up being fired at English soldiers).

Although bellows had been used to feed air to the charcoal from earliest times, the use of water power to feed bellows allowed higher temperatures to be reached. The first generation of blast furnaces followed, in which iron ore was smelted with charcoal fuel. The process began in Belgium in the fifteenth century, but it took another hundred years to reach Britain. In 1575, the Earl of Shrewsbury had a blast furnace built at Goodrich on the west banks of the Wye. A

few years later, the Earl of Essex built one at Lydbrook. The relatively late arrival of blast furnaces in Dean was due to the strong hold on forest activities by the Free Miners. The blast furnace produced a new form of iron – cast iron. The molten iron was tapped from the base of the furnace into a series of channels cut into a bed of sand, the channels arranged in a comb-like form. This form, looking like a sow feeding her piglets, led to pig-iron becoming common as the name of the casts.

The industry expanded in the seventeenth century, particularly after the tree-consuming Wintour furnace had been built at Lydbrook. As

Cannop Pond. Once a source of power, now a beauty spot.

noted elsewhere, it is likely that had it not been for the Civil War, the forest would have disappeared into the Wintour's furnace. Under James I, four furnaces and associated forges, known as the King's Ironworks, were built at Cannop, Lydbrook, Parkend and Soudley. The siting of those works in the forest was a new as well as a royal venture: they were sited close to furnace fuel sources, not ore deposits.

Though the forest was protected after the 1669 Act, iron-making continued, though most of the locally produced pig-iron was shipped along the Severn to forges in the Midlands. With around 16 tonnes of charcoal required to produce one tonne of iron, it is difficult to see how even a coppiced forest could have survived the voracious appetite of the furnaces and the gener-

al requirements for iron, had not the use of coke, rather than charcoal, for furnace fuel been discovered in the first half of the eighteenth century. Since Dean had both coal and iron deposits it seemed well placed for a revival but the nearby south Wales coalfield was able to produce much more coal than even the foreigners in Dean could mine, and Dean coal was found to have very poor coking qualities. However, coke furnaces were built at Cinderford and Parkend, the latter powered by a 15m (50ft) waterwheel. The two storage ponds to power the wheel are now a local beauty spot – Cannop Ponds. The Parkend site produced great quantities of iron, perhaps as much as 200,000 tonnes over its life, but by the end of the nineteenth century smelting had ceased, as a result of dwindling ore deposits and competition from other areas. The Free Miners continued to mine ore until the Second World War, but by then even they had to admit that it was no longer economic to continue.

In addition to coal and iron, Dean had several other minor industries based on the mineral riches beneath the forest floor. Gold was mined, though not very successfully, to the north of Drybrook, and there were wireworks and a tinplate works at Lydney. Lydney was also a shipbuilding centre, as were Newnham, Broadoak, and several of the villages on the Wye. Most construction was of the 'trow' (a flat-bottomed boat), ideal for tackling the shallow waters of the Wye and the tidal Severn. Lydney was also a naval shipyard for a few years until the Admiralty moved its construction to Portsmouth.

Bristol: Slavery and Sugar

English tobacco planters settled not only the east coast of America, but several Caribbean islands as well. By the 1650s the settlers on these islands, and on Jamaica which the English had recently wrested from Spanish control, had begun to shift from tobacco to sugar production. In England, sugar had replaced honey as the sweetener of choice and demand for it was rising rapidly. But sugar production was labour-intensive and shiploads of prisoners soon failed to satisfy the demand for workers. England – and Bristol, the country's second, and leading Atlantic, port – therefore entered the slave trade. It is often assumed that the trade was purely English, but by the mid-seventeenth century it was already a trade with a long history, begun by the Portuguese and taken up by the Spanish and, in a small way, English privateers of the sixteenth century.

Bristol's contribution to this trade in human misery was to create a disciplined and lucrative (if vile) triangle of voyages, from England to West Africa with trade goods such as weapons, metal ware, cloth and alcohol – a much more sophisticated list than the beads and trinkets of

THE CORN STREET NAILS

The four bronze 'nails' in Bristol's Corn Street are trading tables that were set up in the sixteenth or seventeenth centuries. Deals struck on them are believed to be the origin of the expression 'cash on the nail'.

popular imagination – then from Africa to the Caribbean with slaves and from the Caribbean back home with sugar, as well as molasses, rum, coffee and cotton. Back in Bristol, the sugar was refined and cast into loaves for sale. The slaves were taken from the West African coast so that the sea voyage was minimised. The reasons for this were commercial not humane: the shorter the journey, the faster the turnround for the ships and so the greater the profit for their owners. And, equally important, the lower the losses: the 'middle passage' to the West Indies was a

WHITELADIES AND BLACKBOY

Linking Park Street to Durdham Downs is Whiteladies Road, the final uphill section being Blackboy Hill. These names are said to derive from the custom of wealthy Bristolian ladies, who would take the air by promenading along the road accompanied by their black servants, but this story seems to be without any foundation.

dreadful journey that rarely took less than six weeks and frequently took twelve, with a high death rate among the chained up slaves due to dehydration, hunger and disease – all of these exacerbated by poor sanitation and despair. By the time the slave trade ended, it is likely that perhaps 10 million slaves had been transported to the New World.

There are many reminders of the slave trade in Bristol, and some indicate the curious allegiances the trade established. Guinea Street is named after the gold coin which was itself named after Africa's Guinea Coast. The coast provided the gold that underwrote the coin. To prove the connection, some gold guineas carried the elephant and castle of the Royal Africa Company, which had a monopoly on gold, slaves and ivory until 1698. Though London-based, about half the company's owners lived in Bristol. In Corn Street, Bristol's banking street in slave trade times, a plaque notes the founding of the Old Bank, which eventually became part of the National Westminster group. The Old Bank was founded by slave traders.

Surprisingly, Edward Colston, the philanthropist who set up the Colston schools, was also involved in the slave trade. In every other way he appeared a model citizen: Bristol's main concert hall is named after him and there is a statue of him in the Centre, but no mention is made of his position in the Royal African Company or the source of his wealth – sugar from St Kitts. There are also several memorials in the cathedral to prominent Bristolians whose wealth derived from the trade.

Strangest of all is the fact that early members of the Society of Friends (Quakers) were slave traders, including the Frys (who built a chocolate factory at Keynsham, now owned by Cadburys) and the banking families of Lloyds and Barclays. Eventually the Quakers saw the inhumanity of the trade and campaigned vigorously for the abolition, as did John Wesley. The position of the established church was more ambivalent and there is a strong local tradition that when William Wilberforce's 1791 abolition bill was defeated in Parliament the bells of St Mary Redcliffe Church were rung as part of Bristol's celebrations.

The campaign for abolition was begun by Thomas Clarkson in the 1780s and taken up by William Wilberforce. One Bristol campaigner, a friend of both men, was Hannah More who set up one of the early schools in the city (and still has one named after her). Hannah More saved some of her most savage criticism for the Christians who supported slavery, claiming they were 'white savages ruled by lust of gold'.

The slave trade was finally abolished in 1807, though abolition did not lead to emancipation. This curious, unsustainable situation arose from the New World estate owners complaining that they would go out of business and the Government fearing the loss of wealth. It took the worst slave rebellion in Jamaica's history for the Government to change its mind. Appalled by the rebellion, the Government voted for full emancipation in 1834, though it still agreed to a 'transition' period of four years. Only in 1838 were all slaves finally freed.

By the mid-eighteenth century there were twenty sugar refineries in the city. Now almost all that remains of the trade is the Three Sugar Loaves Inn at the bottom of Christmas Steps. This steep, stepped street, one of Bristol's most picturesque, was once a steep and dangerous short cut to the River Frome: the steps were built in 1669 by Jonathan Blackwell, a wealthy wine merchant.

Another local trade, one that has recently undergone a revival (of the famous Bristol Blue Glass) was the production of glass, in part for

Thomas Clarkson
1760 – 1846

Stayed here in 1787 to research the condition of slaves being transported

SEVEN STARS

TREASURE ISLAND

Robert Louis Stevenson set the opening of *Treasure Island* in Bristol because of its reputation as the haunt of pirates. In fact, several of the city's merchants had fitted privateering ships, and made fat profits from doing so. It is said that Stevenson's model for the 'Spyglass' was the 'Hole in the Wall' inn on the corner of Queen Square, so-called because of the spy-hole through which someone always kept watch to warn of the approach of a press gang.

early in the century for local merchants. The street was named after Prince George of Denmark, the consort of Queen Anne. Queen Anne visited the city in 1702, the nearby Queen Square being named for her. Many of the houses in the square were rebuilt after being burned down during riots that preceded the passing of the Reform Act of 1832.

It is said that on Clarkson's visit to Bristol he was shown around by the landlord of the Seven Stars Inn, across the water from Welsh Back, who declined to serve slave traders, a courageous stand at a time when most pubs were recruitment houses for slave-ship sailors. Many men sailed on the slaving ships because of the pay, but there were many who were reluctant to serve because of the suffering of the slaves. It is said that Bristol pubs, but not the Seven Stars, operated a system in collusion with the traders whereby sailors would be given drinks 'on the slate'. When the night ended, the usually drunken sailor would be presented with a bill. Unable to pay, he would be faced with a stark choice – the debtor's prison or signing on a slave ship and having his debt paid by the ship owner.

PARLIAMENTARY REFORM

Prior to the Reform Act of 1832, MPs for Gloucestershire (and the cities of Bristol and Gloucester) were from the wealthy and landowning gentry, predominately the Berkeley and Beaufort families. In the eighteenth century, when the Beauforts were Tories and the Berkeleys were Whigs, the system worked well (for them at least) as they supplied one member each of the two county MPs. By the early nineteenth century, the rising middle class wanted reform, both in terms of representation and also by increasing the franchise. In Bristol in particular there were riots as mobs calling for reform rampaged through the city. The Mansion House was looted and set alight, as were the northern and much of the western side of Queen Square. After the Reform Act, the county's representation was increased to fourteen, though this was reduced to eleven in the second Reform Act of 1885 (four for Bristol, one each for Gloucester and Cheltenham, and five for the rest of the county).

the bottling of West Indian rum. Sand for the glass was mined from caves near St Mary Redcliffe Church, the Redcliffe area supporting many glassworks.

Bristol's best eighteenth-century buildings are in Prince Street. These fine houses were built

One of the most famous buildings in Bristol, the Llandoger Trow Inn in King Street near Welsh Back was created from a terrace of five seventeenth-century houses, reduced to three during the Bristol blitz of the Second World War. The curious name is a reminder of the trows that tied up on Welsh Back after sailing from the Wye valley. Many trows were made at the village of Llandogo on the Welsh side of the river. The inn is said to have been Robert Louis Stevenson's model for the Admiral Benbow Inn in Treasure Island. *The curious rendering of the Welsh name reflects the Bristolian enthusiasm for adding consonants to words ending in a vowel: most famously this resulted in the bestselling Ford car being known locally as the Ford 'Cortinal'. It is claimed that the word trow should rhyme with 'bow', but at the inn and many places elsewhere, it rhymes with 'cow'.*

The County Gentry

Though both the farmers in the wool trade and the poor in the towns suffered, England flourished, and this prosperity was reflected in the increasing elegance of the lives of the gentry.

The reign of Charles II saw the Great Fire of London and a return of the Plague, but it also saw the work of Christopher Wren, Inigo Jones, Rubens and Van Dyck. John Milton and John Dunne wrote their greatest works, while Isaac Newton, who has a claim to being the greatest scientist ever, laid the foundations of a view of the universe that was not revised for three centuries.

The merchant classes built wonderful town houses. Coxwell Street and Dollar Street in Cirencester are both exceptional, arguably the finest examples in the county. An equally delightful collection of houses was built a little

Coxwell Street, Cirencester.

later at Cecily Hill, Cirencester. In Gloucester, Ladybellgate House (birthplace of Robert Raikes), Bearland House, the houses in College Green and also some in Westgate Street date from this period.

There were also great country houses. Badminton House dates from the late seventeenth century. It was the home of the Earls of Worcester, but in 1682 the incumbent Worcester was made the first Duke of Beaufort. Inside the house there are some of Grinling Gibbons' major works. The house stands in Badminton Park, one of the great estates of Britain. The park, which was remodelled by Capability Brown, covers 6,000ha (15,000 acres) and has one of Britain's finest avenues, Great Avenue, which

runs southwards for almost 5km (3 miles) from Worcester Lodge (on the A433 near Didmarton) to the park's northern entrance. Within the estate, St Michael's Church has an array of fine monuments to members of the Beaufort dynasty, most notably that by Grinling Gibbons of the first Duke, who died in 1699.

The mansion of Cirencester Park was built in the early eighteenth century for the first Earl Bathurst, patron of Alexander Pope. It is famously told that after it had been completed the Earl asked Pope 'How comes it to look so oddly bad?' He was correct: despite the attempt at architectural wholeness, the building was not a success, though doubtless that is not the reason it is hidden from the town by one of the largest yew hedges in the world. The huge park behind the house was much more successful, though the plan, with straight rides radiating from a central point, would soon be made to look old-fashioned by Capability Brown's naturalism. Dotted around the park are a number of follies: Alfred's Hall, built in 1721, is one of the earliest such buildings in the country. Another of the follies, Pope's Seat, is named after Alexander Pope.

By contrast to Badminton and Cirencester, the house in Dyrham Park was built by a commoner, William Blathwayt, Secretary of State for War under William III, in about 1700. At the heart of this Baroque mansion is the Great Hall from the previous Tudor mansion on the site. The house stands in over 101ha (250 acres) of parkland,

which Blathwayt kept as a deer park. He also had built what was than considered the finest water garden in Britain, with a dammed lake feeding fountains, a cascade, and a 6m (20ft) water jet. Sadly, the system had become ruinous within 100 years. The deer park and house, the interior of which is virtually unchanged from Blathwayt's time, are now administered by the National Trust.

Painswick House is from the same period, but here the most interesting aspect is the recent revival of the eighteenth-century garden, one of very few in the country not associated with a stately home. The Painswick Rococo Garden has been painstakingly restored from old prints, even down to the use of plants taken from catalogues of the time.

Dyrham Park.

The Gloucestershire Spas

Although the spa at Bath had been in use since Norman times (the waters had, of course, already been exploited by the Romans) it was not until a visit in 1613 by Queen Anne of Denmark, the wife of James I, that taking the waters became part of the social scene. After the disruption of the Civil War, Bath's fortunes rose sharply, particularly after the arrival of Richard 'Beau' Nash. Spas became the latest rage – every town wanted to be one and every county wanted to have one. Gloucestershire was lucky – it had two.

It had been known since at least the fifteenth century that, close to low tide, a strange water bubbled out of the mud of the Avon Gorge in Clifton. However, it was not until the start of the spa boom that anyone took a real interest in it. Even then the water was only bottled, the difficulty of exploiting it in a spa being its position – often below the river surface and in the steep-sided gorge. The water was curious, milky rather than clear and at 25°C (76°F) much cooler than at Bath (though the source was soon termed the 'Hotwell'). However, it rapidly gained a reputation for being a remedy for 'hot livers, feeble brains and red pimply faces', a quite extraordinary and insulting list.

The list of ailments the water treated grew (and the initial list was quietly forgotten), as did its reputation and in 1677 Queen Catherine of Bragança visited the Hotwell. Royal approval was a pre-requisite for the success of a major English spa, and the Hotwell was no exception. Following the royal visit, plans were immediately drawn up for Pump and Assembly Rooms.

After the Pump Room was built – it no longer stands but was, by all accounts, an unattractive building, erected on the cheap – the elegant houses of Dowry Square were constructed for visitors. There was also a small chapel close to the source as the churches of Clifton were too far for the gentry to travel. Spa visitors drank the water, several glasses each morning and evening, but did not bathe in it. The Hotwell water also continued to be bottled and sold, the

sales doing much for the fortunes of the Bristol glassworks. Interestingly, the Hotwell was not in competition with Bath, being seen as a summer spa only, the social scene then moving on to Bath. Not that the Clifton spa could ever have competed with the elegance of Bath: the latter was mentioned in the books of Sheridan and Jane Austen, while the Hotwell could only muster Smollett and Fanny Burney – well-known authors, it's true, but not quite in the same league.

What the Hotwell can claim is to have been the founder of Bristol's theatre. The first to be built for visitors was in Jacob's Wells Road, but soon a larger one, modelled on London's Drury Lane Theatre, was built in King Street. In 1778 it was granted a royal licence and became (and remains) the Theatre Royal. But by the time the theatre was open, the Hotwell was already in decline. The water had been claimed as a cure for consumption (tuberculosis), which persuaded many who were in the advanced stages of the disease to visit. When, as was inevitable, they died, the soaring death rate damaged the spa's reputation. When the Bristol-born poet Robert Southey (who became Poet Laureate in 1813) declared the waters to be of no value in combating the disease, it was the last straw. Spa society was in decline and with Bath's elegance continuing to outshine that of its neighbour, the Hotwell was soon just a name.

In 1704 William Mason, a hosier in fledgling Cheltenham, bought a field at Bayshill with the intention of farming it, but he had done little by 1716. That year he noticed that pigeons were persistently pecking near a trickle of water running at the edge of the field. On investigating he found the birds were pecking at crystals beside the stream. Mason had the water analysed: the results showed a pure mineral water. Mason therefore dug to find the mineral spring: it was in the next field. Mason bought that field, uncovered the spring and erected a wooden shelter over it. Then he stopped. Bath's fame rested on the ability of visitors to bathe in its water – Mason's trickle barely amounted to enough to fill a washbasin.

The Rotunda, Cheltenham.

William Mason's daughter, Elizabeth, was married to Henry Skillicorne, a retired sea captain with a murky past, perhaps even including small-scale piracy. Certainly he had a ready eye for business, and when Elizabeth inherited the Bayshill site on her father's death, Henry set about turning it into a moneymaking spa. True there was not enough water for bathing, but there was enough to drink.

In 1739 Henry planted avenues of lime and elm trees, creating the Upper and Lower Walks. He also erected a picturesque bridge over the River Chelt. In 1740, a Dr Short published his findings on the water, claiming it was superior to any other in the country. The list of ailments the water was claimed to cure was hardly less dreadful than that for Clifton's Hotwell and included 'eruptions, pimples, exudations, scrofulous affections, piles, gravelly disorders and worms'.

Business improved and Henry built a brick wellhouse to cover his asset. As a tribute to the pigeons who had 'discovered' the spring, a stone pigeon sat on each of the house's corners: today a pigeon still sits on top of Cheltenham's crest. The early history of the spring may be read on Skillicorne's 587-word epitaph – the longest in Britain – in the parish church.

Henry's son, William, improved the facilities, even adding limited bathing, but Cheltenham seemed destined to remain a second-class spa until, in 1788, Lord Fauconberg, who had invested money in the Skillicorne holdings, persuaded George III, Queen Charlotte and the three princesses to spend five weeks there. Fanny Burney, one of the ladies-in-waiting, was not impressed, finding the walks were 'clay and sided by common trees without any rich foliage'. Bayshill House, in which they stayed, was small,

The Tudor traveller John Leland described Cheltenham as 'a long towne havynge a market'. At that time the 'town' consisted of little more than one street, what is now High Street. A hundred years later the town had barely changed, still being described as a market town, now housing some 350 families. Another hundred years passes and Henry Skillicorne is planting his avenues of limes and elms. Within a further sixty years the beautiful Regency town which now stands at the foot of the Cotswold Edge had been built.

her own room had only enough space to crowd in a bed, a chest of drawers and three small chairs. As for the queen – 'she is obliged to dress and undress [in her drawing room], for she has no toilet apartment!' To cap it all, Fanny was required to drink her tea in a corridor.

But the king enjoyed the visit, and despite the fact that within a few weeks of leaving Cheltenham he was to have the first attack of the illness that was to plague the rest of his life (was it madness or, as has been more recently conjectured, porphyria?), the reputation of Cheltenham and its waters was secured. Wellington came to see if the water could cure his liver problems, and recommended it to his officers. Visitors increased and building work accelerated. Soon Cheltenham was part of the English social scene, though not everyone was impressed.

In his *Rural Rides* of 1821, William Cobbett wrote that the town was 'a nasty ill-looking place, half clown, half cockney', peopled with 'East India plunderers, West Indian floggers, English tax-gorgers, together with gluttons,

A Caryatid in Montpelier Walk, Cheltenham. The armless ladies are based on their more famous sisters who hold aloft the Erechtheion on Athens' Acropolis. Only two of the ladies are originals, created in terracotta by a London sculptor called Rossi in 1840. The other thirty have been added subsequently, the last – in a somewhat less romantic material, concrete – in 1970.

GUSTAV HOLST

Gustav Holst was born on 21 September 1874 in Clarence Street, Cheltenham (though at that time the street was known as Pittville Terrace). His father was the music teacher at Cheltenham Grammar School and the organist at All Saints' Church. Not surprisingly, Gustav was interested in music from an early age: by the time he was four he was already showing signs of a prodigious talent. He played violin, piano and trombone, sang in the choir, and was having his own music performed by the age of sixteen. At seventeen he became organist and choirmaster at St Lawrence's Church in Wyck Rissington, though this position only lasted a year as he enrolled at the Royal College of Music in London when he was eighteen. From that time on, Holst's life was spent away from Cheltenham, but he returned in 1927 to conduct the Bournemouth Symphony Orchestra playing *The Planets* at the Town Hall.

drunkards and debauchees of all descriptions, female as well as male', here at the suggestion of 'silently laughing quacks, in the hope of getting rid of the bodily consequences of their manifold sins and iniquities'. He returned in the following year and noted with delight that there was less building work in progress. It was 'the desolation of abomination. I have seldom seen anything with more heart-felt satisfaction. The whole town ... looked delightfully dull'. He noted 'it is curious to see the names that the vermin owners have put upon the houses there'. The townspeople were not amused, and burned his effigy.

Skillicorne's Royal Well was sited where the Ladies College now stands. In Cheltenham's heyday there were also other spas. In Montpellier Spa (now occupied by Lloyd's Bank) there was a ballroom-cum-concert hall where Holst's *Scherzo and Intermezzo* was premiered. The Rotunda was added in 1826, architect John Papworth having been inspired by the Pantheon in Rome (Papworth's middle name was Buonarotti – Michelangelo's surname). Inside, the dome is beautifully decorated, and there is a magnificent eighteenth-century Italian marble fountain.

The buildings raised to house the spa visitors have made Cheltenham the finest Regency town in England: Lansdown Crescent with its colonnaded entrances; the houses of the Promenade and Imperial Square, some with beautiful ironwork (the very height of fashion at the time); and the delightful shops of Montpellier Walk with their Caryatids – another reminder of the town's classical influences.

Pittville Pump Room, thought by many to be the finest Regency building in Cheltenham. The Pump Room was intended to be not only a spa, but the social centre of Joseph Pitt's new town.

The best survival of Cheltenham's spa is at Pittville. Pittville was the inspiration of Joseph Pitt who planned a whole new town centred on his Pump Room, a magnificent building, its Ionic columns and design based on the Temple of Illisus in Athens. It has an oval pump room, a ballroom, library and billiard rooms, and the first floor has a balcony from which visitors could watch the activities below them. The Pump Room was (and still is) set in an extensive park where a stream was dammed to create a lake.

Around the park, Pitt planned 600 houses in a complex of terraces and crescents. But the boom ended before work was completed. Prices fell and Pitt was ruined. Of Pitt's planned new town only the buildings of Clarence Square, Pittville Lawn and Wellington Square were completed.

The Wye Tourers

A visitor to Tintern Abbey in the late eighteenth century noted that 'among other things in this scene of desolation the poverty and wretchedness of the inhabitants were remarkable. They occupy little huts, raised among the ruins of the monastery, and seem to have no employment, but begging... As we left the abbey, we found the whole hamlet at the gate, either openly soliciting alms, or covertly, under the pretence of carrying us to some part of the ruins'. The writer engaged an old woman who 'could scarce crawl, shuffling along her palsied limbs, and meagre, contracted body, by the help of two sticks'. She took him to see her house: 'It was a cave, the walls running with water, the floor mud. She had no furniture or utensils, though she did have a bed covered with rags'.

Though describing Tintern, the writer could have been referring to many places in the Wye Valley at the end of the eighteenth century. The writer was William Gilpin, who wrote *Observations on the River Wye and Several Points of South Wales* (1782). He did much to popularise the Wye Tour, the 'Tourers' – moneyed folk – coming in search of the 'picturesque'. This did not mean just a 'nice view', as we might say today, but a real sought-after composition. Not any view could be picturesque: it needed to have certain features, be possessed of foreground, background and colour. The rules were actually laid down and were, perhaps, best expressed by Gilpin who stated his case against nature's ability to compose picturesque scenes succinctly and censoriously: 'Nature is always great in design. She is an admirable colourist also; and harmonises tints with infinite variety and beauty; but she is seldom so correct in composition, as to produce an harmonious whole'.

For the Wye, Gilpin noted that each view comprised the 'area', the river itself; two 'side-screens', the opposite banks; and the 'front-screen', the winding of the river. He noted that the view of the side-screens could be simple or complex, contrasting or folded. The banks could be adorned with one, or more, of four ornaments: ground, wood, rocks and buildings. The proportion of each must be right. The ground, for instance, might be broken or of the wrong colour. The trees might be in the wrong place. And so the rules go on. It really is an extraordinarily complex piece of logical breakdown of the aesthetic. The whole idea seems ludicrous today but was much in vogue at the time, the Wye Tour becoming as much an item on the social calendar as visiting a spa (and bringing some much-needed cash into the area).

In one sense the Tour started in 1750, when Dr Egerton, later Bishop of Durham but then Rector of Ross, and his wife travelled down the river to Tintern. While that was a forerunner, the Tour proper only really existed from 1760 and it did not become popular until after the publication of Gilpin's book and that of Charles Heath – *The Excursion down the Wye from Ross to Monmouth* – in 1799. As befitted the social standing of the Tourers, the Tour was made in a boat rowed by up to six men depending on the size of the party. Apart from trips ashore, no walking was required.

The Tourers were well catered for, an awning kept most of the rain off, and a central table, provided for writing and sketching, frequently groaned under the weight of food and drink provided for the healthy appetites of the occupants. The trip, which was usually only downstream from Ross, cost $1^1/_2$ guineas if Monmouth was the terminal town, this being a day trip, and 3 guineas if the Tourers went to Chepstow, Monmouth then being used for an overnight stop.

The Tour received a boost in the early nineteenth century, when the Napoleonic Wars put an end to European travel. A more stable Europe meant decline for the trade, but there were still people interested in the mid-nineteenth century: in 1865, Prince Arthur, aged only thirteen years, helped to row from Ross to Chepstow in non-stop pouring rain.

CHARLES MASON

One Gloucestershire man who achieved fame far from home in the eighteenth century was Charles Mason, who was born in Sapperton in 1728. Mason was at one time the assistant to James Bradley, the Astronomer Royal, but then emigrated to the USA. There, with Jeremiah Dixon, he helped survey the disputed boundary between Pennsylvania and Maryland, the extension of which was to become the world-famous Mason-Dixon Line.

10. BARGES AND TRAINS

Roads

During the late medieval period, trade in Britain was still extremely localised. As most goods had to be carried by horse or horse-drawn cart, the distance a horse could haul a significant load in a day was one limitation. Another was the state of the roads. Cartwheels made deep ruts, especially when the cart was heavily laden, and horses churned up the soil of unsurfaced roads, as almost all roads were. The combination meant that in wet weather the roads were deep in mud, which made transport slow, if possible at all.

Coastal trade was one answer, and ports such as Gloucester and Bristol improved their facilities. There were also efforts to improve the mileage of navigable rivers, but such attempts often floundered when they encountered opposition from riparian owners, technical difficulties or (and most likely) financial problems. Rivers were also not the complete answer to the problem as many sources and destinations of goods and materials were not served by water. Clearly what was needed was an improvement in the road network.

One problem for road users was that the maintenance, such as it was, of the muddy, rutted highways was the responsibility of the parish through which the road passed, but the large carts and wagons that did most damage were merely moving through and did not usually belong to the parish. The net effect was that the chief destroyers of the roads did not contribute to their upkeep.

Turnpike Roads

This situation was rectified on overused sections of the Great North Road in 1663 when a toll system was introduced. This was the first turnpike (toll-gate) road and remained the only one until 1696. A series of Turnpike Acts then led to a boom in turnpike roads during the first half of the eighteenth century. By 1750 it is estimated that there were more than 5,000km (3,000 miles) of turnpikes, almost all of them in England and mostly heading towards London. Early turnpikes were on existing roads, but they were also added to roads under construction, the combination providing the basis of the present road system.

The first two turnpikes in Gloucestershire were opened in 1698, linking Gloucester to the Cotswold Edge (and on to London), one via Crickley Hill, the other climbing Birdlip Hill (as an aside, it is claimed that a sign erected at the top of Birdlip Hill in October 1901 warning travellers they were approaching the top of a steep hill was the first road sign in Britain). By 1750, there were routes from Gloucester to Bristol and Hereford, and the major Cotswold towns of Stow and Cirencester were linked with Oxford, Bath and Gloucester. In Gloucestershire as elsewhere the standard of the turnpike roads varied enormously. Some were excellent, while others were poorly drained and maintenance consisted of little more than shovelling piles of rubbish into the wheel ruts. Gloucestershire had several of each type. Daniel Defoe in *A Tour through the Whole Island of Great Britain* noted that Birdlip Hill 'formerly a terrible place for poor carriers and travellers' was 'now repaired very well'. Later, the Gloucester–Bristol road was infamously bad: one winter the mud was so deep that a horse almost drowned in it and had to be rescued by brute force – or so it was said.

In general, people acknowledged that the new roads were an improvement, but still resented the tolls levied on users. There were numerous riots in which the toll-gates on the roads were smashed. In Wales such attacks were known as

Stanley Mill, King's Stanley.

Rebecca riots (from an Old Testament quote urging people to rise up and possess the gates of their oppressors – the mob would often wear women's clothes as disguises) but the name does not seem to have been applied to the county rioters who smashed turnpikes around Gloucester in 1734 and Bristol in 1749. Although these attacks were particularly noteworthy because of the size of the armed mob of attackers, the number of turnpikes and the damage done, smaller-scale attacks were actually quite common. Even when roads really did improve as a result of better drainage and surfacing (Cotswold oolitic limestone making an excellent surfacing material), the ill feeling between those who had to pay the tolls and those who collected them did not greatly diminish.

Not only goods but passengers travelled on the new roads: this was the age of the stage coach, a bumpy, tiring, draughty and occasionally dangerous way to travel, but one which for those of us who do not have to tolerate its inconveniences, seems wonderfully romantic. Coach travel required coaching inns placed at the end of each stage of the route. Here, horses could be exchanged, and both horses and passengers could be fed and watered. On longer journeys, passengers could also be accommodated overnight. In 1750 Gloucester and Bristol were three days by coach from London in winter, two long days in summer. The number of inns in Gloucestershire reflects the importance of Gloucester and Cirencester as coaching centres. Set about 15–25kms (10–15 miles) apart, depending on gradients, these fine old inns still cater for the discerning road user unwilling to patronise the new generation of roadside refreshment stops.

As roads improved the coach time to London decreased, falling to one day by 1765 (though by one day the coach owners meant just that, the journey taking about twenty-one hours) and to fourteen hours by the 1820s. The price for the London journey was 30 shillings in 1800, that price halved for 'children in lap' and those outside. The idea of spending twenty-one hours in a coach with a lapful of bored, agitated child fills the author with horror, as does the thought of spending the same time sitting on the top of a stagecoach on a bitter winter day with a strong headwind blowing. Travellers had to face danger as well as discomfort. Some adverts for coach journeys specified 'sober drivers', the clear implication being that such was not always the case. Perhaps drunken drivers were responsible for coaches occasionally turning over, sometimes with fatal results for passengers. There were also robberies, particularly on lonely stretches of road such as the section of Ermin Street between Birdlip and Cirencester.

By the 1830s, new turnpikes were rare and as roads were superseded first by the canals and then by the railways as the main method of

THE ORIGINAL TOM, DICK AND HARRY?

The real highwayman of the coaching era was no romantic hero, having more in common with today's street mugger. One gang who were notorious for robbing the Gloucester to Oxford coach were Tom, Dick and Harry Dunsdon, three brothers from Fulbrook, just over the county border in Oxfordshire. Though the sons of a respectable family, the three rapidly became dangerous criminals.

As well as robbing coaches, the Dunsdons robbed the houses of local gentry. One night in a local inn they were overheard plotting their next crime and the constables were alerted. A shutter for looking at visitors normally guarded a hole in the front door of Tangley Hall, their chosen target, and when an arm appeared through this, feeling for the door key, a constable lassoed it and tied it to the doorhandle. Outside, there was much swearing, followed by a shout of 'cut it' and the arm fell through the hole on to the floor. The door was opened but the brothers had escaped. Dick was never seen again, and it was assumed that he bled to death following the amputation.

The other brothers continued their lives of crime but were eventually caught and taken to Gloucester for trial, where they were found guilty and sentenced to death. It is claimed that the three were the original Tom, Dick and Harry of the popular phrase.

transporting people and goods. As the turnpikes became less important they were abandoned, and no new road improvements were carried out until the arrival of the motor car. Road drainage and surfacing then improved but it was not until the car had become a standard accessory rather than a luxury that new road construction was considered again. Even then, bypasses and the motorway system only appeared after the end of World War II. The M1, Britain's first motorway, was opened in November 1969, Gloucestershire getting its own motorway – a section of the M5 – during the early phase of the programme. Today the M5 allows the county to be travelled from north to south, the long axis, in under an hour, a speed which would astonish those who, 200 years ago, would have considered a day a fair time for the journey.

Canals

The improvements in the carriage of goods and materials that followed the limited improvements to navigable rivers showed what could be achieved by water transport. In the 1760s the logical extension, the digging of a canal, proved to be commercially viable when the construction of the Duke of Bridgewater's Canal halved the cost of transporting coal to Manchester and still made a profit. However, whatever other claims can be made for the Bridgewater Canal, it cannot be said to have been the first in Britain or to have begun the canal age. There were plans in place for the Stroudwater Canal a generation before the Bridgewater opened and there were canals in operation before the Bridgewater's success opened wide the eyes of entrepreneurs. One of the earliest was the Kemmett Canal, a forerunner of the Stroudwater that also started at Framilode, but probably ended around Eastington. The Kemmett used cranes rather than locks to transfer goods between sections of the waterway which were at different heights: as a result goods were packed in containers, making the Kemmett the first user of containers on a British canal. However, handling by crane

caused damage to the containers and the goods they carried, and this was one of the reasons for the canal's eventual demise.

Despite the Kemmett's difficulties, Gloucestershire was quick to realise the commercial opportunities of canals and the Stroudwater, and Herefordshire and Gloucestershire canals opened before the end of the eighteenth century. The more famous Gloucester and Berkeley Canal (now more usually called the Sharpness Canal) linking the city to Sharpness was not completed until 1827.

In an age of mechanical diggers, canal building seems a straightforward exercise, but it was not in the late eighteenth century. Then, before a turf could be cut an Act of Parliament was required defining the construction. The proposed canal then had to be surveyed down to the most minute detail. When work eventually commenced, the canal was dug by hand: the men doing the work were called navigators or 'navvies' for short (the origin of today's, usually pejorative, term). Their only mechanical devices were the pickaxe, the shovel and the wheelbarrow.

The Stroudwater Canal

The Stroudwater Canal symbolises the industrialisation of the Stroud Valley that began with the wool trade. It was dug from Framilode, where a lock allowed transfer to the Severn, to the centre of Stroud, thus connecting the town with the Severn and, via the river and the canals in Herefordshire, to the coalfields in Shropshire and Staffordshire. The price of coal at Framilode was 11 shillings per ton. By the time it had been transported by horse-drawn barge to Stroud the price had doubled. The owners of the Stroudwater managed to reduce the price to 15 shillings. This cheaper method of importing coal enabled the valley to become more competitive than other local towns and so better survive the wool trade crisis. Some idea of the success of the canal can be gauged from the fact that at its peak, the Stroudwater carried over 22,000 tons of coal a year.

The entrance to the Sapperton Tunnel near Coates.

The canal was not built without difficulties, the local mill-owners objecting, successfully in the early years, on the grounds that water losses, especially in the summer months when levels were down, would ruin their businesses. The canal, as completed – it was opened in 1779 – was a little over 13km (8 miles) long and had twelve locks.

The Thames and Severn Canal

Soon afterwards, a far more ambitious scheme was commenced, the building of the Thames and Severn Canal, with the intention of linking Bristol with London. The starting point was Stroud and a link was made between the Stroudwater Canal and the Thames nearly 46km (29 miles) away. This canal was served by forty-four locks, and also by the famous Sapperton Tunnel. The tunnel lies to the east of Stroud and, at 3,490m (3,817 yards), was the longest in Britain at that time. It was 4.5m (15 ft) wide and 4.5m (15 ft) deep, and kept the navvies busy for five years. Some blasting did take place but, as with the rest of the canals, the main work was with pick and shovel. The opening of the Berkeley and Gloucester Canal in 1827 actually helped the Stroudwater, but ultimately the railways caused a decline in trade and profitability. By the 1920s trade had all but disappeared and maintenance was minimal. As a consequence, the canal was derelict by the 1930s and finally abandoned in 1954.

The Herefordshire and Gloucestershire Canal

Often called the Hereford and Gloucester, though the longer name was the official one, this was the last to be dug and the least successful of the county's canals, largely because the reason for its construction, to provide an outlet for the Newent coalfield, was not borne out by subsequent events. The proposed canal was to be 57km (35½ miles) long and from it there was to be a short branch canal to Newent. Because of optimism over the value of the Newent coalfield, it was later decided to take the canal through Newent. This avoided the need for a branch, but took the canal through hilly country requiring the digging of a tunnel at Oxenhall. The decision proved disastrous, the boring of the 2km (1¼ miles) Oxenhall tunnel absorbing almost half the total cost of construction from Gloucester to Ledbury. Even then the tunnel was only 2¾m (9ft) in diameter and when the canal was finally opened it proved to be a bottleneck, which threatened the profits of the waterway. In fact the canal was never really profitable. So long was spent on construction – though parts of the canal were opened when completed – that the railway age had dawned before the final section was completed. A final indignity was the sale of the canal to Great Western Railways, the company using it to carry material for the construction of the Ross, Ledbury and Newent railway (the Daffodil Line), which would put it out of business. By 1883, less than forty years after the last digging had been filled with water, the canal had closed.

The Gloucester and Berkeley Canal

The Severn was such a potentially useful transport artery that the merchants and bankers of Gloucester set themselves the task of finding a way to overcome the problem caused by the narrowing and winding of the river immediately to the south. Ships could only pass the river for a few days close to each month's spring tides and the merchants knew that unless there was more regular traffic, Gloucester would never compete with Bristol. Predictably, they came up with the idea of bypassing that section by canal.

Once the decision had been taken to link the city to Berkeley by canal two things were required – a canal (obviously) and a new basin at Gloucester to accommodate the expected growth in shipping. The decision to go ahead with the project was made in 1792, but financial problems caused, in part, by the Napoleonic wars delayed the start for some time.

Work on the basin started in October 1794, the digging again being done by navvies. By March 1799 the basin was completed and connected by lock to the river, but work on the

The Gloucester and Berkeley (now more often called the Sharpness) Canal at Shepherd's Patch.

Gloucester Docks, with the city's cathedral beyond.

canal had stalled: digging had reached Hardwicke, but money had run out. As a result, Gloucester continued to survive for years on Severn trows sailing up-river to the new basin, although a tramway built between the city and Cheltenham did mean that the new dock made a profit.

Work on the canal began again in 1818 with the great Thomas Telford as consultant engineer. But with the new beginning came a dispute – where should the canal join the Severn? The original plan had been to reach Berkeley, but rising costs and the need to complete the canal as quickly as possible meant that a shorter canal reaching Fretherne was favoured at first. Ultimately this proposal was abandoned in favour of continuing to Sharpness Point. The new digging reached the Stroudwater Canal in 1820, but was not completed until 1827. When the canal eventually opened, the journey from

Sharpness to Gloucester was reduced from 45km (28 miles) to 26km (16 miles) and allowed travel at all conditions of the tide.

As the canal was nearing completion, the new basin at Gloucester was further improved. The first warehouses were built, with more being added right through to the last years of the century. These warehouses stand as a memorial to Gloucester's history as a port and are one of the joys of the renovated dock area. Several have been taken over for new leisure-based facilities, one being the National Waterways Museum, which explores Britain's canal history.

Railways

Road and waterway transport supported Britain's first phase of industrialisation, but were eclipsed after the 1830s by the greater speed and efficiency of the steam-driven trains on the new

---

TRAINS OVER AND UNDER THE SEVERN

In early 1875, contracts were let for the building of a railway bridge over the River Severn. The bridge was opened on 17 October 1879. It linked the village of Purton on the west bank to a point just north of Sharpness on the east side. (Just north of the eastern landfall lies the village of Purton: the bridge could therefore be claimed to link – more or less – Purton and Purton, to the confusion of some and the delight of others.) The bridge was 1,269m (4,162ft) long, including its west bank approach, crossing the river at a point where it was 1,085m (3,558ft) wide. It had two wide spans with a swing-bridge section for shipping, and nineteen shorter spans, all mounted on piers of cast-iron cylindrical columns. For eighty years the bridge survived the river's best efforts to dislodge it and the occasional threat from drifting shipping, but in October 1960, two of the smaller spans collapsed after a pier was hit by a barge in fog. Repair was discussed but the idea was finally abandoned. In 1967 demolition began and in May 1970 the last pier was blown up.

The alternative to going over the Severn was going under it, the choice made by GWR when the company finally grew tired of the suggestion that

its initials stood for Great Way Round when referring to the circuitous journey from Bristol to the south of Wales. Work on the tunnel began in March 1873, the choice of site being not the river narrowing at Aust–Beachley, but a wider point to the south-west. In going from Pilning to Sudbury, over half the underwater section of tunnel was beneath the English Stones, which are exposed for long periods, and the deep water confined to the relatively narrow Shoots channel.. The completed tunnel was 7.5km ($4\frac{1}{2}$ miles) long – the river section being 4km ($2\frac{1}{2}$ miles) – and had a gradient of 1-in-100 to reach a point 10.7m (35ft) below the 24.4m (80ft) deep Shoots channel. Construction was not without incident, the tunnel being flooded several times and once requiring a remarkably brave effort by Alexander Lambert, in a new design of diving suit, to close a valve to prevent the project being thrown into jeopardy. When it was first traversed by train in September 1885, the double-track, brick-lined tunnel was the longest on a British mainline railway. The tunnel is still in operation today, with trains regularly using it to link southern Wales with London, and it is still the longest on the network.

Blackpool Bridge, one of the small number of reminders of the Forest of Dean's railways.

railway systems. The main lines from Bristol to Gloucester, and from both cities to London, were completed between 1839 and 1845. Ironically, the main line from Gloucester to London required a second Sapperton tunnel, the railway running close to the canal it was putting out of business. Gloucester was linked to Cheltenham, the Midlands and the north in 1840, and to south Wales in the 1850s. Though this reiteration of events may imply the easy unification of the systems of several independent railways, such was not the case. Stephenson's standard gauge of 4 feet 8½ inches was used throughout the north of England and it was a track of this gauge that came south to Gloucester. Brunel, following his own path as usual, chose a broad, 7-foot gauge for Great Western and it was that gauge which reached

Gloucester from Bristol. It was thirty years before the battle over size decided in the standard gauge's favour and during that time passengers travelling north from Bristol had to change trains and tracks at Gloucester, a transfer accompanied by 'the chucking of articles... the enquiries for missing articles [and] loading, unloading and reloading'.

The Gloucestershire and Warwickshire Railway linking Cheltenham and Stratford-upon-Avon via Winchcombe was completed many years after the first phase of track building, opening fully only in 1906 (and to Birmingham only in 1908). Of the main lines it is only this last line that no longer survives, yet, ironically, a section of that line is virtually all that remains of steam east of the Severn. Enthusiasts have saved the line near Toddington

BRUNEL

No account of Bristol would be complete without a mention of Isambard Kingdom Brunel. Born in 1806, the son of the French-born engineer, Sir Marc Isambard Brunel, who had emigrated to Britain in 1799. In 1829, a competition was held for the design of a bridge across the Avon Gorge at Clifton. There were twenty-two entries for the judge, the great Thomas Telford, then aged seventy, to consider: Telford rejected them all and proposed his own design. Not surprisingly, Telford was declared the winner. Amid uproar, the decision was declared invalid and a second competition was held in 1830, which was won by Brunel. The reform riots of 1831 prevented an immediate start. Work finally commenced in 1836 only to stop in 1843 when cash ran out. The bridge was abandoned in 1853 but work resumed in the following decade and was completed in 1864, five years after Brunel's death at the age of fifty-three. The bridge remains the most recognisable of all Bristol's landmarks.

After his success in the competition, Brunel was appointed chief engineer of the Great Western Railway (GWR). He was responsible for Bristol Temple Meads station, considered to be one of the true classics of Victorian railway architecture. When one of GWR's directors complained about the length of the Bristol–London line, Brunel suggested making it longer, using a steamer to connect Bristol with New York and so capturing the transatlantic market. The result was the *Great Western*, a wooden paddle-steamer which, despite scepticism, completed her maiden Atlantic crossing in fifteen days in 1838.

More famous was Brunel's second ship, the *Great Britain*: the first iron ship, the first to be screw-driven and the largest by far to have been constructed at the time. The *Great Britain* made her maiden Atlantic crossing in 1845. In 1846 she went ashore in Dundrum Bay, Ireland. Though refloated the same year, the Great Western Steamship Company that owned her was bankrupt and she was sold. For twenty-five years she sailed from Liverpool to Australia but eventually finished up on the Falkland Islands as a coal and wood store. She was saved from this ignominious end in 1970 when she was brought back to Bristol. Having been towed on a pontoon from the Falklands, the *Great Britain* was floated up the Avon, and returned to Bristol 127 years to the day from her launch. Refurbished, the ship is now a major tourist attraction.

Although Brunel is famous for the Clifton bridge, the GWR and the *Great Britain*; one of his more remarkable but lesser-known achievements was the design of a prefabricated hospital for the soldiers in the Crimean War.

on which steam trains run through the 629m (688-yard) Great Tunnel close to Winchcombe. As with all such private ventures, it is hoped that the yardage of open line will eventually increase. In the south of the county there is another small steam operation at Bitton on a short section of an old LMS line.

Beside the main lines there were numerous branch lines and also important cross-country lines, such as that which linked Cheltenham to Andoversford and then Bourton-on-the-Water, and Cirencester to Swindon. Unfortunately, all these branch lines succumbed to Dr Beeching's axe in the early 1960s. The same decade also saw the end of all but the Severnside main line on the east side of the Severn. One of those to go was the line along the Wye valley, the loss of which robbed visitors to Gloucestershire of the pleasure of a train ride along the banks of one of Britain's most beautiful rivers.

Also lost were the Dean railways that had developed from earlier tramways. The nature of the forest, a high, but uneven plateau, precluded the use of canals, but the condition of the roads was becoming increasingly desperate as the forest industries prospered in the eighteenth century. The wagons, laden with coal, made a mess of roads and proper maintenance awkward. When the roads were rutted and muddy, more horses were required for haulage, increasing costs with no return in terms of speed of delivery. In winter, rain and snow often made roads completely impassable. Something had to be done and, between 1809 and 1815, it was – three tram-

Clifton Suspension Bridge. Brunel did not live to see the bridge completed, but his design resulted in the building of Bristol's most famous and well-loved landmark.

roads were built by private companies. Tramroad is now the accepted term for the roads constructed by these companies, but at the time the owners referred to them as either railways or railroads. Each tramroad comprised 'L'-shaped plates along which a flangeless wheeled wagon could be horse-drawn.

The Bullo Pill Company built a tramroad to link Cinderford with the Severn (at Bulls Pill), the Monmouth Railway Company linked Monmouth to Redbrook and Coleford, while the Severn and Wye Railway linked the two rivers by way of the Cannop Valley and Lydney. Each system had as many branches as were required to serve the Dean mines, forges and furnaces. It was these tramroads that formed the basis of the later railway system, though two remained in operation long after all the rest had

succumbed to the steam engine. That at Wimberry Slade continued until the 1930s while the Bixslade road survived World War II, the last horses only being pensioned off in 1947. Great Western took over most of the forest lines when they became true railways, but the Severn and Wye Company remained independent and amalgamated with the company that built the first Severn Bridge of the modern era. The line remained viable until it was closed by an accident in 1960. Today, the only railway left in the forest is that operated by the Dean Forest Railway Company formed, as at Toddington, with the intention of allowing the romance of the steam train to continue to be enjoyed. Trains are run northwards into Dean from Lydney and it is hoped eventually to open the line as far as Parkend.

The Dean Coal Industry

Evidence of smoke-blackened chimneys in Gloucestershire's Roman villas implies that coal as well as wood was being burnt. This is unlikely to have been mined, but in Dean the coal seams occasionally break surface and the Romans would have needed to make little effort to gather coal. There is evidence that they did just that in Lydney. The Saxons and Normans did little more, the abundance of timber in the forest making the use of coal to smelt iron an irrelevance, though coal was certainly dug in medieval times. It is known that in the seventeenth century, experiments were tried using coal rather than charcoal in the forges, but it was not until the advent of steam power in the next century that real attention was paid to Dean's potential as a source of coal.

At first, coal would have been dug from surface mines or shallow pits. This, doubtless, was the reasoning behind the delightfully named 'Strip-and-at-it' mine. But the haphazard nature of finding seams close to the surface ultimately forced the miners underground. Adits were the preferred method of digging, an 'adit' (or drift) being a horizontal shaft (actually, slightly inclined so that water could run out) that followed a seam into a hillside. More importantly, a miner in an adit was granted rights over the seam he was following while a miner in a pit (that is, a vertical shaft) was only granted rights over the coal he was able to remove. The adit's sides and roof were held in place by timber props and, in the more sophisticated mines, there would be a timber floor along which small carts of coal would be trundled. If vertical shafts were dug then the miners would be

Brunel's ship the SS Great Britain *in Bristol's harbour. To the left of the ship is a replica of Cabot's* Mathew, *built in Bristol to re-create the journey to the New World. The* Mathew *has now been added to the list of the city's visitor attractions.*

New Fancy Colliery, Forest of Dean.

As the heading notes, this is the New Fancy Colliery. This and the photograph opposite are postcards from the early/mid-twentieth century. It is somewhat surprising to discover that, in the early twenty-first century, coal mining was thought worthy of postcard status. The reason probably lies not only in the importance of coal as a domestic and industrial fuel but in a romantic view of miners. It was said in the inter-war period that if the English cricket team needed a fast bowler it was necessary only to go to the top of a mine and shout down. Many of Britain's world class boxers also had mining backgrounds.

lowered and the coal raised by a 'whim', a horizontally mounted wheel that would be towed around by a horse, a rope attached to the wheel being fed over a pulley-wheel into the shaft. Later, waterwheels were used to raise and lower the buckets. Water was a continuous problem in the pits, the Dean collieries sometimes having to extract 100 tons of water for every ton of coal. Often water flooded into pits so fast that work had to be abandoned: only with the massive pumping power of steam could water be controlled, and even then it might not be economic to do so.

Conditions for the miners were harsh. Most early mines were worked by a group of Free Miner friends, perhaps just three or four men, who struggled to make a living. In an attempt to solve the problem caused by having so many undermanned mines, Parliament passed an Act in 1838 that allowed 'foreign' investment in Dean with the small mines being amalgamated into larger, more economic ones. But the introduction of mine owners brought Dean the problems that had already arisen elsewhere of men, women and children being forced to work long hours for poor wages. In 1840 a

An extraordinary postcard image probably taken at the Lightmoor Colliery as most other Dean mines had roofs too low to allow ponies to be used. The postcard title seems almost surreal, while the harshness of mining is etched on the faces of the men.

Cheltenham Town Hall. Built in 1901, the year of Queen Victoria's death, to a design by FW Waller, the Hall is in the massive classical style favoured at the time. The style is now seen as ponderous, but at the time was perceived to lend an appropriate gravitas to the building.

Parliamentary Commission was set up to investigate conditions in British mines. In Dean, Commissioner Elijah Waring found boys as young as six employed to operate ventilation doors. They sat in pitch dark for a twelve-hour shift, often with rats scrabbling for their lunch. Older boys also worked twelve-hour shifts towing coal trams, dragging them on their hands and knees through tunnels only 60cm (2ft) high and often deep in water. The Commission led to the 1842 Mines Act, which forbade women, girls, and boys under ten years from working underground. Ironically, the Act was opposed by both the pit owners and the miners, the former because it reduced profits, the latter because it reduced incomes.

Another issue, which showed the pit owners in a rather unflattering light, was mine ventilation. The Dean mines did not suffer the problems of flammable gas that caused problems elsewhere. As a result there was no need for forced ventilation, but its lack meant that the miners frequently worked in the foul air caused by their own presence. One mine owner reasoned that the existence of this foul air could not be a problem – if it were then the miners would not be able to work, but they did. The logic would have been impeccable had it not ignored the fact that if the miners did not work they did not get paid – a strong incentive to work even when suffering from the effects of poor ventilation.

By the end of the nineteenth century the output of the Dean mines was almost 1 million tons annually, with the Foxes Bridge and Lightmoor collieries near Cinderford among the chief producers. Output was maintained throughout the first half of the twentieth century, with a peak of 1.3 million tons in 1938 when, it is estimated, half the male population of Dean worked in the industry. But after World War II it declined sharply and in 1965 the last mine, Northern United, closed. Today, only the tips and the curiously romantic above-ground ruins remain.

The Victorian Era

Improved transport led to increased prosperity, the increase in trade being further fuelled by the expansion of the British Empire. Locally, there was also a revival in the wool trade, at least around Stroud. The mill at King's Stanley was built in 1812 and was one of the earliest to use a metal frame to reduce the fire risk. The mill was a five-storey building, the ground floor built of stone, the rest of brick. Initially, five waterwheels powered it but in 1827 a steam engine

The Winter Gardens, Cheltenham. This delightful building in iron and glass, with brick towers, was built in 1878 in what is now Imperial Gardens. The miniature version of the Crystal Palace was never a rousing success to the dismay of a string of owners. Ultimately the Gardens were taken over by the Town Council and were used for events ranging from auctions to roller skating. By 1939 the Gardens had deteriorated drastically and the possibility that a bomb blast would turn it into a murderous fusillade of glass shards was all the excuse that was needed to ensure its demolition.

The University Tower, Bristol. Standing at the top of Park Street the tower is one of the city's most striking landmarks. Though the tower's neo-Gothic lines are often mistakenly thought to be Victorian in origin, it was actually completed in 1925 during the twilight years of Empire, the Great War having delayed a fitting monument to the charter granted to the city's university in 1909. The tower is 215ft (65.5m) high and houses a bell called Great George.

Woodchester Park Mansion. The mansion is now recognised as one of the most remarkable houses of its period in Britain. It was started (though never completed) by Benjamin Bucknall, a Gloucestershire man, born at Rodborough, who was a friend and admirer of Viollet-le-Duc. It is known that Bucknall consulted the great French architect about Woodchester and there is a legend that French workers were employed on the mansion. After money had run out Bucknall, a Francophile, retired to Algeria. Though curious in many respects – the use of stone for drainpipes for instance – Pevsner is unrestrained in his praise for the mansion, calling it one of the great achievements of nineteenth-century domestic architecture in England.

was installed. By the 1830s it employed nearly 1,000 people. At around the same time, the fine

mill at Ebley and several others were built. But despite the optimism of the mill owners, the wool trade continued to experience successive crises. In 1700 there were about 25,000 people employed in the industry, despite the problems of the preceding decades. By 1800 this number had halved and by 1900 it had fallen to about 3,000. The decline continued throughout the twentieth century: by its end the great cloth mills were empty shells. Today, King's Stanley mill stands forlorn and somewhat neglected, plans to restore it as part of the area's heritage stalled by lack of finance. Ebley mill is now home to Stroud District Council.

In Britain, the Age of Empire more or less corresponded to the reign of Queen Victoria and together they influenced all aspects of British life. Most noticeable today is the effect on architecture. The Victorian establishment believed it had a mission to enlighten, which fuelled not only its imperial ambitions but also its domestic programme. Believing it was creating a new world order, its public buildings were imposing, exuding a muscular dominance that is not to everyone's taste. Good local examples are Cheltenham's Town Hall and Gloucester's Guildhall as well as the great warehouses of Gloucester dock. In Bristol, Great George Street was built in the late eighteenth century/early nineteenth century, but arguably the city's most spectacular buildings from this era are the University Tower and adjacent City Museum/Gallery that were actually completed in the first quarter of the twentieth century. Both buildings were gifts from the Wills tobacco family. The building beyond the museum was inspired by Venice's Doge's Palace. Formerly the university refectory, it is now a restaurant/bar. In the docks area the Arnolfini, Bristol's contemporary art gallery, is a twentieth-century conversion of a fine mid-nineteenth-century tea warehouse.

There are few private houses of the same era. One of the most extraordinary is Sezincote, which was remodelled in the early nineteenth century by Sir Charles Cockerell whose wealth derived from his work with the East India Company. He obviously enjoyed the East, and had the house constructed in Mogul (rather than Hindu) Indian style with oriental gardens, though there were concessions to the British climate – in addition to the onion dome there were also chimney stacks. The park surrounding the house was the work of Humphrey Repton and extends the Indian theme with cast-iron Brahmin bulls, Hindu goats, and clumps of bamboo. The Prince Regent visited Sezincote in 1807, and it is almost certain that it influenced his design of the Brighton Pavilion.

Dumbleton Hall and Lechlade Hall are other good examples of private houses built at this time. Despite the fact that it was never finished, the best, and arguably the finest of its age in Britain is Woodchester Park Mansion. The house was commissioned by William Leigh and designed by Benjamin Bucknall, a friend of French architect Viollet-le-Duc. Work on the mansion was very slow and, after almost four-teen years, stopped altogether when money ran out, but what was completed is remarkable. Everything in the house is of stone – including the drainpipes and the bath – and many of the details – gargoyles, arches – are of breathtaking quality. Curiously, many of the building implements – ladders, huge set squares and the wooden arch formers, can still be seen.

The Victorians also built churches, particularly in the suburbs of expanding cities and towns. In the main, these are solid but somewhat charmless buildings, though George Gilbert Scott's Holy Trinity at Watermoor, Cirencester is a fine church. But in general the Victorians preferred to 'restore' and 'improve' existing churches, some being improved almost beyond recognition and in a style that owes more to misplaced enthusiasm than common sense. Again the work of Scott is (usually) an exception.

The Shambles at Newent is a delightful evo-

Sezincote. This riot of Mogul architecture frequently surprises unsuspecting walkers in the park beside the house. What is less surprising is that the mansion was the inspiration for the Prince Regent's Brighton Pavilion.

EDUCATION

Many of the Norman monastic houses provided basic education, though only for the sons of nobles and gentry. Of these, one of the oldest in the county is King's in Gloucester, which was probably the original choir school of St Peter's Abbey. There had also been a grammar school attached to St Augustine's Abbey in Bristol, and this was refounded at the Dissolution, taking over some of the old abbey buildings. Perhaps as old as Gloucester's King's is the foundation of Katherine, Lady Berkeley, who built a house for one master and two poor boys at Wotton-under-Edge in 1384.

Other early schools in the county include Bristol Grammar School (1532), that built by Richard Pate in Cheltenham (1571), and Queen Elizabeth's Hospital in Bristol, founded in 1586 by John Carr, a soapboiler. In 1634 John Whitson built the first boarding school for girls in Bristol. It was called Red Maids because of the distinctive uniform of the girls, and still retains the name.

By the eighteenth century, many of these private schools were in decline and very few new ones were being established, those of Edward Colston in Bristol being an exception. The first change was brought about by Nonconformist ministers such as John Wesley and George Whitefield, and then by the Sunday school movement of Raikes and Stock.

One of the first schools ('British' schools) of the new movement was at Wotton-under-Edge: its first master was Isaac Pitman. Pitman was born in 1813, the second of eleven children of a clerk in a Trowbridge clothing factory. After becoming a teacher, his first job was on Humberside, but he accepted the Wotton job in order to return to the west of England. The story runs that on the journey south, he fell into religious discussions with a man from Clifton who altered his convictions. Following this change, he was promptly sacked from the teaching post, the local Wesleyan minister telling the congregation that 'if he held such religious sentiments he should expect to be hunted out of the town like a mad dog'. Pitman left the chapel and joined the Church of England. He also set up his own school in Wotton in January 1837, which he ran until 1839. During this period he invented his famous shorthand system, which he taught to his pupils. A plaque on his old house in Orchard Street reads 'In this house Sir Isaac Pitman, b 1813, d 1897, invented his System of Shorthand known as Phonography in the year 1837'.

cation of Victorian town life, but this romantic portrayal is at odds with the disease-ridden, squalid existence of the urban poor. However, the quality of life for all sections of society was improving, nowhere more obviously than in education.

Cheltenham College, a public school for boys, was founded in 1841 and therefore has a claim to being the first Victorian public school. Its delightful buildings, built mostly in Gothic style, stand beside Bath Road and form one of the finest sights in the town. The college also owns Thirlestaine House, across the road from the main buildings, which it bought in 1947. The House, with its classical entranceway, pre-dates the school. It is in the grounds of the college, where Cecil Day Lewis was once a master, that Cheltenham's Cricket Festival is held.

To the west of the Promenade lies Cheltenham Ladies College, founded in 1853, when a group of men, including the principal of the boy's college, decided that there should be an equivalent for the 'daughters of Noblemen and Gentlemen'. The college stands on the site of the old Royal Well. The college buildings, which are imposing rather than beautiful, include a curious onion-dome which can be seen peeping over the Promenade's Regency terrace when it is viewed from the Imperial Gardens. Dorothea Beale, one of the greatest names in the education of girls, was made principal of the college in 1858 at the age of twenty-seven and remained in post until her death in 1906. Cheltenham Ladies College was a revolution in the education of girls, and was soon followed by the Clifton and Redland girls' high schools in Bristol.

Since the 1870s Education Act, the process of education for the majority of Gloucestershire's schools, both primary and secondary, has developed along the lines imposed by central government. The most significant event in tertiary education occurred in 1909 when Bristol University received its charter. The university has since achieved world-renown in many fields, not least physics in which it can claim four Nobel laureates, one of whom, Cecil Powell, received his prize while working there. More recently, Bristol's position as the only university in the extended county has been lost, the former Cheltenham and Gloucester College of Higher Education becoming the University of Gloucestershire on 23 October 2001.

The Arts and Crafts Movement

Industrialisation, while creating a general improvement in living standards, had its down side. The rise of trade unions was one response to the less glorious aspects of factories. Another was the Arts and Crafts movement spearheaded by William Morris. Morris, a designer and craftsman, as well as a poet and writer, lived in Kelmscott Manor, just over the Oxfordshire border from Lechlade, from 1871 until his death in 1896. He was greatly influenced by the scenery of the Cotswolds. While staying at Broadway Tower with his friends, the pre-Raphaelite artists Edward Burne-Jones and Dante Gabriel Rossetti, Morris began his Society for the Preservation of Ancient Buildings as a reaction to the 'restoration' of local churches, which he saw as destroying much that was worthwhile. Morris also reacted against what he saw as the soulless aspects of mass-production. He formed Morris and Company to promote the production of crafted goods that were both beautiful and useful.

Significant members of Morris' movement were the architects and furniture designers Ernest Gimson and the Barnsley brothers, Ernest and Sidney. These three lived in Daneway

Hidcote Manor Gardens.

House, parts of which date back to the thirteenth century. The house stands close to the entrance to the Sapperton Canal Tunnel. The three men are all buried in the churchyard of St Kenelm's Church, Sapperton.

Some of the best works of Morris and his co-workers can be seen in Gloucestershire. Rodmarton Manor was designed by Ernest Barnsley, while Owlpen Manor was restored by Norman Jewson, a co-worker of Gimson and the Barnsleys. Perhaps the finest examples are the stained-glass windows of the church at Selsley featuring designs by several pre-Raphaelite artists including Ford Madox Brown, Burne-Jones and Rossetti. Many claim that the Creation window is the finest product of Morris' stained-glass works.

The Resurrection Window by Edward Burne Jones at Selsley Church.

Kiftsgate Court. Kiftsgate was one of the Hundreds of Saxon Gloucestershire, named for the Kiftsgate Stone which stands beside the road from Dovers Hill towards Broadway. The name translates as Chief's Track, one of the tracks which crossed the Saxon landscape. The Kiftsgate Stone was a moot point, one used for hundreds of years. The Magna Carta was read from it and King George III proclaimed there. The Court which takes the Hundred's name was raised in the late nineteenth century by Sydney Graves Hamilton who brought the complete Georgian façade built by his ancestor Walwyn Graves on Mickleton Manor to the site as a starting point. Despite this remarkable evolution it is the garden beside the mansion which attracts the visitor. The garden was laid out by Heather Muir, but undoubtedly inspired, in part at least, by Lawrence Johnson who was responsible for the nearby Hidcote Manor Gardens.

Today, the Guild of Handicraft Trust can be said to be continuing the Morris tradition. Set up by CR Ashbee, the guild attracted such famous names as Sir Gordon Russell and Robert Welch to the northern Cotswolds around Chipping Campden. The workers at Campden's silk mill maintain the guild's tradition and the shop set up by the late Robert Welch is still in the town's main street.

Though it seems strange to include gardens in the framework of the Arts and Crafts movement, several are seen as encapsulating its essence. Ernest Barnsley designed the gardens as well as the house at Rodmarton Manor. His efforts to create outdoor rooms and so incorporate the garden into the overall design influenced Charles Wade at Snowshill Manor, though this is now more famous for Wade's eclectic (not to say eccentric) collections. Lawrence Johnson followed the same principle in creating the Hidcote Manor Gardens, perhaps the most famous in the county, though the nearby Kiftsgate Gardens run a very close second.

Snowshill Manor.

11. The Twentieth Century

Queen Victoria died in 1901. She had reigned for over sixty years, during which time Britain had industrialised, built an empire and become a world leader. Her death almost coincided with the start of the century in which Britain would lose both the Empire and her status as a world power: Victoria's funeral really did represent the end of an era.

The first years of the twentieth century, the Edwardian age, were the last of the golden years. Edward VII died in 1910 and was succeeded by his son George V. These were years of widespread social reform. Old age pensions were introduced in 1908; the National Insurance Act of 1911 brought in sick pay, welfare benefits and some free medical treatment; and school meals were introduced. With increased leisure time, organised sport became a passion – another thing that the British could teach the world.

Sport

The first county cricket match to involve a Gloucestershire side is now reckoned to have been that on 8–9 July 1862, when a side organised by Dr Henry Mills Grace defeated Devon by an innings and seventy-seven runs in a match on Bristol's Durdham Down. Dr Grace was the father of nine children, five of them boys. One of these, Edward Mills Grace, played in the game. A younger son was William Gilbert Grace, the great WG, who was certainly the best cricketer of his generation and possibly the greatest of all time.

W. G. Grace's reputation is so huge that he overshadows all the others who have played for the county. But there have been other great Gloucestershire cricketers – Wally Hammond, the best batsman in the world in the immediate pre-Bradman era; Gilbert Jessop (named after WG); Charlie Parker, who played only one rain-shortened test, but would surely have played more had he not antagonised the cricketing authorities; and the overseas players, Mike Procter and Courtney Walsh.

The county's main home is the County Ground in Bristol, but matches are still played at other venues, particularly at Cheltenham during the cricket festival. Cheltenham has a particular place in cricketing history, being the only ground to date where a hat trick of stumpings has taken place (in the Gloucestershire v Somerset match of 1893). Remarkably, Mike Procter achieved a very similar (but not unique) feat in 1973 with a hat trick of lbw.

A sport in which the county excels is rugby union, the union code being especially strong in the south-west of England. Both Bristol and Gloucester have teams in the new league's top division and regularly supply players to the national side. The Bristol club was formed in 1888 by an amalgamation of the Carlton Club and Redland Park. The team's first game was a defeat away to Cardiff. Home games were, at first, on the Gloucestershire County Cricket ground at Nevil Road. Now the club shares the Memorial Stadium with Bristol Rovers. Gloucester Rugby Football Club was formed in 1873 playing three matches in its first season and winning them all. The team entered the Gloucestershire League in 1908/9 winning eleven of its twelve matches and finishing at the top of the league. One of their opponents was Bristol, a match they won. The team plays at Kingsholm, once the site of a royal palace.

The Wishing Fish Clock in Cheltenham's Regency Arcade. The clock was designed by Kit Williams, author and illustrator of Masquerade, *a book he published while living in Horsley. The book, with its theme of a real buried treasure, caused a sensation, as did the clock. It is claimed to be the tallest in the world (at 14m – 45ft), and weighs 3 tons. Its array of rolling balls and bubble-blowing fish attracts a crowd every hour.*

WG GRACE

William Gilbert Grace was born on 18 July 1848 at Downend, Bristol. He was educated locally and qualified as a doctor, despite claiming that he preferred not to read books as they ruined the eyes for batting. As a cricketer, his achievements almost defy belief. In 1871 he scored 2,739 runs in the season at a time when no other batsman had ever scored 2,000. In 1874 he scored 1,000 runs and took 100 wickets in eleven matches between 6 July and 12 September. In 1875 he took 191 wickets at 12.92 runs/wicket. That same season also saw him score 344, 177 and 318 not out in three consecutive innings in ten days in August. During the full month he scored 1,278 runs. In 1876 he scored 400 not out against twenty-two men. He regularly threw a cricket ball more than 100 yards.

He scored 126 centuries, more than double the number of any of his contemporaries. His career total of runs has only been beaten by a handful of later players, and it must be remembered that he played many fewer innings. As a batsman he favoured attack, declaring once that he disliked purely defensive shots as he could only get three runs from them. As a bowler he was also formidable – quick when he was young, slower, but more wily, when he was older. He played in twenty-two tests, a small number by modern standards, but there were far fewer test matches in the late nineteenth century. In 1880 he played in the first ever test match between England and Australia. That team also included his brothers EM (Edward Mills) and GF (George Frederick). The three brothers helped Gloucestershire win the county championship in 1876 and 1877, but GF Grace was to die tragically young.

The stories about WG Grace are legion. It is said that notices were put up outside cricket grounds declaring that admission was 6d, but one shilling if Dr Grace played. He is said to have once made a hundred with a walking stick as a bet and to have caught a bird in the slips, so fast were his reflexes. Many of the tales are doubtless apocryphal – though none the worse for that – especially the ones about his gamesmanship. Did he really once decline to walk when clearly out, intimidating the umpire into letting him stay at the crease on the grounds that the crowd had come to see him bat? As with so many stories about the great man, if it wasn't true, it probably should have been.

Both rugby clubs are in the top division of the English league and regularly challenge for European honours. The same cannot be said for football where the local standard is comparatively low. Bristol has two sides – City and Rovers. Bristol Rovers (the oldest club and from the Gloucestershire side of Bristol) have never played in the top division. Bristol City (from the Somerset side of the city) has a better record. Until recently, the two Bristol sides routinely competed for the Gloucestershire professional cup (being the only two professional sides), but have now been joined in the professional ranks by Cheltenham Town who achieved promotion from the non-league ranks. At the time of writing Cheltenham have achieved promotion to the Second Division and are therefore a division above Bristol Rovers. As a lifelong Rovers' supporter, the author finds the current state of affairs almost beyond endurance, particularly as he now lives within easy reach of Cheltenham's ground.

No quick look at sport in Gloucestershire would be complete without a mention of Cheltenham racecourse, home to one of Britain's greatest festivals of racing and the premier jump race of the annual calendar. It is occasionally claimed that the true discovery of Cheltenham's spa followed the recovery of a horse after it had drunk the famous waters. Whatever the truth, it is certainly the case that horse racing was part of the social scene from the spa's early days, though the first races were run on Cleeve Hill. The first Gold Cup was run there in 1819, but unlike today's race it was over the flat (the race was over 3 miles and was won by Spectre).

Racing at Cleeve Hill was eventually discon-

The Gloucestershire County Cricket team which won the County Championship in 1877. Standing (left to right) are WO Moberley, W Fairbanks, GF Grace, FG Monkland, WR Gilbert and M Midwinter. Seated (left to right) are HB Kingscote (the team captain), F Townsend, RF Miles, WG Grace and EM Grace.

tinued following the protestations of a local clergyman, only to reappear in 1831 at Prestbury Park. Although Prestbury has been the home of Cheltenham racing since then the course has not been in continuous use, a gap of fifty years occurring in the nineteenth century when a new owner refused to allow the events. The early races at Prestbury were, like those at Cleeve, over the flat, but within just a couple of years steeplechasing had been introduced. The March festival of racing under National Hunt rules is now Britain's foremost steeplechase meeting, its

most famous races being the Champion Hurdle and the Gold Cup, where the exploits of horses such as Golden Miller (who won five successive Gold Cups), Arkle (who won three Gold Cups from three starts) and Desert Orchid have become legendary.

The other equestrian event for which the county is famous is the three-day event held annually at Badminton, one of the most important dates in the sport's calendar. Competitors frequently include world and Olympic champions.

The first Cheltenham Gold Cup. This painting by an unknown artist of the English school was completed in 1826. It depicts the first race, held in 1819 on Cleeve Hill.

FAMOUS JOCKEYS

The most famous jump jockey was George Stevens, who was born in Cheltenham in 1833, and won the Grand National five times between 1856 and 1870. Stevens lived in Emblem Cottage, Cleeve Hill, naming the cottage after his first National winner. He raced in fifteen Grand Nationals and never once fell, which makes it ironic that he died as a result of a fall during a pleasure ride. The horse he was riding took fright on Cleeve Hill, unseated him and he hit his head on a stone. Stevens died soon after, aged 38.

Famous for his exploits on the flat, Fred Archer, whose parents owned the King's Arms in Prestbury, rode his first winner at the age of twelve (a donkey race in the paddock of Prestbury's Plough Inn) and was champion jockey for the first time when he was just seventeen. At the time, a jockey was allowed to bet, and Archer is claimed to have bought his parents the Andoversford Hotel with the proceeds of one particularly successful punt. Archer won the Epsom Derby five times, but at the age of twenty-nine, having become champion jockey for the thirteenth consecutive season, he committed suicide. He was tall for a flat-racing jockey and it is believed that the endless diets and purges needed to maintain his racing weight had destroyed his health.

The End of An Era

As if to herald the end of the long hot summers of Edwardian Britain (an opinion not necessarily borne-out by meteorological data) Scott died in the Antarctic and the *Titanic* sank in the Atlantic. Fractures were occurring in Britain's position in the world and these accelerated quickly in the aftermath of World War I and the economic decline that followed.

World War II, while less damaging in terms of soldiers' lives lost was far more damaging to property because of aerial bombardment. The blitz of Bristol (not only a major port, but a centre for aircraft production), which began in November 1940, destroyed several thousand homes and damaged as many as 90,000 others. From the southern Cotswolds the glow of Bristol burning could be seen, while from the northern Cotswolds the glow in the sky was the burning of Coventry. Despite its rural nature, the rest of the county did not escape attack. Cheltenham had a particularly heavy raid in December 1940 and many of the county's towns and villages received at least one hit, even if it was a stray bomb. The last bomb to have landed in the county damaged the school and post office in Upper Slaughter.

The remains of St Peter's Church and the tower of St Mary le Port, Bristol. Partly destroyed during the air raids of World War II the ruins have been left as a symbol of the period, though the nearby area, on Castle Green, has been extensively landscaped.

Gloucestershire Takes to the Air

Interestingly, two major industries in the county were air-war related, though not exclusively set up for that purpose. The forerunner of the Gloster Aircraft Company was set up by George Holt Thomas, a man with a passion for flying. In 1910 he obtained licences for the sale of French Forman aircraft and Gnome rotary engines in Britain. Thomas formed the Aircraft Manufacturing Company where he was joined in March 1914 by Hugh Burroughs who had worked at the Farnborough Balloon Factory.

When war was declared, the company looked for premises where aircraft could be built and, as early planes were wooden, chose the wood and metal works of HH Martyn at Sunningend, Cheltenham. In 1917, the two companies merged to form the Gloucestershire Aircraft Company. The loss of wartime contracts made life difficult for the new company, but it survived, in part on foreign orders, but mostly because it was producing competitive planes: the Mars I racing biplane won the Aerial Derby for three consecutive years in the early 1920s and set a British speed record of 196mph (314km/h). In 1925 the company moved to Hucclecote and shortly after changed its name to Gloster – the true spelling of the county had been found to be unpronounceable by foreign customers. Further speed records followed – the biplane record of 277.1mph (443km/h) and a monoplane record of 336.3mph (538km/h) in a Gloster VI floatplane.

The company supplied Gloster Gladiators to the RAF and Sea Gladiators to the Fleet Air Arm, but despite service in World War II, the age of the biplane was over. Gloster was taken over by Hawker Aircraft Ltd in 1934 and built Hurricanes at Hucclecote, production reaching five planes per day at peak production in the early 1940s. Though the Hurricane helped win the Battle of Britain and the war, more important to the future of aircraft was the production of the E28/39 using Sir Frank Whittle's W1 jet engine, which flew from RAF Cranwell on 15 May 1941. The plane was the forerunner of the Gloster Meteor which entered service on 12 July 1944. The first victory for the new jet occurred three weeks later when a Meteor downed a V1 flying bomb, not by shooting it down as its cannons had jammed, but by tipping it over.

Post-war the company made the Gloster Javelin, but cancellation of a supersonic successor by the Government caused an economic crisis. Despite becoming a part of Hawker Siddeley in 1963, the Hucclecote works finally closed in April 1964.

The early years of the Bristol Aeroplane Company closely followed the Gloster story. In 1910, Sir George White of the Bristol Tramways and Carriage Company founded a series of four aircraft companies, one of which was called the Bristol Aeroplane Company. The first plane, a Zodiac of French design, built under licence, was constructed at Filton in 1910. A series of biplanes followed, the Bristol Scout and Bristol Fighter seeing service in World War I. In the inter-war years, several Bristol planes were made for the RAF and foreign air forces, including the Bloodhound and Jupiter. The most famous was the Bristol Bulldog which first flew in May 1927 and was still being produced in 1935. During World War II, the Filton works produced the Blenheim, Beaufort and Beaufighter, and the Bristol Hercules engine powered the Mark II

EDWARD WILSON

Standing on the Promenade, close to the Neptune Fountain, is a statue of Edward Wilson sculpted by Kathleen Scott, the wife of Robert Falcon Scott. Wilson was born in Montpellier Terrace, Cheltenham and spent his boyhood there and at Crippetts Farm on the flank of Shurdington Hill. He was educated at Cheltenham College and then read natural science and medicine at Caius College, Cambridge. As well as a doctor, Wilson was an excellent naturalist and superb artist, and was chosen for the 1901–04 National Antarctic Expedition. Together with Scott and Shackleton, he sledged to a new furthest south record in December 1902. As a friend of Scott, Wilson declined to travel south with Shackleton in 1907. Indeed, he criticised Shackleton for what he saw as a failure to keep a promise not to 'trespass' on ice close to Scott's 1901 base. In 1910 he accompanied Scott back to the Antarctic. During the austral winter of 1911 he was one of the three-man team that made the 'worst journey in the world' to retrieve the eggs of emperor penguins. He was then part of Scott's team, which reached the pole on 17 January 1902 only to find that they had been beaten to it by the Norwegian team led by Roald Amundsen. None of Scott's men survived the return journey – Wilson, Scott himself and Bowers died in a tent just 17.5km (11 miles) from a food depot after being trapped by a blizzard for several days.

Lancaster. All the Bristol planes were highly successful.

During the war years, the company was involved in design work for a bomber capable of carrying 100 tons of bombs for 5,000 miles. This led to the production of the Brabazon, a huge four-engined airliner. Some still claim that it could have been a success, but the vast length of runway it required – the Filton runway had to be extended so far that it cut the Bristol bypass – and the soon-abandoned concept of a 'hotel in the air', doomed it to failure. The future of air travel lay in lighter, faster aircraft such as the Bristol Britannia, which was very successful.

In 1957 the Bristol Company was forcibly

Edward Wilson, in full Antarctic clothing, looks out from his pedestal beside Cheltenham's Neptune Fountain. Behind him are the town's municipal offices, built as five houses in the 1820s.

merged with English Electric and Vickers to create the British Aircraft Corporation which built the highly successful One-Eleven and, most famously, the Concorde. Concorde 01 flew from Filton on 17 December 1971 and entered airline service in January 1976. Unfortunately, it was never as successful as had been hoped because of restrictions on supersonic flights over land. In 1977, the company became part of the nationalised British Aerospace and has had continuing success with the co-operative Airbus projects.

The Gloucester Regiments

The conflicts of the twentieth century and the production of warplanes leads inevitably to thoughts of men in battle. Gloucestershire is home to two regiments that have seen service in

the wars of three centuries. The Gloucestershire Regiment was formed from two early eighteenth-century regiments, the 28th and 61st. The 28th fought with Wolfe at Quebec and in the American War of Independence. Fighting in Egypt in 1789, they famously fought an encircling French army and were granted the unique right to wear a badge on both the front and back of their head wear, an honour they still retain. When, in 1782, regiments were linked to parts of the country for ease of recruiting, these regiments became the North and South Gloucestershire Regiments. They were combined to form the 1st and 2nd Battalions of the Gloucestershire Regiment in 1883, the two battalions being reduced to one in 1948.

Both the 28th and 61st saw action in the Peninsula War, after which the 28th fought at both Quatre Bras and Waterloo. At Waterloo, the 28th was the only regiment Wellington mentioned by name in his dispatches. Later the 28th fought in the Crimean War while the 61st saw action during the Indian Mutiny, Surgeon Reade receiving the regiment's first VC. As the 1st and 2nd Battalions, the regiment saw action in both the Boer War, and World War I when five VCs were awarded. At Dunkirk in 1940, the 2nd Battalion sustained heavy losses, but recovered to play a part in the D-Day invasion. Meanwhile the 1st Battalion fought in Burma. Then, during the Korean War the now-combined Battalion was involved in the famous battle at the Imjin River where, after holding out against overwhelming Chinese numbers, just forty men escaped being taken prisoner. For that action, the battalion was awarded the President's Distinguished Unit Citation by US President Henry Truman.

The second county regiment, the Royal Gloucestershire Hussars, began life in 1794 when volunteer cavalry units of 'yeomen and gentlemen' were formed because of the threat of invasion. With Napoleon defeated and the threat averted, the unit was disbanded, but re-formed in 1834, taking its present name in 1846. It fought in the Boer War, and World War I where it saw action at Gallipoli and Egypt. In 1938, the regiment split into two, one seeing service in the Western Desert campaign of World War II, while the other served in Britain as a training and home defence unit. In post-war army reductions, the RGH was reduced to just eight men (kept on in order to preserve the name), but then amalgamated with other units to form the Royal Wessex Yeomanry of the Territorial Army.

Those wishing to find out more on the history of Gloucestershire's soldiers should visit the Regiments of Gloucestershire Museum, which is housed in the Old Custom House on Gloucester docks.

The Post-War County

Though the aircraft companies were large employers, they were not the only ones to help Gloucestershire recover from the tribulations of half a century of conflict: Listers and Dowty were among several large companies that made the county their base.

In the 1950s, Berkeley was chosen as the site for the world's first commercial nuclear power station. Berkeley power station began electricity production in 1962, a world-first for Gloucestershire. The two nuclear reactors at Berkeley were Magnox reactors with uranium metal fuel in a magnesium alloy can, the reactors cooled by carbon dioxide gas. The reactors were contained in a steel pressure vessel. In 1968, the first Magnox reactors with pre-stressed concrete pressure vessels began operating at Oldbury-on-Severn. Then, in 1989, the Berkeley reactors became the first commercial reactors to be permanently shut down in a managed manner, and to be decommissioned. The fuel and some other radioactive material were removed from the site, but the boiler shells and the graphite core remain: they will need to be off-limits for many decades. The Oldbury reactors are still operating.

Electricity supplied by the grid system into which Berkeley and Oldbury fed their power lit the homes and powered the televisions and fridges of Gloucestershire. In the 1920s, there

---

ZULU WAR HERO

Despite having been born in Churcham, Private Alfred Henry Hook did not serve in the Gloucestershire Regiments. He was in the 2nd Battalion of the 24th Foot (later the South Wales Borderers) and was with them at Rorke's Drift when 153 men defied a Zulu army in January 1879. The incident was the basis of the film *Zulu*, though the film's portrayal of Hook as a malingerer reflects the need for a good story rather than reality. Hook was awarded the VC for assisting wounded men from the mission station's hospital – that part of the story the film did get right. Hook died in 1905 and was buried in Churcham's churchyard.

A study in engineering and modern art – the new Severn Bridge.

were few homes in the county with electricity. In the 1950s, the rural county was still largely without electricity – a decade later there were few homes without it. Another decade and there were few families without a car, car ownership in the county having risen from about 1,700 in 1914 to more than 170,000 by the century's end. The increase in traffic made new roads a necessity: many bypasses were built and the M4 and M5 motorways crossed the county. The elegant Severn Bridge was opened in 1966 to take the M4 across the Severn and Wye to Wales, only to need supplementing by a second, even more elegant bridge a little further south, before the end of the century.

HOW DO YOU SAY MICHAELWOOD?

In an interesting meeting of the modern county with its Saxon roots, an ancient name achieved national prominence after being confined to local usage for a thousand years. The M5 motorway service area at the base of the Cotswold Edge near Berkeley was named after the local woodland – the *mycel* or *meikle*, 'great', wood – of Saxon times. Pronounced mick-ell by the locals, the proprietors of the service area mistakenly turned the name to Michael Wood and so allowed TV and radio presenters, and a million tourists to pronounce it incorrectly.

Spring in a Cotswold beech wood.

Winter in the county.

Studies in modern architecture. Prinknash Abbey (above) which saw a return of monasticism to Gloucestershire and Berkeley Power Station (below), the world's first commercial nuclear power plant and also the first to have been decommissioned.

Laurie Lee's grave in the churchyard of Holy Trinity Church, Slad.

The twentieth century saw the return of monasticism to Gloucestershire when monks from Caldy Island came to Prinknash manor house in 1928. Later, a new abbey, famous for its pottery, was built using 2,500 tons of Guiting stone. In one of those eccentricities at which the English excel, the name of the abbey is pronounced 'Prinage', and not as spelled. The century also saw a re-emergence of Royal Gloucestershire with Princess Anne taking up residence at Gatcombe Park and Prince Charles moving in to Highgrove. Princess Anne, herself a European three-day event champion, brought equestrian events to Gatcombe and further raised the profile of the Badminton event. More controversially, Prince Charles and, later, his sons, raised the profile of the Beaufort Hunt. Fox hunting is currently a hot topic of debate, both in Gloucestershire and the country as a whole, and this is not the forum to discuss its pros and cons. It would, however, be an abrogation of the aims of the book not to point out that in the Berkeley Hunt Gloucestershire is special in being one of only two hunts in England whose hunting 'pink' is actually yellow (the two yellows are actually different, so each in its own way is unique). The Berkeley yellow is worn by members of the Berkeley family and the hunt's joint masters.

Twentieth Century Writers

Laurie Lee was born in 1914 in Slad, a village in a picturesque valley set back from the Cotswold Edge. He was educated at the village school and the Central School in Stroud. Though he published several books of poems and considered himself a poet, he is best known for his prose works, particularly *Cider with Rosie*, his lyrical account of childhood in the Cotswolds of the

1930s. As a writer he divided his time between Slad and Chelsea, but chose to spend his last years in the village of his birth. Before he died, he requested that he be buried in a plot of the local churchyard close to the road, so he would hear the footsteps of men walking to the village pub – this wish was granted when he was laid to rest in May 1997.

Dennis Potter was quite a different writer. He was born in May 1935 at Berry Hill in the Forest of Dean, where, he later recalled, the family's three bedrooms were occupied by his grandparents, his parents, himself and his sister. He went to Christchurch Junior School, then to Bell's Grammar School in Coleford (no longer a school, having become a hotel/golf club in 1973), but also spent time in London before doing National Service and going to Oxford University. Potter wrote books, stage plays and film scripts, but is best remembered for his television plays, being one of the first writers to concentrate on that medium and to explore its potential. Drama series such as *Pennies from Heaven*, *The Singing Detective* and *Blackeyes* broke new ground, but were also criticised for

their heavy emphasis on sex and the perceived exploitation of woman. The debate on the works continues, despite Potter's death from pancreatic cancer in 1994.

In the years that preceded the First World War, the Dean village of Dymock was home to a group of poets whose work has been influential in the development of modern poetry. The first to arrive in the village was Lascelles Abercrombie who came in 1911. John Drinkwater and William Gibson arrived soon after. One of the best known American poets, Robert Frost, came in 1914 as did Edward Thomas and Rupert Brooke, now the most famous of the six 'Dymock poets'. The group produced a quarterly magazine called *New Numbers*, but only four issues had been published before the outbreak of war and Brooke's subsequent death ended the venture. The last issue of *New Numbers* included Brooke's war poems and so secured Dymock a lasting place in the history of poetry.

Ivor Gurney was born in Queen Street, Gloucester in August 1890. He attended the National School and All Saints' Sunday School,

---

BRIAN JONES

Gloucestershire has supplied famous names to the worlds of literature and classical music, so it is good to record that it was also the birthplace of Brian Jones, whose contribution was to the world of popular culture. He was born in Cheltenham in 1942, educated in the town and worked as a bus conductor and record shop salesman before moving to London and becoming a founder member of the Rolling Stones. He left the group in June 1969 and died soon after in a still-mysterious drowning incident. He was buried in Cheltenham's Priors Road cemetery. His grave is a place of pilgrimage for fans, but the council have yet to be persuaded of the merits of erecting a statue or memorial to him in the town. The attitude of the council is in sharp contrast to that of Bristol, where a plaque was recently erected to celebrate the centenary of the birth, in the city, of Nipper, the HMV dog.

CARY GRANT

Archibald Alexander Leach was born in Horfield, Bristol in 1904. As a nine-year old, his father told him his mother had gone on holiday to Weston-super-Mare. In fact she had been committed to a mental home, something the young boy did not discover until 1935 when his father died. Young Archie went to Bishop Road Primary School and Fairfield Grammar School, where he was expelled for stealing. Archie forged his father's signature on a form, which enabled him to join a travelling troupe of acrobats and comedians. Eventually he went to Hollywood, changed his name to Cary Grant and became a legend of the cinema. He was the first actor to break the studio system, freeing himself of a studio contract and becoming a free agent. There are many who think that he ranks with the true greats of cinema. Somewhat belatedly, Bristol has now erected a statue to its famous son.

Script in hand, Cary Grant strides across Bristol's new Millennium Square intent (in statue at least) on reaching the Hippodrome theatre.

Autumn full moon at Westonbirt Arboretum. On such occasions the arboretum is floodlight adding to its attractiveness. Such sites make Gloucestershire a magnet for visitors.

then won a place in the cathedral choir and attended King's School. A gifted musician and scholar, Gurney passed the entrance exams for Durham University and, later, was given a scholarship to the Royal College of Music. He volunteered in 1915 and saw active service in the First World War. In 1918 he was discharged from the army suffering from shell shock, which, it was claimed, was aggravating an existing condition. From then until his death from tuberculosis in 1938, Gurney spent most of his time in mental institutions, attempts at suicide punctuating periods of poetry writing. Much of his poetry was published during his lifetime, but was overlooked as the literary world concentrated on the more famous war poets. With the publication of what was considered his best work in 1997, Gurney's poetry is now being reassessed and he is seen as one of the significant poets of the twentieth century.

Mention must also be made of Beatrix Potter, for despite her not having been either county-born or a county resident, one of her most famous books (and her own favourite) was *The Tailor of Gloucester*, a tale inspired by a local legend concerning the Gloucester tailor John Pritchard and the suit he was making for the city's Mayor, a suit which was finished by a mysterious hand. On holiday in Gloucester, Beatrix Potter heard the story and found the quaint Tailor's House in College Court, a house which is now dedicated to the Peter Rabbit books. Finally, to make up a trio of literary Potters, the Forest of Dean can claim some credit for *Harry Potter* – J K Rowling, the author, moved to Tutshill with her parents at the age of nine.

A New Century

With the rise of Bristol as a centre for local commerce – it now has more residents than the entire old county of Gloucestershire – many of the local towns and villages have become dormitories for the city: the same thing has happened close to Gloucester and Cheltenham. Many lament the change, but the rise in car ownership and general prosperity made such a development inevitable. The growth of cities and their satellite towns at the end of the twentieth century echoes a previous expansion when rural workers abandoned the country in search of work in the towns. The growth can be decried, but it does allow the more far-sighted cities to invest in an architectural future. The excellent Millennium Square in Bristol, set on reclaimed land, was built at a fraction of the cost of some other millennium projects and was clearly better value than many of them.

Another aspect of modern Gloucestershire arouses much debate. The county includes the bulk of the Cotswolds Area of Outstanding Natural Beauty (AONB), smaller parts of the Wye Valley and Malverns Areas, and the Forest of Dean. Inevitably, it attracts visitors and there are many who feel that the growth in tourist-based facilities has created a 'theme park' county. Certainly Bourton-on-the-Water, to take an example, can be overwhelmed by visitors on a

sunny summer's day, and publicity was recently given to a shopkeeper in Stow who felt that the town had been so given over to tourism that it was no longer possible to run a shop for 'ordinary' people. It would be a great shame if tourism was to take over the lovelier of the Cotswold villages completely, effectively destroying what the visitor has come to enjoy; but it would also be a pity if attracting industry into the area, to compete with tourism as a source of income, were to have the same effect.

Gloucestershire as a whole has adapted well to the new Britain in which service-based industries have largely taken over from those based on manufacturing: as a sign of the county's willingness to embrace the realities of the modern world, the Co-op in Cinderford had already modified its supermarket trolleys to take euros long before a debate started on the issue.

Given the sheer beauty and historical interest of Dean and the Cotswolds – and other parts of the county too – it was inevitable that in a more leisured society there would be an increase in visitor numbers. And why not? Gloucestershire is just too good a county to miss.

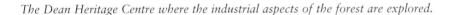

The Dean Heritage Centre where the industrial aspects of the forest are explored.

INDEX

Numbers in italics refer to illustrations in the text.